A
Biographical Dictionary
of
Architects in Ireland
1600–1720

A
Biographical Dictionary
of
Architects in Ireland
1600–1720

ROLF LOEBER

John Murray

© Rolf Loeber 1981

First published 1981
by John Murray (Publishers) Ltd
50 Albemarle Street, London w1x 4bd

Printed and bound in Great Britain at
The Camelot Press Ltd, Southampton

British Library Cataloguing in Publication Data
Loeber, Rolf
A biographical dictionary of architects in
Ireland 1600–1720.
1. Architects – Ireland – Biography
I. Title
720'.92'2   NA996
isbn 0–7195–3832–7

Contents

Introduction

On May 29, 1661 the foundation stone was laid for the largest private house built during the 17th century in Ireland, the Earl of Orrery's country-house and castle Charleville in County Cork. The Earl called himself the 'architect' of his house, for he pretended 'something to engineership'. From then onwards the site swarmed with craftsmen and labourers, and nearby, limestone quarries were opened. A Mr Fennell supervised the hauling of timber from the woods, and transported it by oxen to the site. Limekilns and brick kilns were built. Even a bagpiper was hired to keep the workmen at the kilns awake during the night. The stone work was contracted by William Armstead and Thomas Smith for £4000. A supervising master mason (an Irishman by the name of Lehan) had twelve other masons under him. They were joined by carpenters and bricklayers, most of whom were Irish. In the progress of the building, slaters, plasterers, joiners, glaziers, smiths, turners and carvers were involved, each of whom may have submitted their own designs for parts of the building. They came with their apprentices, often still boys. The co-ordination of such a huge project (Charleville Castle was finally to have fifty-six chimneys) was initially in the hands of two officers, Lieutenant John Greene and Captain William Kenn.

The reason for embarking on a detailed discussion on the building of the now lost Charleville Castle, is that it illustrates the three main sources from which the architectural profession in Ireland emerged in the 17th century. In continuation of the medieval tradition, some craftsmen, especially masons and carpenters, developed designs for whole buildings or parts of buildings, which they usually then contracted to build. A second group consisted of officers, who, like Captain William Kenn, often were skilled in the building of fortifications. The officer-architect, especially shortly after the restoration of the Monarchy in 1660, became prominent in the construction of Irish country houses when only a handful of civilian architects were left in Ireland. The third group consisted of noblemen such as the 1st Earl of Orrery and the well-to-do and professional gentry. Often they were of considerable means, and had travelled abroad; almost all had an official position, as clergyman, lawyer, or farmer of the revenue, and used architecture as a hobby, or as a profession to complement their income. From these three rather diverse groups, the craftsmen, the officer-architects, and the gentlemen-architects, not only did an architectural profession emerge, but their advent signalled a departure from traditional modes of building. Probably each group, in its own manner, contributed

1

towards the introduction of a new, and classically inspired, architecture in Ireland.[1] With the new movement the gothic style survived for a while in the early 17th century, but then succumbed to the change of taste of both architects and patrons. As in England a new breed emerged – the architect who made a conscious study of design, and whose involvement in building was 'supervisory rather than executive'.[2] Each of the three main developments in the Irish architectural profession had its own merits and its own backgrounds.

THE CRAFTSMAN-ARCHITECT

The educational background of craftsmen consisted of a seven-year apprenticeship with a master craftsman. For example, an Anthony Fleming contracted in 1656 with the joiner William Russell of Kinsale to be apprenticed for that period. At the end of his time he would receive over and above his ordinary apparel, one new suit and cloak of broadcloth, one set of tools, and £5.[3] The completion of an apprenticeship conferred upon the newly-qualified craftsman the opportunity to become a freeman of a town and to apply for membership of a guild. The guilds in Irish towns were often a curious conglomeration of professions. In 1657 the plumbers in the city of Cork were incorporated in a guild together with the goldsmiths, saddlers, bridlemakers, pewterers, tinmen, lattin workers, founders, braziers, glaziers and upholsterers.[4] Later in the century more specialized guilds were formed, such as that of the carpenters in Cork (1667), bricklayers and plasterers in Dublin (1671) and joiners in the same city (1700). Each building guild enforced rather strict rules regarding admissions and quality of work,[5] and such enforcement usually carried the authority of the local town council. The number of craftsmen working in the building trades who were admitted as freemen to the city of Dublin more than doubled in the 1630s in comparison with the preceding five decades. Their number again doubled in the 1660s compared with that of the 1630s and finally levelled off at 160 individuals a year for the next three decades. Among these freemen, architects are first mentioned in the 1620s, when twelve were admitted. With the exception of Thomas Lucas, nothing

---

[1] R. Loeber, 'Early Classicism in Ireland, Architecture before the Georgian era' *Architectural History*, 1979, *22*, 49–63.

[2] *Colvin*, 11, 27.

[3] R. Caulfield (Ed.), *The Council Book of the Corporation of Kinsale from 1652 to 1800*, Guildford, 1879, 19.

[4] J. Coleman (Ed.), *Windele's Cork*, Cork, 1910, reprinted 1973, 65.

[5] The nature of the rules of guilds has been little studied. Some evidence is presented in the above sources and in *CARD*. Note that the records of the guild of bricklayers and plasterers were still extant in the 19th century, but their present whereabouts are not known. In the Gilbert Collection of the Public Library, Pearse St, Dublin, is an index of these records written in a 19th-century hand.

is known about them other than their names.[6] Lucas, who was most probably a carpenter by profession, was an architect in the modern sense, for in one of his projects he submitted a design for a building (part of the old front of Trinity College), but left the execution to someone else. Much more commonly, craftsmen designed a part or the whole of a building and then assumed the responsibilities of chief contractor. Of this group the carpenters Andrew Tucker (*c.* 1624) and John Darley (*c.* 1677) are typical examples. The latter's decorated houses once adorned Lisburn in County Antrim. In the South of Ireland John and Richard Hamond designed and executed an elaborate gate for the 1st Earl of Cork's house in 1611. Other examples will be found in the following pages. Craftsmen-architects in Ireland may have used printed pattern-books as well as their own 'book of draughts' from which a patron could choose a pattern. For instance, in 1681, the carpenter Mr Fisher was asked to bring his book of drawings to Sir John Perceval, who was then rebuilding Burton House, County Cork.[7]

As shown in the example of Charleville Castle, the use of Irish craftsmen during the 17th century was very common. Richard Boyle, 1st Earl of Cork and many other patrons relied heavily both on native and imported craftsmen. Many examples of the first category can be found in the following pages: Nicholas Bremagh, James Connor and John Walshe. A further example, Nicholas Cowli, was not only a builder but also a sculptor. In the majority of known cases native craftsmen were used for the execution but not for the design of buildings. Among the exceptions was the mason John O'Brien, who probably both designed and built Shannongrove, a country house in County Limerick, from 1709 onwards. Imported craftsmen frequently supervised the building of a wide variety of structures in the 17th century, ranging from almshouses (see Nicholas Langredg, and Thomas Smith), churches (William Parrett and Father Thadeus Holenus), market houses (William Armstead and someone named Mason), bridges (John Lodden), town walls (Peter Benson and John Lodden) and castles (Daniel Thomas). The first Master of the City Works in Dublin, Richard Mills, came from Gloucestershire. In Dublin a number of English or foreign craftsmen could be found as for example, Abraham Hawksworth and John Herne. Most important in this group was the French carver and designer James Tabary, whose unique work survives in the Royal Hospital, Kilmainham. Another foreign craftsman, the Dutch painter Robert Trotter, supervised building activity at Dunmore House, County Kilkenny, for the Duchess of Ormonde in the 1670s.

On occasion, those who designed buildings were called 'contrivers'.[8]

---

[6] R. Loeber (Ed.), 'Architects and craftsmen admitted as freemen to the city of Dublin, 1464–1485, and 1575–1774'. Unpublished typescript, copy in the library of the National Gallery of Ireland, Dublin.

[7] R. Loeber, 'Early Classicism in Ireland', p. 52. See note 1.

[8] Others named as contriver are one Browne, and Capt. Rudolph Corneille.

Introduction

Thomas Smith, who worked in County Cork in the late 17th century is a case in point, for a number of years after developing the defensive outworks of Burton House, he made designs for the remodelling of the main house. Also included in the following pages are craftsmen who supervised and co-ordinated the building or maintenance of structures, without having been responsible for their design. Often they were called overseers or clerks of the works, as for example Thomas Hand, Charles Lyndon, Thomas Ball, Edward Miller, and William Spike; the latter also acted as Deputy Surveyor-General to William Robinson.

THE OFFICER-ARCHITECT

It is not surprising that military officers with a knowledge of mathematics became interested in the engineering of defence works as a profession. For them, the transition from fortifications to domestic architecture was relatively easy. Whereas in England professional architects or master craftsmen dominated the building market, in 17th-century Ireland the shortage of such individuals provided particular opportunities for the emergence of officer-architects. In Ireland, their numbers were relatively large, because the erection or rebuilding of fortifications was frequent there throughout the 17th century. In 1661, according to one account, only three individuals in Ireland could be called experts on building: the engineer and architect Captain John Paine, John Mills, the Master Carpenter of the Royal Works, and the gentleman-architect Dr John Westley.[9] Not surprisingly, in the following years, a number of officers put up domestic buildings: the Catholic engineer Captain James Archer (who had had previous experience in France) and Captain John Morton were employed by the Duke and Duchess of Ormonde, while Captain William Kenn was patronized by the Southwell and Perceval families in Munster. In the 1660s the engineer and mathematician Miles Symner also emerged as an architect. Not all of the officer-architects are known by name. An unidentified soldier was called to his unit in 1667 before he was able to sign a contract with his partner William Moore for the rebuilding of Rathcline Castle, County Longford. A few years earlier a Sergeant Wynter was considered for repair work at Lismore Castle, County Waterford, for he was a 'professed Freemason'.[10]

The phenomenon of the officer-architect was not confined to the late 17th century. Captain (later Sir) Edward Doddington has been credited with the introduction of the 'English' style of building at Coleraine, County Derry in the early 17th century. The massive proliferation of buildings

[9] Bodl., Carte Ms 31, f. 373.
[10] NLI, Ms 12813(4), f. 787.

during the plantations of Ulster, Leinster, and Munster during this period, probably provided enormous opportunities for the old servitors who remained in Ireland. One of them, Captain Richard Crofte, was overseer of, and possibly designed, the new market house at Bandon, built from 1615 to 1617. Some engineers employed for the fortifications and royal works in Ireland, as for instance the Surveyors-General Sir William Robinson and Thomas Burgh, were also engaged in domestic architecture for private patrons. However, the Directors-General of the Fortifications during the early 17th century (Sir Josias Bodley, Captain Nicholas Pynnar, and Sir Thomas Rotheram) are not known as domestic architects other than for some limited work on the royal residences. Even on these works they were often assisted by private entrepreneurs (see the following section on the Royal Works). One of them was an officer, Sir Edward Brabazon, who planned alterations to Dublin Castle in 1606.

The employment of engineers on domestic projects continued throughout the 17th century and even into the early 18th. Mentioned in the following pages is the work of the civil engineer Francis Nevill, who rebuilt the Town House of Londonderry in 1692, the military engineer Captain Rudolph Corneille, who offered to rebuild Burton House, County Cork in 1710, and Captain Francis Portall, who used his engineering skills to design a dome for St Canice's Cathedral, Kilkenny, in 1722. In short, the officer-architect in Ireland played a major role in the building history of the 17th and early 18th centuries. Only those known for their domestic, civil or ecclesiastical architecture have been included. Biographical entries on other military and civil engineers of the period have been published separately in the 13th volume (1977–8) of *The Irish Sword, The Journal of the Military History Society of Ireland.*

THE GENTLEMAN-ARCHITECT

The architectural profession in Ireland received great impetus from a group of individuals who practised architecture as a sideline, and who can be generally described as 'gentlemen'. A typical example of this group is William Dodson, whose main profession was the farming of the revenue. He, like most of his colleagues in architecture, was familiar with architectural pattern-books, and played an important role in introducing into Ireland classical styles of building described in such pattern-books.[11] His contemporary and rival was Dr John Westley, who combined the position of one of the Masters of Chancery with a career in architecture. By marrying a daughter of John Webb, the pupil of Inigo Jones, Westley made the potential of John Webb's vast experience in classical architecture

[11] R. Loeber, 'Early Classicism in Ireland', p. 58. See note 1.

accessible to Irish patrons. Incidentally, both Westley and Dodson not only provided designs for buildings, but also operated as contractors. Other gentlemen such as Roger Boyle, 1st Earl of Orrery, Thomas Roper, 1st Viscount Baltinglass, and Miles Symner, could be classified either as officer-architects, or as gentlemen-architects. The first not only had access to pattern-books, but also benefited from having been introduced to architecture abroad by his tutor when they were on the Grand Tour in 1637–9. Another gentleman-architect, Richard Jones, 3rd Viscount Ranelagh is only known for his work in England.

Miles Symner and John Johnson became engineers and architects after starting their careers as clergymen. Both prepared the way for the New Learning, a movement also actively promoted in the late 17th century by the gentleman-architect and scientist William Molyneux.

Little is known about the individuals who were responsible for the planning of new towns in 17th-century Ireland. The sparse evidence available suggests that the group of gentlemen-architects in particular left their mark in this respect. William Dodson laid out streets in Oxmantown, near Dublin, and Thomas Burgh prepared plans to alter the main entry into Dublin Castle by changing the lay-out of streets adjacent to the castle.

Most of these gentlemen-architects practised in the late 17th century. Although they usually had more experience in architecture than their patrons, they often had similar interests and backgrounds. It is noteworthy that patrons frequently had pattern-books in their own libraries,[12] and would direct an architect or builder, or even assist in the design of the building. For example, the 1st Earl of Cork, together with Edmund Tingham designed the rebuilding of Maynooth Castle in 1632. The Lord Deputy at the time, Lord Wentworth, who built Jigginstown thought himself 'as pretty an architect as Inigo Jones . . .';[13] however, his efforts and those of the Reverend John Johnson as overseers and those of John Allen as contractor, totally discredited Wentworth's claim. In 1677 the famous scientist and entrepreneur Sir William Petty contemplated the building of a 'great house' in Ireland and started 'contriving many noble palaces on paper'.[14] Occasionally the wife of a patron would direct the building activities. For instance, Lady Barrymore, while attending to the rebuilding of Castlelyons in County Cork in 1641, volunteered her architectural advice for the benefit of a relative.[15] In the North of Ireland, a decade later, Lady Anne Conway professed knowledge of some architectural treatises

[12] R. Loeber, 'Early Classicism in Ireland', pp. 51–2. See note 1.
[13] C. V. Wedgwood, 'The Earl of Strafford and the Fine Arts', *History Today*, 1961, *11*, 663. I am indebted to Mr David Alexander for drawing my attention to this article.
[14] McGill University, Montreal, Osler Ms 7612, f. 65, October 6, 1677, Dublin, Sir William Petty to Lady Petty. I am indebted to Dr T. C. Barnard for allowing me to quote from his notes of this manuscript.
[15] Lady F. Verney & M. M. (Eds) *Memoirs of The Verney Family*, London, 1892–1904, I, 210.

and advised on the rebuilding of Lisburn Castle.[16] The times were not ready yet for gentle-women to become architects. For their husbands, on the other hand, it would have been relatively easy to turn from being a gifted amateur into a gentleman-architect.

THE ROYAL WORKS IN IRELAND

Shortly after King Charles II was restored to the throne in 1660, plans were made by the Lord Justices to fit up Dublin Castle and rebuild the royal lodge, the Phoenix House, which stood in Phoenix Park. The following events are illustrative of how the Royal Works functioned in Ireland. For a list of its members, see Table 1. The change of government did not lead to the immediate dismissal of the 'Overseer of the Public Works', Randall Beckett, who was in charge of the operation during the Commonwealth. However, the main responsibility for the renovation after the Restoration was not given to Beckett, but to four other architects, three of whom had no formal appointment in the Royal Works. The 1st Earl of Orrery and Dr John Westley prepared plans for the extension of Phoenix House. The latter took a wooden model to Whitehall to have it approved there – a not uncommon procedure at the time. Westley subsequently supervised alterations at Phoenix House and Dublin Castle, but for unknown reasons was replaced at the former site by the architect William Dodson (who also did not hold a position in the Royal Works). At Dublin Castle, extensive alterations were undertaken in the early 1660s by Captain John Paine, whose full title was Director-General and Overseer of the King's Fortifications. He was assisted by John Mills the Master Carpenter of Ireland. When a few years later the Lord Lieutenant, James Butler, 1st Duke of Ormonde, started the building of a 'palace', popularly so called, at Oxmantown, it was again Dodson who made the preparations. His patron also employed him on alterations to the other Royal lodge, Chapelizod House on the far side of Phoenix Park. Thus, at this period, the erection of royal residences in Ireland was largely in the hands of private architects. The nominal head of the Royal Works was an engineer, who was usually a military officer, but, on occasion, a civilian. In the early 17th century he was assisted by a Clerk and a Comptroller of the Works, but these positions ceased to exist in the second half of the century. Of all possible crafts, only the position of a Master Carpenter of Ireland was officially instituted, and was held for about thirty years in that century. Other craftsmen employed in the Royal Works did not have fixed salaries, but were paid on the basis of the amount of work done, or on the basis of a contract. Their names often recur, especially during the Surveyor-Generalship of Thomas Burgh.

[16] M. H. Nicolson (Ed.), *Conway letters. The Correspondence of Anne, Viscountess Conway, Henry More, and their friends, 1642–1684*, London, 1930, 17.

Introduction

Due to the scarcity of documentary material little is known about the actual functioning of the Royal Works. The name was used mostly in the early 17th century. Later in the century, Robinson and Burgh were called Surveyors-General of the Fortifications and Buildings. As the name implies, the incumbent supervised both the erection and repair of fortifications and royal buildings. He was usually supervised by the Master of the Ordnance who often had a substantial knowledge of engineering. The amalgamation of the departments which took care of the building of fortifications and of royal residences occurred sometime in the 17th century, but the precise date is uncertain.

A FINAL NOTE

No biographical dictionary can be exhaustive. In fact such a work should be thorough and documented, but cannot provide answers to all questions. The following biographical sketches may inspire others to pursue further research both documentary and in the field. It is hoped that this will lead to a wider appreciation of the Irish heritage and consequently encourage those who would secure the preservation of significant buildings, monuments and sites.

ACKNOWLEDGEMENTS

When in May 1972 the Hon. Desmond Guinness suggested to me the writing of a *Biographical Dictionary of Irish Architects* I had little idea about the amount of work involved. Over the past years he continuously encouraged the work and greatly facilitated its execution. He made it possible for my wife and me to stay in Castletown House, the headquarters of the Irish Georgian Society during the academic year 1972–3; from Castletown House I co-ordinated the project with the participation of experts in the field. I am grateful to Mr Charles E. B. Brett, Dr Maurice Craig, Mr Hugh Dixon, The Knight of Glin, Dr John Harris, Miss Jeanne Sheehy, Dr Edward McParland, and Dr Douglas Richardson for their inspiration, and for their liberal passing on of information. The distribution of work among them freed me to concentrate on the period of greatest interest to me, 1600 to 1720, which has resulted in the present work. Throughout the project I received the generous assistance and advice of Prof. Anne Crookshank, who passed on to me the transcripts she and Mrs Irene Calvert had made of unpublished manuscripts of the 1st Earl of Cork. During the course of the research I benefited greatly from the knowledge of other researchers in architectural history, notably Mr Howard M. Colvin, but also from Mr Paddy Bowe, Mr Shane de Blacam, the late Mr William English, Mr William Garner, Mr David Griffin, Mr David Johnson, Mr Paul Kerrigan, Mr Peter Walsh and Mr Jeremy Williams. I valued much the advice and suggestions of Dr Toby Barnard, Dr John Andrews, Dr Karl S. Bottigheimer, Dr Nuala T. Burke, Dr Louis Cullen, Miss M. Griffith, Mr William O'Sullivan and Dr J. G. Simms. The librarians and staff of numerous libraries in Ireland and England have been of enormous help to me, as have been the owners and caretakers of countless buildings in Ireland. I am particularly indebted to the staff of the Inter-Library Loans' Office of Queen's University, Kingston, Ontario, Canada, for their assistance. Also in Kingston, I owe much to my unofficial tutor Dr Pierre De La Ruffinière Duprey. In the last stages of the manuscript I received valuable assistance from The Knight of Glin, who with the help of Mr Frank Wilson and Miss Siobhan Barry took care of the checking of the sources and references. I am also particularly indebted to Mr John Gibbins for his patience and care in preparing the manuscript for publication. Last, but not least, I owe much to my wife Magda, whose unfailing support and curiosity has much stimulated my research. Without her companionship during my searches for surviving pieces of architecture, this book would never have been completed.

It was largely made possible by the financial support of the Irish Georgian Society, the Paul Mellon Foundation, the Leverhulme Trust, and during its final year, by the Canada Council. This book has been published with the help of a grant from the Canadian Federation for the Humanities, using funds provided by the Social Sciences and Humanities Research Council of Canada.

Eugene, Oregon
June 1980

Abbreviations

APCE	*Acts of the Privy Council of England, 1613–1631*, London, 1921–64.
BL	British Library.
Bodl.	Bodleian Library, Oxford.
CARD	Sir John Gilbert (Ed.), *Calendar of Ancient Records of Dublin*, Dublin, 1889–1944, 19 vols.
Carew	J. S. Brewer & W. Bullen (Ed.), *Calendar of Carew MSS*, London, 1867–73, 6 vols.
Colvin	H. M. Colvin, *A Biographical Dictionary of British Architects*, London, 1978.
Commons Jour.	*Journals of the House of Commons of the Kingdom of Ireland*, Dublin, 1796–1802, 2nd Ed., 21 vols.
CL	*Country Life.*
Craig	M. Craig, *Dublin, 1660–1860*, Dublin, 1969.
CSPD	*Calendar of State Papers, Domestic*, London, 1856–1972, 80 vols.
CSPI	*Calendar of State Papers, Ireland*, London, 1856–1910, 24 vols.
CTB	*Calendar of Treasury Books, 1660–1718*, London, 1904–1957, 32 vols.
CTP	*Calendar of Treasury Papers, 1556–1728*, London, 1868–89, 6 vols.
Dalton	C. Dalton (Ed.), *English Army Lists and Commission Registers, 1661–1714*, London, 1892–1904, reprinted 1960, 6 vols.
Dem.	Demolished.
DNB	*Dictionary of National Biography*, London, 1885–1900, 63 vols.
Gilbert	Sir John Gilbert, *A History of the City of Dublin*, Dublin, 1854–59, 3 vols.
Gilbert Ms	Gilbert Manuscript, Public Library, Pearse Street, Dublin.
Geneal. Off.	Genealogical Office, Dublin Castle, Dublin.
Grosart	A. B. Grosart (Ed.), *The Lismore Papers*, London, 1886–8, 10 vols.
HMC	*Historical Manuscript Commission Reports*, London, 1870 onwards.
IGS	*Irish Georgian Society, Quarterly Bulletin of the.*
JCHAS	*Journal of the Cork Historical and Archaeological Society.*
JRSAI	*Journal of the Royal Society of Antiquaries of Ireland.*
JWAS	*Journal of the Waterford and S.-E. of Ireland Archaeological Society.*
KASJ	*Kildare Archaeological Society Journal.*
Lodge	M. Archdall (Ed.), *J. Lodge. The Peerage of Ireland*, Dublin, 1789, 7 Vols.
Loeber	R. Loeber, 'A Biographical Dictionary of Engineers in Ireland: 1600–1730', *The Irish Sword*, The Journal of the Military History Society of Ireland, 1977, 13, 30–44, 106–120, 230–255, 283–314.
Marsh Lib.	Archbishop Marsh's Library, Dublin.

NLI	National Library of Ireland, Dublin.
PRO	Public Record Office, London.
PROI	Public Record Office, Dublin.
PRONI	Public Record Office, Northern Ireland.
Reg. D.	Registry of Deeds, King's Inn, Dublin.
RIA	Royal Irish Academy, Dublin.
TCD	Trinity College, Dublin.
UJA	*Ulster Journal of Archaeology.*

A

ALLEN, JOHN (–1641), bricklayer, whose family moved from England to Holland in the late 16th century. From there John Allen emigrated to Ireland at the end of Queen Elizabeth's reign as a factor for the Dutch. According to *Lodge*[1] he was very handsome, and had a 'great skill in architecture', which caused him to be 'much esteemed, and consulted by the most eminent of the nobility and gentry in their buildings'. A bricklayer of his name was admitted to the freedom of the City of Dublin in 1630. His major commission was the building of JIGGINSTOWN, CO. KILDARE (fl. 1636) for Sir Thomas Wentworth (later Earl of Strafford), Lord Deputy of Ireland.[2] In this work John Johnson (q.v.) acted as overseer and engineer, but also Wentworth himself may have had a hand in the design for he thought himself as 'pretty' an architect as Inigo Jones. The results, however, ridiculed this claim, for Jigginstown remained conventional and virtually deprived of classical themes. Allen may have participated in Wentworth's other building schemes, as at Dublin Castle and Fairwood, Co. Wicklow, but no evidence to that effect has come to light. In 1636 he was paid for minor works done in Trinity College, Dublin.[3] Swift alludes to Allen's work at Howth Castle,[4] but this and other commissions for private patrons remain obscure. Allen's will was dated 1641, but is most likely not extant any more.[5] The executors of his considerable estate were Abraham Butts and John Rice.[6] Before his death Allen had laid the foundations of his house at Mullynahack, outside the walls of Dublin, which was finished by his son Joshua Allen, ancestor to the Viscounts Allen of Stillorgan.

[1] *Lodge*, V, 181–2.
[2] H.G. Leask in E.M. Jope (Ed.), *Studies in Building History*, 1961, 244–6; M. Craig, 'New light on Jigginstown', *UJA*, 1970, *33*, 107–110; C.V. Wedgwood, 'The Earl of Strafford and the Fine Arts', *History Today*, 1961, *11*, 659–64.
[3] TCD, MUN/P/2/1, f. 7.
[4] F.E. Ball, *The History of the County of Dublin*, Dublin, 1917, 88.
[5] Sir A. Vicars (Ed.), *Index to the Prerogative Wills of Ireland*, Dublin, 1897, 5.
[6] J.W. Stubbs, *The History of the University of Dublin*, Dublin, 1889, 85.

ALLEN, THOMAS (fl. 1624), mason who was employed by the 1st Earl of Cork. In 1624 Allen, his 'son' [-in-law] Thomas Westcomb, and the (? carpenter) Robert Soden contracted for the building of a lodge in the park near LISMORE CASTLE, CO. WATERFORD at a cost of £150.[1] In the following year Allen (here named Allen Mason [sic]), his 'son' Westcomb, and the carpenter Andrew Tucker (q.v.) undertook the building of an almost similar 'castle' at BALLYKNOCK, also CASTLEKNOCK (? CO. TIPPERARY). Subsequent work for the Earl of Cork included a pigeon house at Lismore Castle and a variety of walls and two turrets on the estate.[2] He is lastly noted in 1640.

[1] *Grosart*, series 1, II, 123, 156.
[2] *Grosart*, series 1, II, 159; V, 40; NLI, Ms 6897; Lismore Chatsworth Ms 19, f. 62.

ANNESLEY, FRANCIS, later Viscount Valentia (1585–1660), Comptroller of the Works. Eldest son of Robert Annesley and Beatrix Cornwall. He became a successful civil servant in Ireland, and his life has been treated in detail in the *Dictionary of National Biography* and in *Lodge*[1]. On July 16, 1606 he received a patent for the position of 'Comptroller of all and singular of our works in any of our castles, forts, houses, and other buildings and structures . . .' in Ireland.[2] The patent was granted for life at a fee of £20 per annum.[3] Apparently the payments lapsed, for the fee was restored to him in 1625.[4] His influence on the architecture produced by the Irish Royal Works may have been minimal. None of his account books is known to have survived. As a private individual he participated in the plantation of Ulster, and built two bawns and one 'English' house in Co. Tyrone.[5] In Co. Wexford he received 1,000 acres in the new plantation.[6] Nothing is known about his residence in Dublin. In the Rebellion he and his son claimed that they lost their whole estate in Ireland to the value of £4,000 per annum and £10,000 in personal estate.[7] He was created a baronet in 1619, Baron Mountnorris in 1628, and received a reversionary grant of the viscounty of Valentia in 1620. He married firstly Dorothea, daughter of Sir John Philips, and secondly Anne, daughter of Sir John Perrot, Lord Deputy of Ireland. Their son, Arthur Annesley was created Earl of Anglesey in 1661. He died in 1660, and was buried in Thorganby Church, Yorkshire. The position of Comptroller of the Irish Royal Works lapsed after the death of Francis Annesley.

[1] *Lodge*, IV, 109–117.
[2] R. Lascelles, *Liber munerum* . . ., London, 1824, II, 106.
[3] *Lodge* IV, 109; elsewhere this is mentioned as amounting to £26. 13*s*. 4*d*. (*Carew*, 1603–24, 182).
[4] *CSPI*, 1625–32, 54, 686.
[5] *Carew*, 1603–24, 229, 415.
[6] BL, Add. Ms 4756, f. 123[v]
[7] Bodl., Clarendon Ms 22, f. 1667.

ARCHER, JAMES, Senior (fl. 1632–?1680), military engineer and architect. Little is known about the background of this Roman Catholic, native of Kilkenny,[1] only that he was a kinsman of the merchant Patrick Archer.[2] He is not to be confused with the James Archer who was one of the surveyors of the Strafford and Civil Surveys.[3]

Sometime about 1672 Archer summarized his life: by then he had served six years as an ensign and lieutenant, and twenty-four years as a captain. During the latter period he was for fifteen years governor of a 'place' in France. Together with other Royalists he most likely had left for that country after the Irish Rebellion, for his estate in Ireland was disposed of by the Cromwellians.[4] In the French service he had much experience as an engineer, and was present at the siege and defence of many unidentified places.[5] He presumably met the Marquis (later Duke) of Ormonde in France, who was to patronize him afterwards. At the Restoration Archer returned to England, but was sent, together with Capt. Arthur, by Lord Arlington to France and the Low Countries to collect intelligence on the negotiations between these powers and disaffected Irishmen, for which he was paid £100. He recollected later that he was directed by Lord Muskerry, son of the Earl of Clancarty, to his house in France by the command of the Duke of Ormonde, but that he was '3,000 *l*. the worse for it'.[6]

Archer probably returned to England before January 1664, for a 'Mr Archer', an 'old servant' of the Duke of Ormonde brought some papers to Lord Anglesey, who reported that Archer was financially unable to bring over his family into Ireland.[7] Presumably on the outbreak of the Dutch War in 1665 Archer was sent out again as secret agent to France, leaving England before October of that year.[8] This time he was to present himself as one of the disaffected Irishmen, and to provide officials with false information about weak coastal defences in Ireland, and the support which an invading army could expect there. In Paris he met the deputy of the French

Minister Colbert, and other officials including the Dutch ambassador, with whom he talked about the landing of troops at Valencia Island in Co. Kerry, and at Dover and Portsmouth.[9] He returned to England, probably in July 1666, where Lord Arlington brought him to Charles II. In Archer's words, the King told him "Captaine Archer Je vous remersie du soyn que vous avez de mes interests & Je suis fort satisfaiet de Votre Conduite en Cest Rencountre cy & Je vous promett que vous y treuverez votre Coumpt."[10] He possibly stayed on in Oxford to meet a French Jesuit and a Colonel Cusack for he wrote from there to Ormonde on January 8, 1665[–6] concerning information on suspected Irishmen such as Edmund O'Reilly, the titular Primate of Armagh, and Sir James D'Arcy. He complained that since his return he had not been paid a penny, and requested from Ormonde an allowance, to prevent the suffering of himself and his family.[11] As a Catholic Capt. Archer may have acted a double role for in October 1665 the Primate O'Reilly solicited Archer's assistance in order to return to Ireland before his death.[12] Shortly afterwards he received some relief by his appointment as engineer on the English Establishment. However, his salary was less than that of the two foreign engineers working there, who did not have to travel abroad, facts about which he complained bitterly.[13] On September 20, 1666 he wrote to Arlington from Holyhead, where he was waiting for a boat to take him to Ireland.[14] Two years later he was still in Ireland where he oversaw repairs on the residences (and a bridge) of the Duke of Ormonde. On October 5, 1669 by command of Charles II and Ormonde he was forced to leave Carrick-on-Suir in order to survey and oversee the Island of Jersey and its fortifications for which he was paid £100.[15] He was subsequently granted by Charles II the post of Royal engineer with an annuity of £150 out of the English Ordnance. About 1672, payment had not been forthcoming, and a memorandum relates his suffering, for he had, prior to leaving for Jersey, sold his house and goods in Ireland to the value of £500, which had led to the 'Totall destruction' of his family.[16] He stayed in London on February 17, 1671, from where he instructed Lord Ossory, son of the Duke of Ormonde about fortifications in general, so that Ossory could judge the fortifications while travelling in Ireland. For that purpose Ossory was to use the 'little instrument' which Archer had given him formerly.[17] Early in 1673 Archer was sent to Guernsey, to inspect the results of the disaster there caused by lightning;[18] he surveyed the fortifications on the island and promised to return to London within ten days in order to present his findings. During this time, as also since the Restoration, he had been in close contact with Henry Bennet, Earl of Arlington. Between 1666 and 1670 Arlington altered his English country house Euston Hall, in Suffolk, and gave it French characteristics.[19] As Archer was one of the architecturally inclined few in Arlington's circle who were familiar with French architecture, it seems not impossible that he could have furnished designs for Euston Hall, but no definite evidence has come to light so far. Between April 1672 and September 1674 Archer petitioned Arlington for payment of his salary as engineer; at the same time he petitioned the King, for the fulfilment of the latter's promise, made at Oxford, to take care of him in his old age.[20] Little is known about Archer's activities from 1673 to 1677, but in the latter year he re-emerged in Ireland, where he was recommended by the Duke of Ormonde to the 1st Earl of Orrery (q.v.) in order to assist William Robinson (q.v.) who had less experience in fortifications than Archer, with the extensive rebuilding of Rincurran (later Charles) Fort, near Kinsale.[21] Orrery had a high opinion of Archer, and found him 'very diligent, frugal, faithful and industrious ...'.[22] Archer was occupied with Rincurran Fort for nearly two years. Apart from his regular salary he also received in February 1678 £20 from the secret money account.[23] Nothing is

Archer

known about his subsequent career. He possibly died in 1680 after having been engineer for 26 years to Charles II.[24] He was survived by his wife Anne, whose last petition for the arrears of her annual pension of £100, is dated 1703.[25] James Archer had five children, three at least of whom also became engineers. His eldest son Major Francis Archer was slain at the siege of Maastricht in 1676,[26] while in the service of the Prince of Orange.[27] James Archer junior became an engineer in Virginia.[28] The youngest son Walter Archer, in 1678, received an allowance, as had his brothers Francis and James earlier, to travel in order to improve his knowledge of fortifications.[29] Both James and Walter died prematurely, however, one at the siege of Cork, the other in the service of King William III.[30]

[1] R. C. Simington (Ed.), *The Civil Survey, a.d. 1654–6, County of Waterford*, Dublin, 1942, 504, 513.
[2] Bodl. Carte Ms 221, f. 213.
[3] W. H. Hardinge, *A Memoir on Manuscript mapped and other Townland Surveys in Ireland*, Dublin, 1863, 47, 60, 97.
[4] PRO, SP 29/338, f. 138.
[5] *HMC. 6th Rep.*, 731.
[6] PRO, SP 29/338, f. 138.
[7] *HMC, Ormonde*, n.s. III, 142.
[8] Bodl., Carte Ms 221, f. 213.
[9] Bodl., Carte Ms 34, f. 530ᵛ–2.
[10] Bodl., Carte Ms 34, f. 532ᵛ–4. See also PRO, SP 29/338, f. 138 for another version.
[11] Bodl., Carte Ms 34, f. 529.
[12] The Franciscan Fathers, *Father Luke Wadding*, Dublin, 1957, 209; Bodl., Carte Ms 221, f. 213.
[13] PRO, SP 29/338, f. 138.
[14] *CSPD*, 1666–7, 144.
[15] Bodl., Carte Ms 160, f. 47ᵛ; *CSPD*, 1670, 14, 705.
[16] PRO, SP 29/338, f. 138.
[17] *HMC, Ormonde*, n.s., III, 311.
[18] *CSPD*, 1672–3, 470, 510, 549; *HMC, 11th Rep. App. V*, 20.
[19] O. Hill & J. Cornforth, *English Country Houses, Caroline*, London, 1966, 229.
[20] *CSPD*, 1673–5, 80–1; PRO, SP 29/338, f. 138.
[21] *HMC, 6th Rep.*, 731.
[22] *HMC, Ormonde*, n.s. IV, 260.
[23] Bodl., Carte Ms 38, f. 512.
[24] *CSPD*, 1680–1, 136; *CTB*, 1689–92, pt. IV, 1493.
[25] BL, Add. Ms 21137, f. 15.
[26] *CSPD*, 1676–7, 238.
[27] *HMC, 6th Rep.*, 731.
[28] *CSP Colonial America & W. Indies*, 1675–85, *passim*.
[29] *CSPD*, 1678, 536.
[30] BL, Add. Ms 21137, f. 15.

CARRICK-ON-SUIR, BRIDGE, CO. TIPPERARY. Near the Ormonde residence, Archer in November 1668 finished one half of the bridge in ten weeks, and cleared the river Suir at this place from rocks in order to make it navigable for ships and thus stimulate commerce at Carrick-on-Suir. He was offered £3 for his work, but found this too little. He planned also to erect an ice-house near Ormonde's residence there, where he had already carried out some minor repairs (*HMC, Ormonde*, n.s. III, 288–90).

CLONMEL, LORD ORMONDE'S HOUSE, CO. TIPPERARY. On January 12, 1669 Ormonde planned to live at his house at Clonmel, and ordered the dining room to be enlarged, the roof raised, stables and offices to be built, etc., adding that 'Capt. Archer may be the fittest man to contrive the thing and oversee the worke ...' (Bodl., Carte Ms 50, f. 1). The house was out of repair in 1686 (BL, Landsdowne Ms 1153). An inventory is mentioned in *HMC, Ormonde, n.s. VII*, 509. Dem.

KILKENNY CASTLE. On January 28, 1669 Lady Ormonde ordered the roof of the old hall of the Castle to be repaired by the carpenter [?Giles] Taylor; she mentions that 'Archer' was to oversee the work, which probably refers to Capt. James Archer (*HMC, Ormonde*, n.s. III, 440).

KINSALE, CO. CORK, RINCURRAN (later CHARLES) FORT. From 1677 till at least 1679 Archer oversaw the erection of the fort, designed by William Robinson (q.v.) and the Earl of Orrery (q.v.). Archer seems also to have been actively involved in the planning of the fort and the making of contracts for materials and workmen (Bodl., Carte Ms 70, f. 461; NLI, Ms 2379, f. 17).

ARMSTEAD, WILLIAM (fl. 1664), a contractor. When the 1st Earl of Orrery (q.v.) planned to build sod works at Castle Park Fort in 1666, near Kinsale, the only man fit to do them was, according to Orrery, the man working on his ponds[1] at his house at Charleville (now Rathluirc, Co. Cork). This was most likely William Armstead, who was later employed by Orrery to work on Rincurran Fort, together with Thomas Smith (q.v.), his partner for many years. Armstead and Smith also worked on the Orrery estate at Charleville, where both were paid in 1667 for work on Orrery's schoolhouse in the town of Rathluirc,[2] and it seems likely that Armstead also functioned as comptroller in Orrery's household, for in many of Armstead's letters to Orrery estate matters were discussed.[3] Armstead's name is present on Orrery's rent roll for 1674, and in 1680 after Orrery's death, Armstead and Smith inquired of his widow, the Dowager Countess of Orrery, about the lease of Ballismuttan, near Shandrum, 4 m. SW. of Rathluirc.[4] Armstead's last known documented involvement with building is recorded in the *Egmont Papers*. On February 29, 1681[-82] the steward of Sir John Perceval wrote about the slow progress of Perceval's residence, Burton House in Co. Cork. Thomas Smith had contracted for the rebuilding of this country house, but Perceval's steward mentions in his letter that 'Mr Armstead and Smyth' had surveyed the (? mason's) work, and found that they (? the masons) had all been overpaid.[5] In 1682 the 2nd Earl of Orrery had also died, and Armstead and Smith requested of his mother, the Dowager Lady Orrery, payment of £600 which they had lent to her son two years earlier; Armstead had received a lease from him, but both lease and money were politely refused.[6] On the Orrery rent roll of 1685 Armstead was the person who paid for the lands of Kippane the highest rent of all of Orrery's tenants. Two years later he had brought his financial conflict about his lease with Lady Orrery to the High Court of Chancery.[7] It is possible that he died shortly afterwards. He had married a Sarah Simpson in 1664.[8] The Dublin joiners, Francis and Thomas Armstead (fl. 1700),[9] may have been his relatives.

[1] T. Morrice, *A Collection of the State Letters of R. Boyle, the first Earl of Orrery*, London, 1743, 164.
[2] NLI, N6268–6271, Pos 7074–7077.
[3] NLI, N6268–6271, Pos 7074–7077.
[4] E. MacLysaght, *Calendar of Orrery Papers*, Dublin, 1941, 228–9.
[5] BL, Add. Ms 46958B, f. 241. See also Add. Ms 46958C.
[6] MacLysaght, *op.cit.*, 132, 275*ff*; NLI, Mss 34, f. 367; Ms 35, ff. 433, 466.
[7] MacLysaght, *op.cit.*, 310, 325; NLI, N6268–6271, Pos 7074–7077.
[8] H. W. Gillman, *Index to Marriage License Bonds of the Diocese of Cork and Ross ...*, Cork, 1896–7, 4.
[9] *JRSAI*, 1922, 162.

KINSALE, CO. CORK, RINCURRAN (later CHARLES) FORT. Having probably worked at the nearby Castle Park Fort in 1666, in March 1667[-68] Armstead and Thomas Smith presented their first proposal to finish Rincurran Fort (*HMC, 6th Rep.*, 778), which had been renovated by Roger Boyle, Earl of Orrery (q.v.) the year previously. Their proposal was not accepted, but in 1672, under the engineer in chief, Capt. Paulus Storff (q.v.), they erected all the stone work (except the gate and its ornaments), for which a contract was drawn up on January 29, 1671[-72] between Orrery and Armstead and Smith (NLI, Ms 2355, f. 67–8).

They were to employ 40 masons, and their account in 1673 amounted to £789 1*s*. 8*d*. (NLI, N6268–6271, Pos 7074–7077). When in 1678 the fort was expanded after the designs of William Robinson (q.v.), Armstead and Smith concluded a contract for the stonework with Robinson and the overseer Capt. James Archer on March 12, 1677[-78], which among other things stipulated that either Armstead or Smith had to attend at the building (BL, Add. Ms 28085, f. 196ᵛ). It seems likely that both partners were still involved at later repairs of the fort, for they both addressed a letter from the fort to Lady Orrery on March 30, 1680 (MacLysaght, *op.cit.*, 228).

CORK, ST FINBAR'S CATHEDRAL. On April 5, 1677 the Chapter of the Cathedral decreed that £20 should be given as a gratuity to Armstead and Thomas Smith in consideration for their 'laudable care' in building the tower of the Cathedral (R. Caulfield, *Annals of St Fin Barre's Cathedral*, Cork, 1871, 40). Replaced.

RATHLUIRC, formerly CHARLEVILLE, CO. CORK, SCHOOLHOUSE, built by Armstead and Thomas Smith (q.v.) for the Earl of Orrery (q.v.) in 1667 (NLI, N6268–6271, Pos 7074–7077).

ATTRIBUTION

RATHLUIRC, CO. CORK, CHARLEVILLE CASTLE, had been designed by the 1st Earl of Orrery (q.v.). When Orrery sent for the two people with whom he had contracted for the building of Rincurran Fort in 1671, he mentioned that these men, being 'good artists', had more than £4,000 of Orrery's money for building for him (*HMC, Ormonde*, n.s. IV, 100–1). There is little doubt that the men referred to were Armstead and Smith, who most likely had executed a greater part of the stone work of Charleville Castle from 1661 onwards, although their names occur only occasionally in the sparse surviving accounts. Dem.

B

BALL, THOMAS (fl. 1668). From 1668 till at least 1673 he acted as overseer for the building of the Blue Coat School in Oxmantown, near Dublin (Dem.). The craftsmen involved were Ralph Allen, William Rothery, and Paul Fleeson, masons, John Savage and John Greene, carpenters, Robert Massy and Thomas Reynor, joiners, William Robinson, and Isaac Chalk, plasterers.[1]

[1] C. Lucas, *A Narrative and an Accompt Concerning the Hospital on Oxmantown-Green, Dublin . . .*, Dublin, 1749 *ff*; King's Hospital, Palmerstown, Co. Dublin: Blue Coat School Account Books (I am greatly indebted to M/s L. Whiteside for allowing me access to these manuscripts, and for giving me valuable advice); NLI, Ms 13659(4); *CARD*, IV, 495.

BALTINGLASS, 1st Viscount, see Roper, Sir Thomas.

BANNISTER, JOHN (fl. 1619–1649), Master Carpenter of Ireland. He was admitted to the freedom of the City of Dublin in 1611,[1] and obtained a patent for the office of Master Carpenter in Ireland on January 15, 1619, 'for the reparation of Our castles and houses, and for the erecting of other buildings and works . . .'.[2] He presumably worked under supervision of the Clerk of the Royal Works, Samuel Molyneux (q.v.). Curiously enough, John Bannister's name does not occur on most lists of the Irish Establishment,[3] nor is his name evident on known accounts of the Works. A John Banister [sic], carpenter, died in Dublin in 1649 when his will was proved.[4] The position lapsed during the Commonwealth and was reinstated in 1661 by the appointment of John Mills (q.v.).

[1] *CARD*, III, p. 9.
[2] *Royal Engineer's Journal*, 1909, *10*, 126.
[3] As for example in 1622, *cf.* Kent County Library, Sackville Ms ON 8541.
[4] *Appendix 26th Report of the Deputy Keeper of the Public Records in Ireland*, Dublin, 1895, 34. A will abstract in the Geneal. Office (Ms 290, p. 32) may possibly refer to him. However, there were certainly more individuals of this name. A John Bannister was admitted as freeman in Dublin in 1628 (this could have been his son). A Capt. John 'Banistre' is noted in Ireland in 1646 (*CSPI*, 1633–47, 451).

BECKETT, RANDALL (also **RANDOLPH**) (fl. 1633–1673), Overseer of the Public Works. He is first noted in 1633 when elected as Steward to the King's Inn in Dublin, after which he had 'a mixed career of open impudence or concealed fraud . . .' as Under Treasurer of the Inns till at least 1657. In 1637 he is mentioned in connection with the newly built summer house in the gardens of the Inn, but this, and later payments to him, are unclear indicators of Beckett's architectural skills.[1] During the period of the Commonwealth, Beckett was appointed Overseer of the Public Works (?1653). The official patent, however, has not been found. For this position he received a daily stipend of 3*s*. 3*d*. till as late as August 8, 1660. By then he was only involved in minor repairs on the wash-house at Kilmainham bridge, Phoenix House, the King's Bench, the Armoury, the stables of Dublin Castle, and the Custom House.[2] At the Restoration he lost the position in favour of Capt. John Paine (q.v.) and Capt. John Hallam (q.v.), although the last recorded payment to him in relation to Royal Works occurred in 1663. In 1665 he petitioned the Duke of Ormonde regarding the recovery of debt.[3] He made his will on January 28, 1673 (proved March 7, 1673), in which he mentioned his wife Anne, his son William, his daughter Hanna who was married to Thomas Crowe, and another daughter married to Richard Reynell.[4]

[1] B. T. Duhigg, *History of the King's Inns ...*, Dublin, 1806, I, 158–163, 368, 370; PROI, Lodge Ms, Members of the King's Inns, p. 132–3.
[2] *HMC, Ormonde*, n.s. III, 385.
[3] *HMC, 9th Rep. App. II*, 170.
[4] Geneal. Office, Ms 281, f. 6.

DUBLIN, CUSTOM HOUSE. Erected in 1638–40; Beckett and John Mills were paid in 1656 a number of times for finishing the building (*Analecta Hibernica*, 1944, *13*, pp. 292, 294), in order to house the Privy Council, Court of Exchequer, Treasury, and Pells Office. Decorative painting in the Council Chamber was executed by Richard Carney, Ulster King at Arms. In 1663 Beckett received £35 7s. 6d. for more repairs at the Custom House (Bodl., Carte Ms 52, f. 264). Burned 1711.

PHOENIX HOUSE, CO. DUBLIN. Beckett and John Mills were paid several times in 1656 for work at this former Royal lodge (*Analecta Hibernica*, 1944, *15*, 292, 294), which probably involved the addition of a wing to the house for Henry Cromwell. In 1662 Beckett received another payment of £69 10s. 3d. for repairs at the Parliament House (also Chichester House) and Phoenix House (Bodl., Carte Ms 52, f. 262), where he probably assisted Dr John Westley (q.v.) in the rebuilding. Dem.

DUBLIN CASTLE. Beckett and John Mills were paid for repairs on one of the towers of the Castle, and the 'burnt' stores, probably also in the Castle, in May and June 1656 (*Analecta Hibernica*, 1944, *15*, 292, 294).

DUBLIN, TOWN HOUSE. After 1633 he obtained a lease of land on the King's Inns property, and erected there a house of 10 hearths (Duhigg, *op.cit.*, I, 369; *57th Rep. Deputy Keeper of the Public Records in Ireland*, 1936, 562).

BENSON, PETER (fl. 1614–1642), a tiler and bricklayer from London,[1] who tendered successfully for the building of the walls of Londonderry in 1614 for the Irish Society,[2] after the 'model' designed by either Sir Edward Doddington (q.v.) or Capt. Panton, and overseen by John Vaughan. In addition, as chief mason he was in charge of the masons putting up houses within the walls. By 1618 the walls and gates were finished at a cost of at least £10,757, and even the critical Sir Thomas Phillips could find little fault with them. As late as 1624 Benson petitioned the King for £1,157 2s. 10d. as his arrears in this work. Benson's fame spread quickly, and in 1615 was recommended for the building of the castle at Lizard in Co. Derry for the Ironmonger's Company. A surviving plan in the records of the Company shows a residence of 60 foot length within a fort with four flankers surrounded by a ditch.[3]

As an undertaker Benson was granted 1,500 acres at Shraghmiclar, near Lifford, in Co. Donegal, on which he built, according to the survey of 1622 'a house slated of lyme and stone, and Birch Timber 58 foot long, 20 foot wide, with 2 Returnes, the one 36 foot long and 20 foot wide, the other 28 foot long, and 18 foot wide, being a storie and a half high, which house is compassed with a Bawne of lyme & stone 120 foot square, with 4 Flankers, 12 foot square a peece, the Bawne and Flankers 9 foot high, wherein the said Benson, his wife & Familie inhabite.' Like most settlers, Benson founded a nearby village 'of 10 houses & Cottages, whereof 3 are stone houses: 50 foot long a peece, one of them covered with thatch, the other two not covered ...'. The plan of Lizard Castle, and the description of Shraghmiclar Castle show an asymmetrical appearance within a bawn.[4] In 1621 he is mentioned among the first burgesses of the new charter of Londonderry,[5] and in 1639 became Mayor of the City. He died on August 24, 1642 as recorded in the Derry Cathedral register.

[1] Most of the following information is from C. D. Milligan, *The Walls of Derry*, Londonderry, 1948, I, 26 *ff.*
[2] C. A. Chart (Ed.), *Londonderry and the London Companies*, Belfast, 1928, 45–6.
[3] G. Hill (Ed.), *An Historical Account of the Plantation in Ulster ...*, Belfast, 1877, 442; J. Nicholl, *Some Account of the Worshipfull Company of Ironmongers*, London, 1851, 415, 420–2; *CSPI*, 1615–25, 382–3. Notice that this plan little corresponds with the contemporary view of the Ironmongers' buildings published in D. A. Chart (Ed.), *Londonderry and the London Companies, 1609–1629*, Belfast, 1928, pl. 21. There the buildings are identified at Agivey rather than Lizard.
[4] Hill, *op.cit.*, 514–5, BL, Add Ms 4756, f. 115.
[5] M. C. Griffith, *Irish Patent Rolls of James I*, Dublin, 1966, 164, 538.

BIRKETT, GEORGE (fl. 1614), bricklayer and builder from London. He was sent over to Ulster *c.* 1614 by the Drapers' Company of the city of London to build the castle at Moneymore, the Drapers' plantation in Co. Derry.[1] The castle became a long building with curvilinear gables inside a large bawn, or court, defended by two flankers.[2] It was almost finished by 1620.[3] However, the construction of the bawn was weak and, according to a report of the preceding year, did not allow the construction of a moat.[4] Nearby six stone and six timber houses had been erected by 1620, one of which was occupied by Birkett, his wife and children. Also in the little village lived the carpenter James Bodkin,[5] who in all likelihood assisted in the building of the smaller houses and the castle. Presumably as part of his payment, Birkett received a lease of 15 acres and the residence, on the conditions that he would enclose the 15 acres with trees, provide himself with arms, and pave the street in front of his door.[6] As late as 1632 he was living at Moneymore as appears from a letter in which he complained that his right to the house and the land was disputed by the new agent of the Drapers. He stated that he had expected to receive more employment in his trade on the Drapers' estate, which did not take place for 'so longe atyme'.[7] Little is known about Birkett's work for other patrons. He was appointed 'Surveyor' by the parishioners of Donoghenry, near Stewartstown, Co. Tyrone, to repair their ruined parish church, but its stones were taken away for another purpose.[8] Consequently Birkett may have failed to obtain benefit from the commission. His later life remains obscure.

[1] T. W. Moody, *The Londonderry Plantation*, Belfast, 1939, 322.
[2] E. M. Jope, Moyry, Charlemont, Castleraw and Richhill: fortification to architecture in the north of Ireland, *Ulster Journal of Archaeology*, 1960, 3rd series, *23*, Fig. 9; C. Falls, *The Birth of Ulster*, London, 1936, opp. p. 196; Moody, *op.cit.*, 301–311; *CSPI*, 1615–25, 384.
[3] A. H. Johnson, *The History of the Worshipful Company of the Drapers of London*, Oxford, 1922, IV, 527.
[4] Moody, *op.cit.*, 305.
[5] Johnson, *op.cit.*, 527, 545.
[6] Moody, *op.cit.*, 317.
[7] Guild Hall, London, Drapers Archives under 'Manor of Drapers', July 31, 1632, George Birkett to the Drapers' Company.
[8] NLI, Ms 8014 (viii).

BODLEY, Sir JOSIAS (*c.* 1550–1617), Director-General of the Fortifications and Buildings in Ireland. Although his life has been treated in the *Dictionary of National Biography* much new information has come to light since.[1] He was born at Exeter in about 1550. His father, the youngest son of John Bodley and his wife Joan Hone, took his whole family (including his later famous son Thomas) to Wesel and Geneva, where Josias received his early education. It is said that this brought him into contact with illustrious scholars such as Calvin, Chevallier, and Beza. At the accession of Elizabeth I the family returned to England after which he studied at

Merton College, Oxford, but left without taking a degree. As has been suspected by former biographers, he went to Danzig in Poland, where the English ambassador noticed 'Mr Bodligha's' son in 1581 in relation to commercial interests.[2] However, he chose a military career, and in 1615 he could boast of having had three apprenticeships in the army, and these may have included continental experience. Little is known about his early life as a soldier. By 1586 he was in the Earl of Leicester's army in the Low Countries, when he and his two servants were stationed at Leyden.[3] From the Netherlands he was sent to Ulster in 1598 as a captain in the army under Sir Samuel Bagnell in order to take part in the campaign against the Earl of Tyrone. Bodley and his company of foot were first stationed at Newry, and later at the new fort of Mountnorris. He took part in skirmishes at Carlingford and Loghrorcan, and won the praise of the Lord Deputy Mountjoy. Whether he was asked to design or build one of a number of the forts which Lord Mountjoy erected in Ulster in 1600 remains unclear. In the following year Bodley had to resign as governor of Newry in order to join the army in Munster, where the war had moved. Under the Lord President of Munster, Sir George Carew, he took part in an attack on the Spaniards who had landed at Kinsale. There he distinguished himself as a 'trenchmaster generall', although he is said to have acted as chief engineer, and undoubtedly was in charge of the building of the siege forts.[4] In the same year, 1601, he donated to the Bodleian Library an astronomical sphere and a quadrant, which may be taken as a sign of his interest or skill in mathematics. After the defeat of the Spaniards in Kinsale he is said to have been at the sieges of Baltimore, Berehaven and Castlehaven, all in Co. Cork.[5] In January 1602 he went to England with a recommendation by Lord Mountjoy to the Privy Council. In that year two new forts were built, Castle Park and Halebolin, but their design was left to Paul Ive. Bodley did not have any involvement in these projects. He returned to Ireland in the same year and was once more stationed in Ulster, now as governor of Armagh. In 1603, however, Bodley and his company were transferred to the City of Waterford where the governor was Sir Richard Moryson, later Vice-President of Munster. From 1604 to 1606 he held the governorship of the nearby fort of Duncannon. For his good services he was knighted by Lord Mountjoy on March 25, 1604. In 1603 or 1604 he, Sir Arthur Chichester and the Dutch engineer Levan De Rose selected the sites of the citadels to command the cities and ports of Waterford, Cork and Limerick.[6] In 1605 he went to England with plans for these which presumably were presented to King James I. He returned with orders to start building the citadels of Waterford (St Patrick's Fort) and Cork and other fortifications, but had to resign the governorship of Duncannon and the command of his Company of foot. In return for the latter he received a pension. Initially he was engaged on fortifications in Ulster, where he finished Mountjoy Fort, but seems to have interrupted his work for, from at least as early as April 1606, he was in London, probably to promote his own interests, for his payments had not been forthcoming.[7] He was badly missed by the Lord Deputy Chichester who urged his return to complete the fortifications in Ireland. Finally, in 1607, Bodley obtained, as the first military officer in Ireland, the post of Superintendent of the Castles in Ireland at a daily stipend of 20 shillings, and returning to Ireland at the end of that year as 'the Agent' of the English Privy Council to superintend the fortifications at Cork, Limerick, Waterford and Kinsale.[8] His new position, however, was not a patent, but part of the yearly Establishment, which caused him to run into debt.

On his return, until the end of 1608, he rode more than 700 miles inspecting fortifications and garrisons in Munster (accompanied by the Lord President Sir John Danvers)[9] and in Ulster. Bodley's report on the latter is now in the British

Library.[10] In the supervision of the fortifications he was assisted by two Dutch engineers, Levan De Rose and Joyes Everard. Bodley became responsible for the strengthening of the coastal fortifications against a foreign attack, which led him to finish the forts of Duncannon in Co. Wexford, Halebolin, Elizabeth Fort, both near Cork, St Augustine's Fort, near Galway, and to improve Limerick Castle.[11] He was also instrumental in the building of the town walls of Coleraine for the City of London. In the case of works in Co. Cork Samuel Molyneux (q.v.), Clerk of the Royal Works, later sought to replace Bodley, but was unsuccessful, despite his being recommended by the Lord Deputy Chichester. Little is known about Bodley's activities between 1608 and 1611. A sparse note by Sir Francis Bacon in the summer of 1608 shows that a Mr [? Inigo] Jones was to introduce Sir Josias Bodley to him. He perhaps wanted Bodley's expert advice, for Bacon completed his 'Certain Considerations touching the Plantation in Ireland' in that year.[12]

In 1611 Bodley was still busy finishing the forts in Munster and Galway.[13] In that year he petitioned 'some competent allowance during the few days [sic] that he has to live . . .' but offered nevertheless optimistically to survey all the forts in Ireland.[14] It was not until January 29, 1613 that he finally received a patent creating him Director-General and Overseer of the Fortifications and Buildings in Ireland for life at his former salary. This position was an amalgamation of his former office with that of the supervision of the Royal Works. This made him apparently from then onwards the superior of Samuel Molyneux, Clerk of the Works (q.v.).

In March of that year he returned to England, presumably to attend the funeral of his brother Thomas Bodley, which took place on March 29. Thomas bequeathed Josias a meagre £100 and leaseholds in London, and a release from debt of loans. In November Bodley, still in London, was requested by the Lord Deputy Chichester to inform the Privy Council regarding the sites and plans of the proposed citadels at Cork and Waterford,[15] but both remained unfinished at the end of Bodley's career. He went once more to England in March 1614, together with Sir Arthur Chichester and Sir John Davies.[16] Evidence is lacking to show that Bodley in his last three-and-a-half years was involved with fortifications. In summarizing his career, because all his work on fortifications was limited to alterations and improvements, his skill as an engineer is hard to assess. Only six drawings by him, which have been identified by Mr W. O'Sullivan, are known. They are the plans of the Castle of Limerick, and the forts near Cork, Waterford and Galway.[17] Nothing is known about his involvement in the repairs of the Royal Works such as Dublin Castle. Whether he acted as a private architect is unclear. However, the enormous amount of building activity in the plantations of Ulster, and the relative lack of skilled architects there, makes it likely that he became involved in domestic architecture.

A major part of Bodley's professional duty was the surveying of lands. In government accounts he is mentioned as 'surveyor and overseer of the plantations to be made in Ireland'. His first survey, with William Parsons the Surveyor-General of the Lands, took place in 1609 and covered the six escheated counties in Ulster. This, he later claimed, was 'his invention wholly', and only accomplished by himself and his assistants who completed the survey, from which maps were produced, in sixty-seven days.[18] Three years later, with John Ball, he covered Ulster again, this time in order to survey the new plantations.[19] He received the thanks of James I, who instructed that Bodley should survey the planations in 1616.[20] In September 1614, however, Bodley was appointed by the Lord Deputy to inquire into the progress of the London Companies' plantations in Co. Derry. Again, his report was presented to James I.[21] Bodley brought out his last report on the City of London's plantations in 1616.[22] Finally, in March of the year of his death, he surveyed 16,500 acres in Co. Wexford for the new plantation there using the improved technique of measuring with the chain.[23]

He died unmarried on August 22, 1617, and was buried four days later in Christ Church Cathedral, Dublin. A contemporary recalled that 'his last memorable action was drinking to his friends in a cup of Kanary [wine]'. After his death the office of Director-General passed to Capt. Nicholas Pynnar (q.v.) and Sir Thomas Rotheram (q.v.). Bodley left no will, but made his executor the Lord Deputy Sir Oliver St John,[24] who had been his immediate superior as Master of the Ordnance. One can only speculate about who inherited Bodley's papers as he was only survived in the male line by the sons of his deceased brother Miles. No portrait of Bodley has been identified. He left a number of letters, most of which are now among the Irish State Papers in the PRO. The extent of his estate is unknown. Although he was considered in 1610 as a possible undertaker for the new planations in Ulster, he failed to obtain a grant, a fact about which he complained bitterly. He was often in financial difficulties. On several occasions he successfully sought the help of the English Secretary of State, Sir Ralph Winwood, who by marrying Sir Thomas Bodley's stepdaughter in 1603 became related to him. Bodley wrote a playful description in doggerel Latin of a journey to Lecale in 1602, which was popular as late as 1634. His 'Observations concerning the fortresses of Ireland, and the British Colonies of Ulster' has been mentioned as among the Clarendon Mss but has not been found,[25] and may be similar to his report on the forts and garrisons in the north of Ireland now in the British Library.[26]

---

[1] Much of the following information is derived from W. P. Pakenham-Walsh, 'Capt. Sir Josias Bodley', *Royal Engineers' Journal*, 1906, 253–64, supplemented with the *Biographia Britannia*, 1778–93, 2nd ed., II, 393–4.

[2] *CSP Foreign*, 1583, 582.

[3] R. C. Strong & J. A. Van Dorsten, *Leicester's Triumph*, Leyden, 1964, 110.

[4] F. Moryson, *An Itinerary*, Glasgow, 1907, II, 15; PRO, A.O. 1/288/1082. I am indebted to Dr John Andrews for showing me this last source. See also 'A Letter from a Souldier of good Place in Ireland' (1602), printed in A. F. Kinney (Ed.), *Elizabethan Backgrounds*, Hamden, Conn., 1975, 352.

[5] *Biographia Britannia*, 1778–93, 2nd ed., II, 393.

[6] *Analecta Hibernica*, 1938, *8*, 141; PRO, A.O. 1/289/1085.

[7] *HMC, Salisbury*, XVIII, 380.

[8] BL, Add. Ms 11402, f. 138.

[9] PRO, SP 63/223, f. 375–6.

[10] BL, Lansdowne Ms 156, f. 335–6ᵛ, published in *UJA*, 1910, series 2, *16*, 61–4.

[11] Between 1607 and 1609 he was paid over £6,666 for this purpose (PRO, A.O. 1/290/1088).

[12] J. Spedding (Ed.), *The Letters and the Life of Francis Bacon*, London, 1868–90, IV, 66, 110.

[13] *HMC, Salisbury, XXI*, 305–6. See also footnote 26.

[14] *CSPI*, 1611–14, 154–5.

[15] *Analecta Hibernica*, 1938, *8*, 122.

[16] R. Bagwell, *Ireland under the Stuarts*, London 1909, I, 127.

[17] TCD, Ms 1209, ff. 11, 48, 59, 65, 71. He is also known to have drawn a large trout caught in Tyrone (D. B. Quinn, *The Elizabethans and the Irish*, Ithaca, 1965, 166).

[18] PRO, A.O. 1/290/1088; J. H. Andrews, 'The Maps of the Escheated Counties of Ulster', 1609–10, *Proceedings of the Royal Irish Academy*, 1974, *74*, section C, No. 4.

[19] PRO, A.O. 1/290/1090. The survey was printed in *HMC, Hastings*, IV 159–182; (the original is now in the Huntington Library, San Marino, California, Ms HA 13964). See also T. W. Moody, *The Londonderry Plantation, 1609–41*, Belfast, 1939, 159–165.

[20] A. H. Johnson, *The History of the Worshipful Company of the Drapers of London)*, Oxford, IV, 505–7.

[21] J. Brett, *The Story of the Irish Society*, London, 1921, 63.

[22] C. D. Milligan, *The Walls of Derry*, Londonderry, 1948, pt 1, 35; Moody, *op.cit.*, 177.

[23] *HMC, Buccleuch and Queensberry*, I, 190, 193–4.

[24] *Grosart*, series 2, II, 102.

[25] *Biographia Britannia*, 1778–93, 2nd ed., II, 394. Information kindly provided by Mr W. O'Sullivan.

[26] BL, Lansdowne Ms 156, ff. 335–6ᵛ; between 1611 and 1613 Bodley was paid for viewing the forts in the provinces of Leinster, Connaught and Munster (PRO, A.O. 1/290/1090) which may have led to this

report. A survey of the Munster forts is in Bodley's letter to Lord Carew, endorsed 1611 (Lambeth Palace, Ms 629, f. 146–7).

MOUNTJOY FORT, CO. TYRONE. In 1605 Bodley completed this fort which had been started by either Josias Everard or Levan De Rose (*CSPI, passim*).

DUNCANNON FORT, CO. WEXFORD. Probably from 1608 onwards until 1611 he reinforced the bulwarks, raised a mount and executed repairs (*CSPI, passim; Carew*, 1603–24, *passim*). Bodley's drawing of the fort is in TCD, Ms 1209, f. 11.

CORK, HALEBOLIN FORT. The unfinished fort was completed between 1608 and 1611 by Bodley, who erected a castle in its centre, lodgings for soldiers, and executed a number of repairs (*CSPI, passim; Carew*, 1603–24, *passim*).

KINSALE, CASTLE PARK FORT. Bodley finished the uncompleted fort by erecting a square tower in its centre, and two 'castles' at two opposite flankers, and reinforced the ramparts (*CSPI, passim; Carew*, 1603–24, *passim*). Bodley's drawing of the fort is in TCD, Ms 1209, f. 48.

LIMERICK CASTLE. Between 1608 and 1611 Bodley reinforced the foundation of its towers and erected a bulwark on the town side (*CSPI, passim; Carew*, 1603–24, *passim*). Bodley's drawing of the fort is in TCD, Ms 1209, f. 59.

GALWAY, ST AUGUSTINE'S FORT. Between 1608 and 1611 this fort, which had started to slide, was stabilized by Bodley who enclosed it with two stone walls, made parapets, ditch, and lodgings within (*CSPI, passim; Carew*, 1603–24, *passim*). Bodley's drawing of the fort is in TCD, Ms 1209, f. 71.

CORK, ELIZABETH FORT. Bodley presented in 1605 and in 1613 a plan for this citadel, which had been demolished ten years earlier. The fort remained uncompleted until 1624 (*CSPI, passim; Analecta Hibernica*, 1938, 8, 150–1, *JWAS*, 1899, 5, 152). Bodley's drawing of the fort is in TCD, Ms 1209, f. 48.

WATERFORD, ST PATRICK'S FORT. Bodley's plan for this citadel is mentioned in 1605 and in 1613 and survives at TCD, Ms 1209, f. 65, and has been published in *Loeber*, pl. 6. The fort remained uncompleted until 1625 (*CSPI, passim*).

COLERAINE, TOWN WALLS, CO. DERRY. After 1610 Bodley built the town walls of sods on behalf of the City of London (*CSPI*, 1615–25, 501).

BOUGHTON, WILLIAM (fl. 1642), directed the making of outworks about St Augustine's Fort, near Galway in 1642[1]. In January of the following year he was sent by the governor of the fort, Capt. Anthony Willoughby, to England to report to the Parliament on the weakness of the fort. He may have been a civilian for he is mentioned without a military rank.[2] Possibly he can be identified with the Boughton who worked for the Earl of Clanricarde on the building of Portumna Castle, Co. Galway in the early 17th century.[3]

[1] *HMC, 13th Rep. App. I*, 84.
[2] It seems less likely that he can be identified with the Capt. Boughton, who was stationed in Dublin in 1643–4 (*HMC, Ormonde*, n.s. I, 158).
[3] M. Craig, *Portumna Castle*, Dublin, 1976, 4–5.

BOYLE, ROGER, Baron Broghill, and 1st Earl of Orrery (1621–1679). He was the third son of Richard Boyle, 1st Earl of Cork, and Catherine, daughter of Sir Geoffrey Fenton. Roger Boyle's life as soldier, statesman and playwright has been extensively described in the *Dictionary of National Biography*, and in K. M. Lynch's biography *Roger Boyle, first Earl of Orrery* (Knoxville, 1965). His career as a gentleman-architect and engineer only is described here. He grew up in Ireland, where he was created Baron Broghill at the age of six. On the vast estates of his father he must have witnessed the almost continuous improvement of residences which occupied his father for many decades. His early impressions about these are not known. As a youth he was educated at Trinity College, Dublin, and travelled through France, Italy and Switzerland in 1637–9. He was accompanied by his brother Lewis, Viscount Kinalmeaky and a French tutor, who had been selected by Sir Henry Wotton, the author of *The Elements of Architecture* first published in 1624. Abroad, Broghill visited not only the chief cities, but fortresses and arsenals also. In Geneva he studied mathematics among other subjects, 'especially the knowledge of the sphera and of the architecture'.[1] Otherwise little is known about his exposure to ancient or contemporary architecture in Europe. He married Margaret, daughter of the 2nd Earl of Suffolk in 1641. He returned to Ireland on the very day that the great Rebellion started, and took immediate command in the army. In February 1643 he and his brother Richard, Viscount Dungarvan, were employed by their father to make entrenchments around the town of Tallow in Co. Waterford.[2] In the following year Broghill gave instructions for the repair of the town walls of Youghal,[3] which he possibly supervised personally. Presumably in 1648 he became Lieutenant-General of the Ordnance in Ireland, which office undoubtedly brought him in close contact with engineers such as William Webb, Miles Symner (q.v.) and the future Master Carpenter of Ireland, John Mills (q.v.).[4] Possibly during this period he saw to the restoration of Dunboy Fort, near Berehaven in Co. Cork. On the execution of Charles I, he left the army, and retired to his English estate at Marston in Somersetshire. However, he accepted a general's command from Cromwell in the war against the Irish, and returned to Ireland actively participating in the war. During this time he built the fort at Bantry and other garrisons to defend the coast of Co. Cork for which he received at least £150.[5] Whether he himself prepared designs for these fortifications remains unclear. In 1658 he resided at Ballymaloe in Co. Cork, which, together with other estates, had been granted to him. He failed to persuade Cromwell to accept the Crown, and after the latter's death took steps to invite Charles II to land in Ireland. His reversion to the Royalist cause was accepted without much resistance, and he, with Sir Charles Coote and Sir Maurice Eustace, were appointed Lord Justices of Ireland on October 26, 1660. Soon Broghill received other Royal awards, including the title of Earl of Orrery, and subsequently the office of Lord President of Munster. Orrery had hoped to become Lord Lieutenant of Ireland, but this post was given to the Duke of Ormonde. In the autumn of 1661 Orrery stayed at the Royal residence, Phoenix House, and prepared plans for alterations there for the reception of Ormonde. Prior to this he had been his own architect for the building of Charleville Castle in Co. Cork, which he used as his official residence as Lord President. Presumably emphasizing the defensive characteristics of Charleville Castle and not so much its architectural features, he wrote to Ormonde that he pretended 'something to engineership'.[6] If Orrery had any more notions about architecture, except the need for symmetry (as he urged for Phoenix House), this has not come to light so far. His contact with professional architects seems to have been peripheral. For example, in 1665 when Orrery's play *Mustapha* was performed in London, the scenes had been designed by Inigo Jones's pupil John Webb.[7] Orrery might have met Webb through Webb's son-in-law, Dr John Westley, himself a gentleman-architect, who supervised the alterations of Phoenix House. From December 24, 1660 onwards Orrery was Governor of Limerick City and its citadel. In 1666 he petitioned Ormonde for a lease of part of the island at Limerick, promising that he would build on it, 'which would be an enlargement, beautifying, and strengthening of the city . . .',[8] but it is unclear whether these plans were realized. Elsewhere, he claimed to have made three new citadels in the cities of Cork and Limerick without being allowed a penny for his work,[9] but there is little evidence of these fortifications. After the Restoration, Orrery's concern for the fortifications in Co. Cork derived mainly from his anxiety about a Dutch or French invasion in Ireland. He reported on the state of these forts in 1666,[10] but was to devote over twelve years of his life with defence works at Rincurran (later Charles) Fort, Kinsale. He collaborated intensively with Capt. James Archer (q.v.) and William Robinson (q.v.) on this fort, the stonework of which was contracted by William Armstead (q.v.) and Thomas Smith (q.v.), the first of whom was presumably comptroller in Orrery's household. Archer asked Orrery's advice at least once about the fort, and this Orrery considered merely as a compliment for his skill in engineering.[11] He presumably was familiar with some of the contemporary published works on fortifications, for in his play *Mr Anthony* he alludes to the engineers, the Chevalier Antoine Deville and Adam Friedrich Freitag.[12] Thoughts about building must have kept Orrery busy till the year of his death in 1679, for Sir Philip Perceval relates that he went to dine at Castlemartyr in Co. Cork after which Orrery 'kept me ... discoursing of ordinary things, as building and husbandry.'[13] Whether Orrery ever designed houses for his numerous relatives remains unknown. His brother, the famous physicist Robert Boyle lived most of his life in London, where Dr Robert Hooke designed a house for him. Another brother, Richard, 1st Earl of Burlington and 2nd Earl of Cork, similarly employed Hooke, while his London residence, Burlington House, was supposedly designed by Sir John Denham, the English Surveyor-General. Burlington also rebuilt Lismore Castle, Co. Waterford in 1662–3, where he employed Miles Symner (q.v.). A brother-in-law of Orrery was Richard Jones, 3rd Viscount Ranelagh (q.v.), who later became an enthusiastic gentleman-architect. Orrery wrote many plays, but as far as is known, no treatise on architecture or fortifications. The first volume of his *Treatise on the Art of War*, published in 1677, was to be followed by a second volume, which might have dealt with defence works, but this was not finished at his death on October 16, 1679. He was buried in St Mary's Church, Youghal, where a baroque wall monument was erected for him. Orrery's portrait has been published by his biographer Lynch.

[1] L. Stone, *The Crisis of the Aristocracy, 1558–1641*, Oxford, 1965, 698, where quoted from *Grosart*.

[2] *Grosart*, series 1, V, 221; series 2, V, 120.

[3] R. Caulfield (Ed.), *The Council Book of the Corporation of Youghal ...*, Guildford, 1878, 547.

[4] *HMC, Ormonde*, II, 244.

[5] *Lodge*, I, 183.

[6] T. Morrice (Ed.), *A Collection of the State Letters of R. Boyle, the first Earl of Orrery*, London, 1743, 31.

[7] W. S. Clark, *The Dramatic Works of Roger Boyle, Earl of Orrery*, Cambridge, Mass., 1937, I, 39.

[8] Morrice, *op.cit.*, 144.

[9] O. Airy (Ed.), *Essex Papers*, Camden Society, 1890, 8. Orrery recommended repairs of St John's Castle in Limerick in 1663, but employed an unknown person to prepare the estimates (Morrice, *op.cit.*, 67). The Ormonde papers contain two other unsigned estimates for the improvements of fortifications at Limerick (not dated, but late 17th Century), which may have been prepared during Orrery's governorship. One estimate totalled £9,464 10s. 6d., the other £12,602 4s. 11d. (NLI, Ms 2490, ff. 109, 115).

[10] Morrice, *op.cit.*, 145 ff.

[11] *HMC, 6th Rep.*, 732.

[12] Clark, *op.cit.*, II, 810, *n*. 119.

[13] *HMC, Egmont*, III, 81.

BEREHAVEN, CO. CORK, DUNBOY FORT. In 1666 Orrery claimed that he had built this fort (which had been in existence from at least 1602), but that it had been demolished by the 'usurpers' [sic] (*CSPI*, 1666–9, 92). Redesigned by Thomas Burgh (q.v.) in 1702.

BANTRY, CO. CORK, BANTRY FORT. Orrery claimed in 1666 that he had erected this fort during the last Dutch War (1652–4); receipts for more than £80, dated 1652 for finishing the fortification, signed in unintelligible handwriting, are among the *Orrery papers* (NLI, N6268–6271, Pos 7074–7077). Orrery described the fort in 1666 as small but regular, consisting of four small bastions, the faces of which were 48 feet long, and the flanks 18 feet, etc. (Morrice, *op.cit.*, 145). Orrery seemed to have re-fortified the fort in 1672 (*HMC, 6th Rep.*, 318). It was demolished in 1689 (*CSPD*, 1694–5, 94), but presumably Rudolph Corneille (q.v.) designed new plans for it.

RATHLUIRC, CO. CORK, CHARLEVILLE CASTLE. Orrery made the designs for this castle, the first stone of which was laid on May 29, 1661. Overall supervision, in the absence of Orrery, was in the hands of Sir St John Brodrick, but the overseers on the site were Capt. William Kenn (q.v.), one Lieut. Greene, and possibly Robert Fennell. The contractors for the stone work were in all likelihood Thomas Smith (q.v.) and William Armstead (q.v.). This vast house was burned in 1690 (Morrice, *op.cit.*, 31; NLI, N6268–6271, Pos 7074–7077.)

PHOENIX HOUSE, CO. DUBLIN. On December 28, 1661 Orrery designed the hall and chapel to this Royal residence, to make it symmetrical, and planned a stable for the Duke of Ormonde. Whereas there seems to have been a question that Dr John Westley was already on his way to England with [? other] plans of Phoenix House, it is unclear whether Orrery's or Westley's designs were finally executed. Dem. 1735. (Morrice, *op.cit.*, 31; Bodl., Carte Ms 52, f. 288; BL, Add. Ms 15893, ff. 243–7.)

KINSALE, CO. CORK, CASTLE PARK FORT. In 1666 Orrery assisted the Irish Master of the Ordnance, Sir Robert Byron, with putting the fort in a posture of defense against a foreign attack (*HMC, Ormonde*, n.s. II, 226 *ff.*), which consisted of making a breastwork, built of sod and earth, seven foot high and twenty foot thick, on top of a twenty-foot high rampart. According to Orrery the only man fit to execute the sod work, was a man working at Orrery's ponds [at Charleville] (Morrice, *op.cit.*, 164). This was most likely William Armstead (q.v.) (NLI, Ms 13192). A year later, Orrery presented Ormonde with proposals to redesign the fort drastically, but only smaller changes seem to have been implemented such as the building of a blockhouse at Rincurran (see below), two batteries each of ten cannons, a boom, and a number of other works (*CSPI*, 1666–69, 396, 406, 441–2).

KINSALE, CO. CORK, RINCURRAN (later CHARLES) FORT. From 1667 onwards Orrery constantly oversaw the improvements on the site, which included the building of a block house with a platform for 20 cannon (*CSPI*, 1666–9, 396, 406, 441–2; *CSPID*, 1672–3, 477). At the conclusion of the Dutch War, building activity at the site stopped, but in April 1672 Orrery pressed the Lord Lieutenant the Earl of Essex, to have a Fort Royal erected at Kinsale (Airy, *op.cit.*, 4). Subsequent work again involved Orrery, but now the engineer in chief was Capt. Paulus Storff; the stonework was then and later contracted by William Armstead and Thomas Smith. The last major expansion of the fort took place in 1677–8, when William Robinson (q.v.) prepared plans, and Capt. James Archer (q.v.) oversaw the works on the site. Again Orrery gave continuous guidance about the desirable properties of the fort, which at one stage led to a dispute between Orrery, and Robinson and Archer, which was solved by the sending of Robinson with his plans to England for approval (*HMC, Ormonde*, n.s. IV, 165 *ff.*). Although in the British Library there is a map [by ?Thomas Phillips] of Kinsale Harbour which shows a proposed landward extension of the fort, which is inscribed 'designed by the Earl of Orrery' (BL, King's Maps 52, f. 24), no evidence has come to light that Orrery was indeed mainly responsible for the design of this star-shaped extension.

CASTLEMARTYR CASTLE, CO. CORK. In 1672 Orrery moved from Charleville to Castlemartyr, and executed alterations to make it 'English like' and 'a good house for his younger son' (Lynch, *op.cit.*, 201). Plundered in 1688. Orrery's marks on this building are difficult to identify nowadays among remains which date partly back to the early 17th century.

MARSTON HOUSE, SOMERSETSHIRE. Rebuilding of this seat owned by Orrery took place in 1676–7 (NLI, N6268–6271, Pos 7074–7077).

BRABAZON, Sir EDWARD (*c*. 1550–1625). He was the oldest son of Sir William Brabazon, Lord Treasurer and Lord Justice of Ireland, and Elizabeth Clifford. His life has been described by *Lodge*,[1] who has pointed out that Sir Edward made himself serviceable to the English in England and Ireland both as a soldier and as an official. In 1606 the Earl of Salisbury 'allowed' him to be employed for the alterations of Dublin Castle, presumably to prevent the occurrence of a gunpowder plot in Ireland. Sir Edward surveyed the building with an eye to altering the hall, building a main wall separating the east from the west part of the castle, and improving its defensibility.[2] An unsigned sketch, by one Wattson [sic] of the proposed alterations by Sir Edward, formerly tentatively dated 1609, is in the National Library of Ireland.[3] In May 1606 a plan was formulated to build a new hall in the castle to accommodate the parliament and the courts. Sir Edward claimed he could direct the works at a cost of £400.[4] This amount suggests alterations to existing structures, rather than the erection of a new building, to allow the removal of the courts from St Patrick's Cathedral to the hall of the castle. However, King James I directed the courts to be located elsewhere,[5] and the clerk of the Royal Works in Ireland, Samuel Molyneux (q.v.), built them near Christ Church Cathedral in 1608. Contemporary records suggest that Sir Edward's proposed alterations to Dublin Castle were not made.[6] No other building projects by him are known. He was created Baron Brabazon of Ardee in 1616. He married Mary, daughter of Sir Thomas Smith of Mitcham, Surrey, by whom he had several children, among them William, who later became 1st Earl of Meath. Sir Edward Brabazon died in 1625 and was buried in St Catherine's Church, Dublin. A tomb in that church which he had erected for his father is now only known from a drawing.[7]

[1] *Lodge*, I, 271–3.
[2] *HMC, Salisbury*, XVIII, 348, 381; see also *JRSAI*, 1974, 1–4, 6–7.
[3] The sketch is printed in G. A. Hayes-McCoy, *Ulster and other Irish Maps, c. 1600*, Dublin, 1964, pl. XVIII; its misattribution in date is mentioned on p. 29.
[4] Hayes-McCoy, *op.cit.*, 29; *HMC, Salisbury*, XVIII, 381.
[5] J. Lodge (Ed.) *Desiderate Curiosa Hibernica*, Dublin, 1772, I, 488–9.
[6] R. Loeber, 'The Rebuilding of Dublin Castle: thirty critical years 1661–1689' *Studies* 1980, *69*, 45–69.
[7] Geneal. Off., Monumenta Eblanea, p. 17. The inscription is spelled out by T. Dineley in NLI, Pos 7515.

BRIDGES, EDWARD (fl. 1695), architect and builder from Kinsale. On August 30, 1695 he is first mentioned as a builder when £30 was due to him by bond from William Brown for work done to the town house of Sir Robert Southwell in Kinsale.[1] In the following year Sir Robert gave a lease of land near Charles Fort, Kinsale to Bridges for 21 years,[2] which could have been as a payment for building work done. Bridges is again mentioned, but now as architect, in a conveyance of a house by Richard Harrison of Cork in December 1699.[3] In 1705 and 1707 Bridges executed repairs at Charles Fort, Kinsale, and was paid by Thomas Burgh (q.v.) a total of £73 6s.[4] He became 'sovereign' of Kinsale prior to 1709.[5]

[1] BL, Add. Ms 9714, f. 116ᵛ.
[2] BL, Add. Ms 9714, f. 150.
[3] NLI, Ainsworth Report on Private Collections, No. 13, Perry Papers.
[4] PRO, W.O. 55/1984.
[5] *Commons Jour.*, 1703–13, 621.

BROWNE, ? (fl. 1720), 'contriver' who is mentioned in the Inchiquin papers of 1720[1] during the period in which Dromoland Castle in Co. Clare was rebuilt for Sir Donat O'Brien. A surviving book of drawings of the Dromoland estate does not clarify Browne's part in the rebuilding, in which also the Surveyor-General Thomas Burgh (q.v.) may have been involved. Dromoland was rebuilt *c.* 1826.

[1] NLI, Ms 14369, f. 30, under date November 23, 1720, when Brown received £2 6s. I have been unable to find other references to him in the Inchiquin account books.

BROWNE, JAMES (1598–?1669), bricklayer. On May 6, 1640 Browne and the bricklayer Robert Pavier, concluded a contract with the Provost of Trinity College, Dublin, for the stone and brickwork of the north building of the College,[1] and on December 20, 1640 they made another contract for building the Provost's lodgings.[2] Browne is mentioned as a member of the Corporation of Carpenters in Dublin in 1656.[3] In 1665 the bricklayers James and Thomas Browne, and the plasterer William Robinson, were to report on the condition of Phoenix Park wall built by Henry Gamble and William Dodson (q.v.).[4] James Brown's [sic] name is mentioned in the charter of the newly established Corporation of Bricklayers and Plasterers in 1670.[5] He was obviously of some means when he made his will in 1669 at the age of 71, with bequests to his brothers Peter and Robert, and also to a number of other relatives. His wife Grace was to receive the profits of his houses,[6] presumably including a lot on St Stephen's Green which had been assigned to the mason [sic] James Browne in 1664.[7] None of Browne's works seem to have survived.

[1] TCD, Ms MUN/P/2/1, ff. 22–3.
[2] TCD, Ms MUN/P/2/1, f. 24.
[3] PROI, Corporation Records, Beseeches XIII.
[4] *HMC, 10th Rep. App. V*, 5.
[5] *CSPI*, 1666–9, 782.
[6] Geneal. Off., Ms 290, f. 47.
[7] *CARD*, IV, 305.

BROWNE, THOMAS (fl. 1655–1687), a bricklayer who was admitted to the Freedom of the City of Dublin in 1655. In the following year he is mentioned as a member of the Corporation of Carpenters in Dublin.[1] He received several payments between 1659 and 1660 for making a new gable end and for brickwork in the churchyard of St Catherine's Church, Dublin.[2] With the churchwardens of St Werburgh's Church, Dublin, he made, on April 21, 1662, a contract (where he is mentioned as a mason) for the extensive repair of the walls and roof of the chancel of the church. Browne was to be reimbursed £220 for the work and probably had a supervisory function during the building for he had to pay all the carpenters, masons, and glaziers for their work.[3] Browne is mentioned in 1665 when he, together with James Browne (q.v.) and the plasterer William Robinson, were to report on the wall of Phoenix Park.[4] He probably is the same Thomas Browne, named in 1685, a builder and churchwarden of St Werburgh's Church, Dublin, who lived in Dame Street.[5] When in 1679–81 another series of repairs were carried out at St Catherine's Church, Dublin, the 'mason' Thomas Browne was paid on several occasions, the last time for 'making walls & balls' probably for the church gate in 1681.[6] Browne may have followed designs by the Surveyor-General William Robinson (q.v.), who was probably consulted during the rebuilding of the church. Browne died intestate in 1687.[7] The year before his death, his apprentice, the bricklayer James Browne, received the freedom of the City of Dublin.[8]

[1] PROI, Corporation Records, Beseeches XIII.
[2] PROI, Ms 5122, ff. 16, 22, 29 to the amount of £17, 8s.
[3] TCD, Ms 2063.
[4] HMC, 10th Rep. App. V, 5.
[5] S. C. Hughes, The Church of St Werburgh, Dublin, 1889, 145.
[6] PROI, Ms 5122, ff. 145, 179, 193, 204.
[7] Appendix 26th Report of the Deputy Keeper of the Public Records in Ireland, 1895, 100.
[8] Geneal. Off., G. Thrift, Roll of Freemen.

BURGH, THOMAS (1670–1730),[1] one of the first Irish military engineers. He was the son of the Rev. Ulysses Burgh (Dean of Emly, and later Bishop of Ardagh) of Drumkeen, Co. Limerick, and Mary, daughter of William Kingsmill, of Ballibeg, Co. Cork.[2] After education at Delany's School in Dublin he entered Trinity College, Dublin on November 22, 1685. Before the outbreak of the Williamite War in 1689 he probably joined his father who fled to London. Together they presumably returned to Ireland in King William III's army, for his father, by then Dean of Emly, is mentioned among those in William III's forces before Limerick.[3] This is corroborated by the fact that on March 8, 1689 a Thomas Bourk [sic] was commissioned as Lieutenant in Lord Lovelace's Regiment of Foot, which served with the Duke of Schomberg's army in Ireland.[4] Packenham-Walsh[5] mentioned that Thomas Burgh on February 27, 1691 was appointed to the Irish Engineers. However, his name is notably absent from lists of engineers serving in Ireland during the period.[6] At the end of the war he joined the Royal Regiment of Foot under the Earl of Orkney, left for the continent, and received a commission as captain (dated at Lembecq, August 1, 1692). He served at the battles of Steinkirk (1692), Landen (1693), and the siege of Namur (1695). At the last place he was employed as an engineer[7] presumably supervised by the Dutch commander of the Train of Artillery, John Wynant Goor. In 1697 he is mentioned (as Thomas Bourk) as one of the twenty-five engineers of the King's Company of Engineers,[8] and in that year became third engineer on the Irish Establishment, although keeping his former position.[9] Little is known about his work in the next three years under the Surveyor-General William Robinson (q.v.). Burgh replaced Robinson on July 10, 1700, at a salary of £300 per annum,[10] bypassing the second engineer on the Irish Establishment, Rudolph Corneille (q.v.). On February 12, 1701 he became Barracks overseer in Ireland, a commission which was renewed subsequently several times, the last time on February 14, 1728.[11] Under his care the building of barracks was expanded all over Ireland, the rebuilding of Dublin Castle (started by William Robinson, q.v.) was advanced considerably, and numerous coastal fortifications were improved, although, as in the case of the barracks, it is often difficult to determine whether it was Thomas Burgh, or other engineers of the Irish

Ordnance who were responsible for their design. In 1704 he was admitted as a Freeman of the City of Dublin. He beautified Dublin with a number of large public buildings, notably the Custom House, the Library of Trinity College, Dr Steevens' Hospital, the Linen Hall, the Royal Barracks, and other smaller buildings. In 1721 he acted as a consultant to the City for the creation of a basin for the water supply, for a pedestal for King George I's statue on Essex bridge, and he carried out several unidentified public works for which, in 1723, he was awarded plate to a maximum value of £50.[12] Burgh also seems to have had an interest in navigation for, about 1704, he made a report on the lighthouses in Ireland,[13] and in 1707, as a member of the Dublin Philosophical Society, he presented a paper on the improvement of Dublin Harbour by means of dredging and the building of a fortified basin to hold ships.[14] In 1725 the Lord Lieutenant and Council ordered Burgh and Capt. John Perry to take soundings and make a chart of Dublin Harbour, but their resulting proposals were rejected by the Ballast Board. However their map of the Harbour was published by Perry in 1728.[15] Among drawings from the Ordnance Office, now photocopied in the National Library of Ireland,[16] is a plan of a sluice dated 1726, designed by Burgh, and drawn by his assistant Michael Wills, which was part of one of Burgh's schemes to improve inland waterways in Ireland. In 1704 Burgh was paid for the excavation of a canal to serve as a fishpond in Phoenix Park, and this was to include sluices.[17] In 1729 he planned to survey the river of Newry and the Bog of Glynn in order to prepare an estimate for making a navigable passage from Newry to Lough Neagh, a project which had been attempted before him by Capt. Francis Nevill (q.v.). Burgh feared competitors, for which purpose he published an advertisement in Faulkner's *The Dublin Journal* (August 2–5, 1729) in order to advise the general public. At this time he had developed a plan for supplying the City of Dublin with coals from Co. Tyrone, which caused Francis Seymour to write a pamphlet commenting on this.[18] Burgh's interest in coal mining dated from at least as early as 1721 when he and his partner the Hon. Richard Stewart received the first £2,000 of a total of £8,000 from the Irish government for their operation of a colliery at Ballycastle, Co. Antrim.[19]

In the course of his career Thomas Burgh was involved with several building operations for private clients, although the exact nature of his involvement cannot be ascertained as most of the buildings have disappeared. In 1702 he advised on the building of garden walls at Kilbrew, Co. Meath, the estate of the Quartermaster-General Richard Gorges.[20] In 1703–4 he checked accounts during the renovations of Archbishop William King's residence in Dublin, probably St Sepulchre Palace,[21] the rebuilding of which he possibly supervised. Seven years later he made a model for the porch of Marsh's Library towards St Patrick's Cathedral.[22] Burgh's part is rather vague in the rebuilding of a residence for the O'Brien family, presumably at Dromoland, Co. Clare in about 1719.[23] Sometimes his involvement was limited to the surveying of a house before its sale, as it was with Sir John Perceval's Dublin town house in 1714.[24] His architectural style was restrained and was nothing like the exuberant baroque of his English contemporaries Sir John Vanbrugh or William Talman. Burgh's sober style was only notable by its massing of different portions of buildings on different planes, by arcading on the ground floor, and by the use of a central front of five bays often crowned by a large pediment as at the Armoury, the Royal Barracks, Dublin Castle, Dr Steevens' Hospital, the Customs House, the Linen Hall, and Ballyburley House. He did not introduce Palladian ideas into his buildings, except at his own house at Naas, nor did he subscribe to *Vitruvius Britannicus*, but employed a kind of classicism whose derivation and origin are undetermined. For the lay-out of Dublin Castle he followed very closely the designs attributed to the former Surveyor-General William Robinson (q.v.). In one of his best designs, the library of Trinity College, Dublin, he misjudged its position by having the projecting wings join the older buildings of the Library quadrangle. The most prestigious project, a design for the Irish Houses of Parliament, Burgh lost in 1728 to the newcomer Edward Lovett Pearce.[25] Burgh, although schooled as an engineer, became an architect, but his importance did not spread beyond Ireland. He combined a number of military appointments with civic functions. From 1706 to 1714 he held the important office of Lieutenant of the Ordnance of Ireland,[26] which together with the Surveyor-Generalship made him the most influential officer in the Irish Ordnance. He was granted the rank of Lieutenant-Colonel on April 11, 1706. In addition, he was from 1707–14 a captain in Brasier's Regiment of Foot,[27] High Sheriff for Co. Kildare in 1712, and M.P. for Naas from 1713 to his death in 1730. He became a governor of the Royal Hospital, Kilmainham, in 1707,[28] and from 1717 onwards he acted as a trustee of Dr Steevens' Hospital.

During Burgh's Surveyor-Generalship a number of French engineers were employed for varying periods, and among these were Rudolph and John Corneille (q.v.), Jacques Wibault, Jean Thomas, and Peter Gilbert de Pagez (q.v.). The extent of Burgh's influence on them or their influence on him is unknown. A personal assistant, or deputy, of Burgh seems to have been Michael Wills who also acted as his draughtsman. Burgh seems generally to have had good relationships with the craftsmen whose names recur in most of his projects. Significantly perhaps, he became executor of the wills of at least two of these: the bricklayer Francis Quinn (d. 1728)[29] and the painter Isaac Chalk (prob. 1701).[30]

Burgh married on July 10, 1700 Mary, daughter of the Rt Rev. William Smyth, Bishop of Kilmore, and by her had five sons (Thomas, Theobald, Ulysses, John, and Richard) and four daughters (Mary, Dorothea, Catherine, and Elizabeth).[31] In 1715 he leased a church pew in the parish church at Naas and from 1716 onwards held another pew at St Mary's Church, Dublin.[32] He had his townhouse at 37 Dawson Street (now rebuilt). Burgh dated his will July 27, 1726; he died on December 18, 1730, and the will was proved on March 8, 1731 but no copy has been located. Burgh possessed a country estate at Oldtown, Co. Kildare[33] where his descendants still live. Two portraits of Thomas Burgh are among the paintings at Oldtown, Co. Kildare. His letters have only turn up incidentally in several collections. His drawings are equally rare, and some of these at Oldtown House disappeared mysteriously a number of years ago, but, fortunately, photographs of them have now been deposited in the National Trust Archive, Dublin, while Photostats of drawings from Burgh's office are in the National Library.[34] Burgh published a pamphlet entitled 'A Method To Determine the Areas of Right-Lined Figures Universally. Very Useful for Ascertaining the Contents of any Survey ...', Dublin, 1724',[35] for which Parliament granted him the sum of £1,000 in 1723.[36]

---

[1] I am particularly grateful to Major J. H. de Burgh for allowing me to examine his family papers. Mr Peter Walsh and Dr Edward McParland have been so kind as to pass on to me some information regarding Thomas Burgh's works hitherto unknown to me.

[2] B. Burke, *Genealogical ... history of the landed gentry ...*, London, 1875, I, 175. Much of the following is based on E. de Burgh's 'History of the Oldtown branches of the de Burghs', Ms in Oldtown, Co. Kildare; W. P. Pakenham-Walsh, 'Lieutenant-Colonel Thomas Burgh, Chief Engineer of Ireland, 1700–1730', *Royal Engineers' Journal*, 1907, 6, 69–74; *Craig*, 94–99. Note that Pakenham-Walsh mentioned William Kingsmill as of Ballyowen, Co. Tipperary. Much pioneering work on Thomas Burgh was done by the Knight of Glin, in his 'The Irish Palladians', unpublished thesis, Harvard University.

[3] M. Lenihan, *History of Limerick*, Dublin, 1866, 222–3n.

[4] *Dalton*, III, 76.

Burgh

[5] See footnote 2.
[6] *Dalton,* III, 184.
[7] *Ibid.,* III, 241; V, 48.
[8] *Ibid.,* IV, 171.
[9] W. Porter, *History of the Corps of Royal Engineers,* London, 1889–1915, I, 61.
[10] *CSPD,* 1700–2, 17, p. 480.
[11] J. L. J. Hughes, *Patentee Officers in Ireland . . .,* Dublin, 1960, 19.
[12] *CARD,* VII, 153, 187, 215.
[13] *HMC, Ormonde,* n.s. VIII, 89.
[14] K. T. Hoppen, *The Common Scientist . . .,* London, 1970, 193, 195; *CARD,* VI, 613–6; BL, Sloane Ms 3329, f. 141; Ms 4815.
[15] C. Haliday, *The Scandinavian Kingdom of Dublin,* Dublin, 1884, opp. p. 249, 249n.
[16] NLI, Art Dr 29.
[17] TCD, Ms 1180, f. 179; Gilbert Ms 205, f. 68ᵛ; PRO, W.O.55/1984.
[18] Cambridge University Library, Bradshaw Coll., Hib. 3.730.1¹⁴.
[19] *Commons Jour.,* 1715–21; 1723–30.
[20] R. Gorges, *History of the family of Gorges,* Boston, 1944, 230.
[21] TCD, Ms 751(2). The overseer was Henry Lee.
[22] M. McCarthy, 'Archbishop Marsh and his library', *Dublin Historical Record,* 1975, *29,* 10. This porch has not survived.
[23] J. Ainsworth (Ed.), *Inchiquin manuscripts,* Dublin, 1961, 145.
[24] BL, Add. Ms 47027, f. 153.
[25] *Commons Jour.,* V, 617; The Knight of Glin, 'The Irish Palladians', unpublished thesis Ms, n.d., p. 58; PROI, M 3036.
[26] R. Lascelles, *Liber munerum,* London, 1824, I, 103.
[27] *Dalton,* VI, 252.
[28] PROI, RHK 1/1/2, p. 22ᵛ.
[29] PROI, Preg. Wills.
[30] Geneal. Off., Ms 290, p. 122.
[31] Ms notes by Col T. J. de Burgh, Oldtown, Co. Kildare.
[32] NLI, p. 4576.
[33] St Mary's Church, Dublin, Vestry book, p. 129.
[34] NLI, Art Dr 29.
[35] Cambridge Univ. Library, Bradshaw Coll., Hib. 5.724.1.
[36] T. J. Kiernan, *History of the Financial Administration of Ireland to 1817* London, 1930, 165.

ROYAL BUILDINGS

CHAPELIZOD HOUSE, CO. DUBLIN. Burgh was paid in 1709 for works at this Royal lodge at a cost of £1,540 19s., another £1,238 15s. in 1713 (which included repairs of Dublin Castle), while a last repair was approved in 1718 (*CTB,* 1709, *pt.* 2, 479; Marsh Lib., Ms Z.2.1.10, p. 18; TCD, Ms 751(2), 751(3); Gilbert Ms 205, f. 74). Dem.

DUBLIN, HORSE GUARDS' STABLE. Burgh prepared after 1703 an estimate for building new stables at a cost of £389 14s., when the old stables near the old Council Chamber became ruinous (Gilbert Ms 205, f. 67). The question of its replacement or repair was referred to Burgh in 1718 and 1719 (TCD, Ms 752; PROI, Ms 1A 52. 143). Dem.

DUBLIN, CHICHESTER HOUSE. Burgh supervised periodic repairs at this Parliament House from 1701 till at least 1714 (*Commons Jour.* 1703–13, 2nd ed., 662–6; Marsh Lib, Ms Z. 2.1.10, p. 19). Dem.

DUBLIN CASTLE. In 1704 the Lord Lieutenant the Duke of Ormonde mentions repairs to the Castle at a cost of £1,037 6s. (NLI, Ms 992, f. 61), which were to be executed presumably by Burgh. In the following year Burgh was paid for building a riding house, new stables, coach houses in the 'castle yard', while the building of a bagnio was started for the Duke of Ormonde in the south-east corner of the Castle. The workmen employed were, the bricklayer Francis Quin, the mason John Whinnery, the smiths Robert Greenway and David Thomas, the painter and plasterer Isaac Chalk, the joiner John Sisson, the carpenter Edward Miller, the slater Robert Wharton, and the glazier Andrew Rock (Gilbert Ms 205, f. 74; PRO, W.O. 55/1984; *HMC, Ormonde*, n.s. VIII, 245). In 1710 Burgh prepared plans to facilitate the entrance to the Castle by widening Cork Hill (then an extension of Dame Street) and making a new main passage into the Castle, east of the present one (which would have been very much off-centre, but in line with the Blind Quay). However, even as late as 1718 the new entrance into the Castle was contemplated, but remained unrealized (Gilbert Ms 195, ff. 1, 5, 9, 12, 18, 21, 35; PROI, Mss M 3036; 1A 52. 143; *Commons Jour*. 1703–13, 2nd ed., 753, 832, 868; TCD, Ms 752). The destruction by fire of the old Council Chamber (in Essex Street) in 1711 was followed by Burgh's estimate of £3,337 7s. 9d. for building a new one which was to become the east range of the Upper Yard, 'of the same form' as William Robinson's lodgings for the Chief Governor. This building was started in 1712 (*Commons Jour*., 1703–13, 2nd ed., 847, 863–4; T. Thorpe, *Catalogue of Southwell Manuscripts*, London, 1834, 253, 367, 369). The poor condition of the armoury in Dublin Castle led Burgh also in 1711 to draw up a plan (BL, Eg. Ms 917, f. 214, published in *Loeber*, pl. 9) and estimate for an armoury of seven bays (*Commons Jour*., 1703–13, 2nd ed., 844, 864) to be built in the Upper Yard (as the west range) at a cost of £3,459 5s. 8d. In 1714 an estimate of the costs needed to finish the building was requested (*PROI*, Ms IA 52. 143; *CTB*, 1712, pt 2, 193). Burgh presented in 1711 an estimate for erecting at a cost of £3,710 3s. 3d., offices of the Treasury (i.e. Receiver-General), of the Pells, Auditor-General, Surveyor-General of the lands, Commissary-General, Barracks, and Registry of wills and deeds, etc. Although Burgh objected to situating these offices in the Lower Castle Yard, they were built there after 1712, when a total of £20,512 14s. was granted for the erection of these offices, the Armoury, and the Council Chamber. Burgh received a final payment for these works in 1717 (per warrant dated 1715) (*Commons Jour*., 1703–13, 2nd ed., 865–6; 1715–21, 337; 1723–30, 307–8; PROI, M 3036; Thorpe, *op.cit*., 367; PRO, SP 63/375, f. 375). He was ordered to make more alterations in 1718 (TCD, Ms 752), which presumably refer to additional buildings in the Lower Castle Yard where the Barrack Office was built (TCD, Ms 752; PROI, Ms 1A.52.143; *Commons Jour*., 1715–21, 770). Burgh may have carried out more works at the Castle after 1718.

DUBLIN, OLD COUNCIL CHAMBER AND TREASURY, ESSEX ST. In 1705 and 1707 Burgh supervised alterations (PRO, W.O. 55/1984; T. Thorpe, *Catalogue of Southwell manuscripts*, London, 1834, 369; *Commons Jour*., 1703–13, 372). Dem.

DUBLIN, PARLIAMENT HOUSE. Burgh was invited in 1723 to estimate the cost of replacing Chichester House as a seat of the Irish Parliament. Five years later he was requested to present a plan, which was ultimately rejected in favour of one prepared by Edward Lovett Pearce. The nature of Burgh's design is unknown (*Commons Jour*., 1723–30, 42, 528, 617; NLI, Art Dr 29).

PUBLIC BUILDINGS

DUBLIN, CUSTOM HOUSE. A warrant was issued in 1704 to pull down the old Custom House and rebuild it according to Burgh's estimate of £3,317 16s. By 1706 more than double this amount was wanted for its completion, which, then included an additional storey, a new watch house, and storehouses. The Custom House was pulled down in 1815. Its design showed a close resemblance to Daniel Stalpaert's Magazine for the Admirality in Amsterdam (*CTB*, 1704–5, 281; 1705–6, pt 3, 675; *CARD*, VI, 330–1; *Gilbert*, II, 139; *Craig*, 94 & pl. 28).

DUBLIN, FOUR COURTS. In 1705–6 Burgh supervised alterations to this building designed by William Robinson (q.v.) (PRO, W.O. 55/1984; Gilbert Ms. 205, f. 68). Dem.

DUBLIN, TRINITY COLLEGE LIBRARY. Plans for this library were formulated in 1709. In the ensuing year Burgh presented an estimate for £7,140 (excluding the wainscotting). The foundation was laid in 1712, but its exterior was not completed until 1723, and it was 1733 before the interior was finished. The total cost is said to have been £17,000. Ceiling and arcade altered. (A. Crookshank, *The Long Room*, Dublin, 1976; Pakenham-Walsh, *op.cit.*, 72–4; J. W. Stubbs, *History of the University of Dublin*, Dublin, 1889, 176).

DUBLIN, TRINITY COLLEGE, various buildings. In 1710 the building was started of an anatomical theatre and chemical laboratory, supervised by Burgh. In 1720 he certified work at the new kitchen, a year later, work at the 'new' buildings adjoining the kitchen; and in 1725 the charge for an additional roof adjoining the chapel (Crookshank, *op.cit.*; TCD, Mss 1750; MUN/P/2).

DUBLIN, DR STEEVENS' HOSPITAL. Burgh submitted a plan for this building in 1718. Work began the next year, and was supervised by Burgh. Clerks of the works were Thomas Hand (1720–9), Charles Lyndon (fl. 1729–31), and Michael Wills (1731–7) (T. P. Kirkpatrick, *The History of Doctor Steevens' Hospital, Dublin*, Dublin, 1924, *ff.*).

DUBLIN, LINEN HALL. Erected from 1722 onwards. Although no mention is made of Burgh drawing its plans, he inspected its progress on several occasions. The overseer was James Byrne. Dem. about 1918 (*Precedents and Abstracts from the Journals of the Trustees of the Linen and Hemp Manufacture*, Dublin, 1784, pp. 58, 74, 85; L. M. Cullen, *Merchants, Ships and Trade, 1660–1830*, Dublin, 1971, 18).

DOMESTIC ARCHITECTURE

OLDTOWN, CO. KILDARE. Burgh acquired land at Naas from 1696 onwards. He leased a portion of the church at Naas in 1715, which may have coincided with the erection of his country house in a Palladian layout of which only two pavilions were completed. One of these survives. A drawing of one wing was formerly at Oldtown, and was published in M. Beace-Jones, *Burke's Guide to Country Houses*. Vol. I: Ireland. London 1978. 229. (NLI, p. 4576; Oldtown Mss, T. J. de Burgh, *History of Oldtown*, 1924; E. de Burgh, *History of the Oldtown Branches of the de Burgh's*).

CHURCHES

DUBLIN, ST MARY'S CHURCH. In 1704 Burgh inspected John Whinnery's masonry in this church which had been designed by William Robinson (q.v.). Burgh probably subsequently oversaw the completion of the church for in 1720 he was granted half a pew by the parish because of 'his many good Services' (Vestry Book, pp. 33, 129).

DUBLIN, ST WERBURGH'S CHURCH. The design of this church has been ascribed to Burgh, on the ground that he signed payments for its building from 1716 onwards; Allesandro Galilei has also been mentioned as its designer. However, the façade was very likely neither Burgh's nor Galilei's, but was based on da Volterra's Santa Chiara in Rome. R. Loeber, 'Early Classicism in Ireland: Architecture before the Georgian Era.' Architectural History, 1979, *22*, 56–60, pl. 12a. In about 1713 Burgh prepared a 'Draught and Directions' for its rebuilding which at that date may already have incorporated da Volterra's design. Overseer during the building was Richard Mills (BL, Eg. Ms 1772, p. 112;

PRO, SP 63/373, f. 68; TCD, Ms 2063; S. C. Hughes, *The Church of St Werburgh*, Dublin, 1889, 26: *CL*, January 25, 1973, 210; H. A. Wheeler and M. J. Craig. *The Dublin City Churches*, Dublin, 1948, 38–9).

DUBLIN, ST LUKE'S CHURCH. Burgh's order in 1716 for digging (presumably the foundations) is mentioned in the churchwarden's account, but no clear proof has been forthcoming that Burgh designed this church, which was finished in 1716. Altered in 1835 and 1884 (*CARD*, VI, 555; H. A. Wheeler and M. J. Craig, *The Dublin City Churches*, Dublin, 1948, 32–3).

MILITARY BUILDINGS AND FORTIFICATIONS

DUBLIN, ROYAL BARRACKS now COLLINS BARRACKS. Burgh started laying out the Royal Square for one regiment of foot in 1701, and the work neared completion in 1707. Housing for an additional regiment of foot and three troop of horse was planned in 1706 at a total cost of £21,534 4s. 7d., which was to be 'plain and useful without any unnecessary Ornament' (PRO, T 1/100, f. 186). These further buildings, the Horse Square and the Small Square, were started in 1707, and were almost finished by 1709. The chapel to the barracks was in question in 1723, and Burgh may have had a hand in it. He supervised on-going repairs and other works at the barracks until 1725 at least (*Commons Jour.*, 1715–21; 1723–30). A plan and elevation of these barracks, showing Burgh's work, was copied by John Bastide in 1722, and is now in the PRO (W.O. 78/1921). Another plan of the (?Royal) Horse Barracks was drawn by Michael Wills (NLI, Art Dr 29; for sources see *CARD*, VII, 284–5; *The Irish Sword*, 1957–8, *3*, 72–3; P D. O'Donnell, 'Dublin Military Barracks', *Dublin Historical Record*, 1972, *25*, 141; NLI, Ms 993, ff. 90, 160, 163, 234; I am indebted to Comm. P. D. O'Donnell for his assistance in providing information regarding these barracks).

CHARLEMONT FORT, CO. ARMAGH. Starting in 1701 Burgh spent £120 12s. 9d. on building drawbridges and gates; in 1704 and 1712 a total of £622 13s. 8½d. was expended, while Burgh is also mentioned in 1718–19 as having submitted an estimate for repairs (*CSPD*, 1702–3, 78; Gilbert Mss 91, f. 50v; Ms 205, f. 42; Ms 206, f. 22(1); TCD, Ms 752).

BEREHAVEN FORT, CO. CORK. In 1702 Burgh prepared a plan for this fort, which was built subsequently to protect the trade with the West Indies. A James Fountaine received a payment for its building sometime after 1707. A drawing from Burgh's office of the fort is in the NLI, Art Dr 29 (S. W. Singer (Ed.), *The Correspondence of Henry Hyde, Earl of Clarendon*, London, 1828, II, 432; *Commons Jour.* 1703–13, 2nd ed., 406; Gilbert Ms 205, f. 74).

KINSALE, CHARLES FORT. From 1702 till 1709 Burgh was paid on several occasions for small repairs, which included the erection of the present rusticated main gate. The builder about this time was Edward Bridges. Major renovations took place in 1712 at a total expense of at least £1,926, which was followed by an estimate for repairs as late as 1719 (*CSPD*, 1702–3, 78; Gilbert Mss 205, ff. 66, 68; 206, ff. 19, 22 (1); *CTP*, 1709, pt 2, 58; *CTB*, 1712, pt 2, 215; *CTB* 1716, pt 2, 203; *TCD*, Ms 752).

KILMAINHAM, ROYAL HOSPITAL. Burgh was paid for various repairs from 1702 until his death, and these included, among others, the building of the steeple (1703–5; presumably after the design of William Robinson, q.v.), and a report on the garden (1717). In 1707 Burgh replaced Edward Miller who had acted as Overseer of the Works in the Hospital (PROI, RHK 1/1/1–4).

CARRICKFERGUS CASTLE, CO. ANTRIM. From 1704 to 1706 and again in 1715 Burgh was paid on separate occasions for repairs, for which the engineer Jean Thomas

Burgh

was consulted in 1705 (*HMC, Ormonde*, n.s. VIII, 174; Gilbert Ms 205, ff. 42, 68; *CTB*, 1716, pt 2, 203).

LIMERICK, FORTIFICATIONS. From 1704 onwards Burgh was paid for the repair of the Guard House and Magazines; other repairs followed, after which he reported on the fortifications in 1713, and six years later estimated repairs to the value of £1,250 which were carried out by the engineer De Pagez (q.v.) (Gilbert Ms 205, ff. 42, 66, 68; PROI, Ms 1A 52, 143, *CTB*, 1712, pt 2, 215; *CTB*, 1716, pt 2, 203; TCD, Mss 752; 1179, ff. 107, 143; *Commons Jour.*, 1703–13, 405; 1723–30, 311–12).

MUTTON ISLAND FORT, GALWAY HARBOUR, CO. GALWAY. After 1707 Burgh inspected the fortifications at this island which had been built for the protection of the India fleet in 1702. Although the work was supervised by a Lt-Col. Nicholson, the plans probably came from Burgh's office (*Commons Jour.*, 1703–13, 405; BL, Add. Ms 37, 531, f. 21; J. Hardiman, *The History of the Town and County of Galway*, Galway, 1820, 228; Gilbert Ms 205, f. 42).

DUBLIN, ARSENAL. In 1707 Burgh made a rough draft for a magazine at the back of Dublin Castle, which was to cost £5,000, but he preferred a drier and safer location in Phoenix Park. Three years later Burgh and the Lord Lieutenant, the Duke of Ormonde, presented in person to the Treasury Board in England two estimates for an arsenal, one of £64,085 16*s.*, the other of £31,850 5*s.* 6*d.* The latter was approved, and subsequently payments were made to an Alexander Denton for its construction in Phoenix Park. A considerable sum was misspent, a scandal arose, and the work stopped in 1711. However, by 1714, Burgh had erected an armoury at Dublin Castle of which a plan survives (*Loeber*, pl. 9) (*HMC, Ormonde*, n.s. VIII, 294–5; *CTB*, 1710, pt 2, pp. 6, 259; PRO, T 1/100, f. 188; 33rd Report Dep. Keeper of PROI, 1901, 56; *CTB*, 1711, pt 2, 153; *CTB*, 1714, pt 2, 321; *Commons Jour.*, 1703–13, 730–1, 807, 847, 861–3; BL, Eg. Ms 917, ff. 212–13, 218).

LONDONDERRY, FORTIFICATIONS. Burgh was paid £270 9*d.* in 1709 for repairs. The magazine was rebuilt in 1712, and the work was overseen by Giles Gifford. In the same year Burgh issued a report on the fortifications there (*CTB*, 1709, 58; PROI, M 3036; Gilbert Ms 206, f. 19).

KILMAINHAM, INFIRMARY AND MADHOUSE to the Royal Hospital. In 1711 Burgh presented an estimate for a madhouse, but it was only in 1730 that this building and an infirmary were erected at a total cost of £793 11*s.* 11¼*d.* Burgh's death in December of that year may have preceded their completion. His assistant was Michael Wills (PROI, RHK, 1/1/3, f. 263; 1/1/4 ff. 125ᵛ, 127ᵛ, 150; T.P.C. Kirkpatrick, *A Note on The History of the Care of the Insane in Ireland*, Dublin, 1931, 12–13; *Commons Jour.* 1731–7, 45).

KILMAINHAM, POWDER MAGAZINES. In 1713 Burgh presented an estimate for building two powder magazines for £7,486 4*s.* (*CTB*, 1712, pt 2, 193; *HMC, Ormonde*, n.s. VIII, 294–5; *Commons Jour.*, 1703–13, 866–7), which were to be erected in the grounds of the Royal Hospital, Kilmainham (PROI, RHK 1/1/2, f. 192ᵛ–3ᵛ).

ATTRIBUTIONS

BARBAVILLA, CO. WESTMEATH. Burgh may have had a hand at the start of this country house for his relative William Smyth (The Knight of Glin, 'The Irish Palladians', unpublished thesis Ms, Harvard University, n.d., pp. 25, 26*n.*, 41; NLI, Smyth Mss, which the author was unable to examine).

CELBRIDGE, CO. KILDARE, OAKLEY PARK (formerly CELBRIDGE HALL). Built for Arthur

Price, Vicar of Celbridge, *c.* 1720 (M. Craig and the Knight of Glin, *Ireland Observed*, Cork, 1970, 29).

GALWAY, former MAYOR'S HOUSE. Very similar in design to Oakley Park (see above), dating from *c.* 1720.

BALLYBURLEY, CO. OFFALY. This country house, built for the Wakely family, had a pedimented front of five bays. Burnt 1888 (*History of the King's Country*, 1890, n.p.).

CELBRIDGE, COLLEGIATE SCHOOL, CO. KILDARE. Erected for the Conolly family in 1730. May have been planned as a quadrangle with an arcade on the inside, but was only partially completed (Craig and the Knight of Glin, *op.cit.*, 29).

KILLESTER, CO. DUBLIN. Built for Chidley Coote, who as lieutenant of the Ordnance from 1695–1706 was a colleague of Burgh. Killester was a wide-eaved house of one storey with Serliana windows in its wings. Dem. (NLI, IARA, AD 2477).

C

CHATTERTON, JAMES (fl. 1671), mason, who worked in 1671 at the rebuilding of Castle Island, Co. Kerry, the residence of Lord Herbert of Cherbury, probably together with John Seawell (q.v.) (now ruined). In the same year Chatterton and Seawell were said to have erected the steeple of St Fin Barre Cathedral, Cork,[1] which work was in fact built by William Armstead (q.v.) and Thomas Smith (q.v.). The steeple was taken down in 1865. A mason, James Chatterton, made his will in 1733,[2] and may have been Chatterton's son. Another possible relative, the mason Thomas Chatterton, is noted in Cork in 1713 (see John Coltsman (q.v.)).

[1] W. J. Smith (Ed.), *Herbert Correspondence*, Cardiff & Dublin, 1968, 198–9.
[2] Geneal. Off., Ms 393, f. 96.

COBB, PETER (fl. 1612), master carpenter from the city of London, who was sent by the city to Londonderry. He and the master carpenter Jarman are first noted in the Ulster plantation in November 1612 where they were employed at a salary of 18*s.* per week.[1] Cobb and Jarman oversaw the carpenters who were working on the new stone houses at Derry. Peter Benson (q.v.) was the main contractor for the masonry. Cobb and Jarman's price was higher than that of their colleague Anthony Lipsett. However, they were allowed to execute the work, but had to give up their salary (then amounting to 15*s.* per week).[2] Between 1611 and 1616 a total of 215 houses were built in the town under the patronage of the City of London.[3] It seems possible that Cobb and Jarman left Derry before 1628, for their names are absent on a list of freeholders in the town of that date.[4]

[1] T. W. Moody & J. G. Simms (Eds.), *The Bishopric of Derry and the Irish Society of London, vol. 1. 1602–70*, Dublin, 1968, 85, 89.
[2] C. D. Milligan, *The Walls of Derry*, Londonderry, 1948, part 1, 26.
[3] T. W. Moody, The *Londonderry Plantation*, Belfast, 1939, 275.
[4] R. G. S. King (Ed.), *A Particular of the Houses and Families in Londonderry, May 15, 1628*, Londonderry, 1936.

COLTSMAN, JOHN (fl. 1713), builder and stone-cutter who executed a number of public works in the City of Cork. Nothing is known about his background. It seems likely that he designed his own buildings. One of these, the South Gate Bridge, formerly adjoined a fairly classical façade of the actual gate which may also have been his work.

CORK, SOUTH GATE BRIDGE. Built in 1713 by Coltsman and Thomas Chatterton, mason (R. Caulfield (Ed.), *Council Book of the Corporation of the City of Cork*, Guildford, 1876, 364, 373; J. Coleman (Ed.), *Windele's Cork*, Cork, 1910, reprinted 1973, opp. p. 20).
CORK, NORTH GATE BRIDGE. Built by Coltsman in 1717. (Coleman, *op.cit.*, 28).
CORK, CHRIST CHURCH. Built in 1720 by Coltsman; interior remodelled and West front rebuilt by G. R. Pain (M. Craig & The Knight of Glin, *Ireland Observed*, Cork, 1970, 35).

CORNEILLE, RUDOLPH (fl. 1690), Huguenot military engineer, who became second engineer on the Irish Establishment. He was born in Medemblik in Holland (the year is unknown), the son of Rudolphe Gideon Corneille and his wife Anne,[1] who presumably were refugees from France. It seems likely that he was trained in the Dutch army, which brought him to Ireland, where he is noted in 1690 and where he served as an engineer in King William III's Train of Artillery under John Wynant Goor.[2] A number of his drawings have come to us. The earliest is dated 1691, and represents the batteries at Kinsale and suggestions for their improvements.[3] Otherwise nothing is known about Corneille's activities during the Williamite War. His performance was probably satisfactory for on March 1, 1692 he was given the post of second engineer.[4] Subsequently, until 1705 he had a very busy career, which focussed around the improvement of fortifications and the building of barracks.[5] Contemporary records suggest that government officials valued his judgement; occasionally he shared work with other engineers such as Jean Thomas and Jacques Wibault, who held auxiliary positions in the Irish Ordnance. However, he failed to succeed his superior Sir William Robinson (q.v.) as Surveyor-General in 1700, and was bypassed by the third engineer Thomas Burgh (q.v.). Corneille went to England for his naturalization, which he obtained in 1699.[6] Three years later together with Thomas Southwell he inspected the harbours of the coast of Munster from Berehaven to Dingle[7] with a view to erecting fortifications. Subsequently Corneille may be associated with plans to build fortifications at Bantry (see below). His reputation as a builder reached even private patrons, such as Sir John Perceval, later Earl of Egmont. In August 1710 Corneille visited the Perceval estate of Burton, Co. Cork, accompanied by Sir John's relative, the Secretary of State, Edward Southwell. Corneille as a 'contriver' offered to rebuild the burnt-out shell of this country house for £2,000,[8] but subsequently only the stables were turned into a dwelling, and Corneille's name does not re-occur among the records. No other of his domestic works have come to light. Little is known about Corneille's engineering works after 1705. He may be responsible for a document 'Pensées sur L'Arsenal de Dublin'[9] which concerned the arsenal undertaken by his superior Thomas Burgh (q.v.). He renewed his patent on June 1, 1715,[10] and on September 15, of the next year was succeeded as second engineer by his son John Corneille Sr. As was common for engineers, Corneille was a commissioned officer, and served from July 1, 1695 as a captain in Sir John Hanmer's Regiment of Foot.[11] He represented Tralee in the Irish House of Commons. Rudolph Corneille is last noted in October 1717 when he attended the baptism of his grandson in Dublin.[12] The date of his death is unknown, and his will has not been located.

[1] W. A. Shaw (Ed.), 'Letters of Denization and Acts of Naturalization for Aliens in England and Ireland, 1603–1700', *Huguenot Society*, 1911, *18*, 282. I am indebted to Mr L. M. Hoogeveen for his search in the records of Medemblik, which unfortunately did not shed any more light on the Corneille family.

[2] *Dalton*, III, 184, where he is named Rotoffe Corneille.

[3] PRO, MPF 105, 106.

[4] *Dalton*, III, 186 n. 4.

[5] See also S. W. Singer (Ed.), *The Correspondence of Henry Hyde, Earl of Clarendon*, London, 1828, II, 438.

[6] Shaw, *op.cit.*, 282; *CSPD*, 1699–1700, 86.

[7] BL, Add. Ms 37531, ff. 29ᵛ, 35ᵛ; *CSPD*, 1703–4, 284.

[8] BL, Add. Ms 46964 B, ff. 28, 107ᵛ, where his name is spelled Cornely.

[9] BL, Eg. Ms 917, f. 218.

[10] PROI, M 2539, f. 161.

[11] *Dalton*, III, 186 n. 4.

[12] J. J. Digges La Touche, 'Registers of the French Conformed Churches of St Patrick and St Mary, Dublin', *Huguenot Society*, 1893, *7*, 34.

BARRACKS

LIMERICK, BARRACKS. In 1693 Sir Cyril Wyche concluded an agreement with a John Burton to build barracks for 1,400 men at Limerick. It is unclear whether Corneille designed the buildings. A drawing surviving and presumably from his hand (not dated) shows the soldiers' barracks within the citadel of Limerick, which was a smaller structure (*CSPD*, 1693, 227; The drawing is in a collection at Castletown House, Celbridge, Co. Kildare).

CORK, BARRACKS, begun by September 1698 close to Elizabeth Fort. Dem. (T. Thorpe, *Catalogue of Southwell Manuscripts*, London, 1834, 199; J. Coleman (Ed.) *Windele's Cork*, Cork, 1910, 31; C. Walton, *History of the British Standing Army, 1660–1700*, London, 1894, 718 n).

WATERFORD, BARRACKS. In July 1698 the 'King's engineer' (most likely Rudolph Corneille) contracted with workmen for the erection of the barracks, which seem to have been located close to St Patrick's Fort. Dem. (S. Pender (Ed.), *Council Book of the Corporation of Waterford, 1662–1700*, Dublin, 1964; Walton, *op.cit.*, 718 n).

KINSALE, BARRACKS. Corneille expected in 1698 to start the building of the barracks, but his plan of these, dated 1701, suggests that they were built a few years later. Dem. (T. Thorpe, *Catalogue of Southwell Manuscripts*, London, 1834, 199; the plan was published in *JCHAS*, 1938, *43*, opp. p. 82).

FORTIFICATIONS

KINSALE, CHARLES FORT. He proposed to alter the batteries at this fort in 1691 (published in *Loeber*, pl. 10). From 1694 onwards Corneille was involved with the rebuilding of this fort, in which he followed basically the original outline. Corneille is mentioned in 1713 in relation to the building of a powder magazine at the fort (*CSPD*, 1694–5, 54; TCD, Ms 1180, f. 281–2; a signed plan, dated 1694–5 is in NLI, 15 B 14(11); another one dated 1695 is mentioned in *CSPD*, 1695, 357; Plans by a French hand associated with Corneille are in BL, King's Maps 52, ff. 25–8, one of these (f. 28) is dated 1692 and shows proposed outworks for Charles Fort and Castle Park Fort; see also PROI, Wyche docs., 2nd series, f. 174; Staffordshire County Library, D 1778/V/3).

LIMERICK, FORTIFICATIONS. From 1694 onwards Corneille was employed in the repair of the existing work, and the making of an estimate for building a new citadel. Three years later a plan of this was sent to England. Evidence is lacking that Corneille carried out these projects (*CSPD*, 1694–5, 107; Bodl., Carte Ms 170, f. 134; PROI, M 2454; drawings in a French hand associated with Corneille are in BL, King's Maps 54, ff. 13, 15–17, 19, and in Castletown House, Celbridge, Co. Kildare; a memorandum and estimate (without date) in French are most likely his (now in PROI, Wyche docs., 2nd ser., ff. 171, 173)).

BANTRY, CO. CORK, FORTIFICATIONS. Together with Thomas Southwell, Corneille selected this site for two forts to protect the harbour. Four plans were made, one of which may be in NLI, Ms 174 (PROI, Wyche docs., 2nd ser., f. 170).

COWLI, NICHOLAS (fl. 1626) mason and sculptor, who erected a bridge at Holycross Abbey, Co. Tipperary, over the river Suir in 1626 under the patronage of James Butler, Baron Dunboyne and his wife Marget Brien.[1] Cowli sculptured a tomb of a member of the O'Kennedy family at Lorrha in the same county.[2] Another tomb, for Maurice Hurley, formerly at Emly, Co. Tipperary and dated 1632, is known from a drawing by Thomas Dineley.[3] It was sculptured by Patrick Kearing (also named Kerin) in partnership with Nicholas Cowli. They had their workshop probably in Co. Tipperary or Co. Limerick. As was not unusual for sculptors, they took building work in times when commissions for monuments were scarce. The tombs of Cowli and Kerin formed a school of sculpture distinctly different from those elsewhere in Ireland. Both sculptors had a good knowledge of classical themes which they incorporated in monuments. Cowli's contribution to sculpture has been discussed elsewhere in some detail.[4]

[1] A. Cooper, *An Eighteenth-century Antiquary . . .*, Dublin, 1942, 25.
[2] J. Gleeson, *History of the Ely O'Carroll Territory*, Dublin, 1915, 261.
[3] NLI, Pos. 7515.
[4] R. Loeber, Sculptured Memorials of the Dead in Early 17th-century Ireland: A survey from *Monumenta Eblanae* and other sources (submitted to the *Proceedings of the Royal Irish Academy*).

CRAWLEY, BENJAMIN (fl. 1713). He probably was a professional builder who in 1713 prepared his first estimate for the building of Castle Durrow, Co. Leix, for William Flower. Two years later he was employed by Flower, to oversee the building of the residence, on a salary of £40 per year, of which £15 was to be spent on Crawley's debt due to William Flower. The building of Castle Durrow took from 1716–18. It seems unlikely that Crawley produced the designs for it. Workmen on the site included the joiner John Rudd, the mason Barnaby Demane [or ?Demave], the plasterers John Tompson and Thomas Lett, and the carpenters John Owen and John Coltman. Although it seems likely that Benjamin Crawley oversaw other building works, nothing is known about his further career.[1]

[1] *IGS*, October–December, 1973, *16*, 103–6.

CROFTE, RICHARD (fl. 1597–1629),[1] a Captain who became a contractor for town walls and buildings. He is first noted in 1597 when he was ordered to cross from England to Ireland with 100 soldiers levied in the counties of Montgomery and Radnor[2] to take part in the Tyrone War. Three years later he served under Sir Arthur Chichester at Carrickfergus.[3] At the end of the war he moved to County Cork. Subsequently, he held the position of Scoutmaster until 1610.[4] In 1612 his name occurs as one of the twelve original burgesses of the new Corporation of Bandon,[5] where he had his residence. He held several positions in the town, such as Chief Magistrate (1615), Provost (1617), and Captain of the town militia.[6] He seems to have been knowledgeable in engineering, for he supervised the building of the town walls and gates of Bandon from 1620 to 1622 possibly after the design of Christopher Jefford. After 1622 Crofte was replaced, for unknown reasons, by the mason John Lodden (q.v.). No works of Crofte are known besides those executed for the Earl of Cork. He died September 7, 1629, and was buried in Christ Church, Kilbrogan, in Bandon, where a brass tablet commemorates him.

[1] His name is sometimes spelled Croftes. I have been unable to ascertain whether he was a grandson of Sir James Croft, who came to Ireland in 1551 to inspect the Munster forts. Sir James was Lord Deputy of Ireland for about two years. His son Edward married Ann, daughter of Thomas Browne of Hillsborough, Norfolk, and their sons were Sir Herbert Croft (the catholic writer), William and Richard (*DNB*). The latter may be identified with the Richard Crofts who was one of the planters of the English colony in Jamestown, Virginia before 1608 (P. L. Barbour (Ed.), *The Jamestown Voyages under the First Charter, 1606–1609*, Cambridge, 1969, I, xxv, 222 *ff*; II, 382).
[2] HMC, 15th Rep. App. 10, 61; PRO, A.O. 1/287/1081.
[3] F. Moryson, *An Itinerary*, Glasgow, 1907–8, II, 345.
[4] PRO, A.O. 1/290/1088–9; the position was suspended for some years (*CSPI*, 1606–8, 12).
[5] *CSPI*, 1611–14, 293.
[6] G. Bennett, *History of Bandon*, Cork, 1869, 37, 72.

Curld

COOLFADDOE, BANDON, CO. CORK, MARKET HOUSE. Built from July 1615 to January 3, 1617 for Richard Boyle, later Earl of Cork, at a cost of £117 (*Grosart*, series 1, I, 27, 140; II, 102).

BANDON, CO. CORK, TOWN WALLS. The first stone was laid on June 19, 1620 by the Earl of Cork, and from then onwards, until the autumn of 1622, Crofte acted as chief contractor for the work (*Grosart*, series 1, I, 251 *ff*; II, 25, 63, 73). Drawings of one of its gates (published in *Loeber*, pl. 11) can be associated with the work of Crofte or of John Lodden (TCD, Ms 1209, f. 40; NLI, Ms 16 L 9).

CURLD, JOHN (fl. 1709). He is only known through his plans and elevations for Castle Coole, Co. Fermanagh, a country house which he designed for James Corry in 1709, on, for that time, traditional lines. He probably was an experienced architect for his draftsmanship is skilled.[1] Curld's house was later replaced by the current Castle Coole.

[1] *Irish Architectural Drawings, Exhibition Catalogue*, Dublin & London, 1965, No. 33. His drawings are among the Drawings Collection of the Irish Architectural Record Association in the NL1.

CURTIS or **CURTEIS, RALPH** (fl. 1625), builder who was patronized by the 1st Earl of Cork. Curtis seems to have specialized in the building of bridges. In 1625 he was paid for the building of a timber bridge at Cappoquin, Co. Waterford. A year later he built a bridge at Fermoy, Co. Cork. This bridge was swept away by a heavy flood in 1628, which also damaged a large part of the bridge at Cappoquin.[1] Nothing is known about Curtis's later career.

[1] *Grosart*, series 1, II, 162, 182, 187, 278.

D

DARLEY, JOHN (fl. 1664). A mason and a carpenter of this name is mentioned in late 17th-century records. The mason John Darley is first noted in 1664 when he was paid a total of £17 for work on the wall and one tower of Lisburn Castle,[1] Co. Antrim (the seat of Edward, 3rd Viscount Conway). When in 1671 40 tons of marble arrived at the Conway estate at Portmore, Co. Antrim, Sir George Rawdon wrote to Lord Conway that John Darley could not work with it, for he was only a mason.[2] In 1675, a John Darley of Arnos Vale, Co. Down, and George Darley of Dublin, stone-cutter were bound to the Rev. Dr Thomas Leland, bursar of Trinity College, Dublin, to pay him £345 2s. 1d. before June 24, 1677,[3] presumably for building work at the College. On February 28, 1677 Sir George Rawdon mentions the 'famous' carpenter, John Darley – possibly not the same individual as the mason John Darley – who was a Quaker.[4] This John Darley was later greatly praised by Conway's comptroller at Lisburn, who said that the carpenter encouraged much more those that have money to build than ever Sir George Rawdon has done, and that all those that built before he came are 'ready to hang themselves to see his work and designs, but he is a little of a Quaker'. He was then building a great house for William Benson in Lisburn, which was 'very fine work, set out to the street with medallions and cornice'. Another inhabitant pulled down the upper part of his newly built house for this carpenter to re-erect it with a projecting 'handsome architrave and cornice'. Darley was also building a three-storey house for himself, which was to be 'a fine piece of work'.[5] The town of Lisburn went up in flames in 1707, which probably destroyed Darley's work. The possible family relationship of John Darley to the stonemasons Arthur, George, Henry, Hugh and Moses Darley is not clear from available documents.

[1] *CSPI*, 1663–5, 442.
[2] PRO, SP 63/330, f. 204.
[3] TCD, MUN/P/1, f. 485–6.
[4] *CSPD*, 1676–7, 575.
[5] *CSPD*, 1677–8, 228–9.

DE KEYSER, WILLIAM (1603–?), sculptor and architect. He was the son of the Dutch architect and sculptor Hendrik De Keyser. For a number of years he worked with his father in Amsterdam, where he executed some very competent carvings.[1] De Keyser left for England in 1621, where he was possibly apprenticed to his brother-in-law Nicholas Stone who practised as a carver and master mason. While in England De Keyser married Walburga Parker. Some monuments ascribed to him were probably executed during this period.[2] He returned to Amsterdam in 1640, but after a period of eighteen years went back to England. In 1661 he was paid for making a drawing of the intended palace for King Charles II at Greenwich. He remained in London at least as late as 1678, but little is known about his work during this period. Three years later he or his son (see below) was working in Ireland. He presumably had been introduced to the Lord Lieutenant, the Duke of Ormonde, by Ormonde's agent in London, the Earl of Longford. The latter wrote on December 24, 1681: 'I am very glad Mr De Keizar has performed soe well wth yr Grace about the fountaine, if he finishes it according to the first designs, I am sure it will succeede all workes of that kinde in the Kingdome'.[3] The fountain, in all likelihood, was intended for the Duke's Kilkenny Castle. A contemporary drawing shows a fountain erected in Hugh May's [q.v.] Waterhouse, which was built at this time. It consisted of a large round gadrooned basin with a metal crown hanging over it.[4] Another fountain was erected in the garden in 1682 and is mentioned by the architect William Robinson as being at least 22 feet high.[5] It is not known for certain whether De Keyser knew Hugh May, but it seems quite possible that De Keyser, coming over from England, may have aided in the execution of May's design. Neither fountain survives.

It seems likely that De Keyser set up a workshop in Dublin. In 1683 he agreed with the city fathers to carve two statues for the Tholsel, representing Charles I and Charles II. The statues (or perhaps their replacements?) are now in the crypt of Christ Church Cathedral, and show rather mediocre craftsmanship. A last notice of De Keyser occurs in 1685 when he was paid for the statues, which he made two feet taller, after the shorter ones had not met with approval.[6] His skill as a draftsman may have brought him commissions for buildings from Irish patrons, but this is not confirmed by surviving records. It is not known when and where he died. There is no evidence that his son Hendrik Willemsz De Keyser also came to Ireland though he is known to have executed works at Bishop Auckland at Durham Castle in 1663–4.[7]

[1] Much of this account is based on *Colvin*, 257, and on the sources mentioned by him.

[2] *Walpole Society*, VII, 33.

[3] NLI, Ms 2417, ff. 183, 238.

[4] Drawing by Thomas Dineley published in the *Journal of the Kilkenny Archaeological Society*, n.s. 1862–3, *4*, 103–109.

[5] Bodl., Carte Ms 54, f. 74.

[6] *CARD*, V, 271, 291, 319, 354. Photographs of the statues have been published in *IGS*, April–September 1970, *13*, 20–1, where one has been mistakenly identified as James II instead of Charles I.

[7] Durham University Library, Mickleton & Spearman Mss, No. 13564.

DE PAGEZ, PETER GILBERT (fl. 1690–1721), French military engineer, who served during the Williamite War in Ireland. The nature of his service there has not come to light. Subsequently he served in Flanders,[1] and was appointed a gunner in the Peace Train in 1698.[2] He went to Portugal five years later,[3] and from 1706 to about 1710 served in Spain.[4] There he fortified Alicante, but quarrelled with its governor Major-General John Richards, who wrote 'Captain Pagez has taken a foolish occasion to be angry with me because I will not allow him to be another Vauban ...'. Afterwards he was promoted to Lieutenant-Colonel and served in Port Mahon and Gibraltar.[5] It is likely that by March 1711 he had returned to London, where he was in contact with Sir John Perceval.[6] In the next year De Pagez's petition for his pension on the Irish Establishment was allowed.[7] On January 31, 1712 Sir John Perceval's relative Edward Southwell wrote from London, mentioning 'Pagez's draughts'.[8] Southwell was then building the country seat Kings Weston, near Bristol in England, after the design of Sir John Vanbrugh. A plan of Southwell's house at Spring Garden in London carries an endorsement in French,[9] which may be from De Pagez's hand.[10] Much later, Southwell endorsed a drawing of the levels in the garden of Kings Weston with 'August 1720 Coll.pagez...'.[11] These pieces of evidence suggest an advisory role which De Pagez undertook as landscaper if not as architect over a good number of years. Perhaps it was through him that Southwell was to follow the French fashions by copying the sphinx carrying a cherubin from the gardens of Versailles to be erected at Kings Weston.[12] While it is known that several members of his family went to nearby Bristol, De Pagez left for Dublin in 1715.[13] Two years later he was appointed engineer for the fortifications at Galway,[14] but it is unknown what share De Pagez and John Corneille, Sr and Thomas Burgh (q.v.) had in this. In 1718–19 he was engineer to the fortifications of Limerick, which were altered extensively at this time.[15] One of his interests was the ports of Ireland about which he wrote a memorandum.[16] He made his will at Carlow in 1721.[17] He had married Anne Esther de Goulaine, and their short-lived son, born in 1717 and named Thomas was baptised in the French Church in Dublin, with Captain Thomas Burgh (q.v.), the Irish Surveyor-General and De Pagez's superior, acting as godfather.[18]

[1] *CTB*, 1711, pt. II, 343.

[2] *Dalton*, VI, 43 *n*. 3.

[3] *Ibid.*, V, 122 *n*. 34.

[4] *CTB*, 1711, pt. II, 344.

[5] Cited in W. Porter, *History of the Corps of Royal Engineers*, London, 1889–1915, I, 128–9, 135; see also *CTB*, 1710, pt. II, 344; *Dalton*, VI, 47.

[6] BL, Add. Ms 47026, f. 121.

[7] *CTB*, 1711, pt. II, 186.

[8] PROI, Ms I A 52, 142, 31 January 1711–12, London, [Edward Southwell] to Joshua Dawson (extract of letter, original destroyed).

[9] K. Downes, 'The Kings Weston book of drawings', *Architectural History*, 1967, *10*, p. 17, dr. no. 10. Downes (p. 17) states that Edward Southwell died in this house in 1730. Elsewhere, however, is noted that this house was sold to one Mr Pitts in 1710 for £2300 (T. Thorpe, *Catalogue of Southwell Manuscripts*, London, 1834, 627).

[10] I have been unable to compare the handwriting of De Pagez with that of the drawing. I am not aware of other Frenchmen with whom Southwell had artistic contacts at this period.

[11] Downes, *op.cit.*, 22, dr. no. 43. Note that the endorsement on the drawing states 'August, 1720 Coll. pages's Levells of Kings Weston Garden, from the House to the top of the Hill' (Fig. 36), and not 'pages Levells' as stated in the text.

[12] Downes, *op.cit.*, Fig. 22.

[13] C. E. Lart, *Huguenot Pedigrees*, London, 1924, 74–5.

[14] PRO, SP 63/375, f. 417, February 6, 1715.

[15] TCD, Ms 1179, f. 107; *Commons Jour.*, 1715–21, 543, 737.

[16] PROI, M 3036. Only a reference to this memorandum survives, which did not carry a date.

[17] Sir Arthur Vicars (Ed.), *Index to the Prerogative Wills of Ireland . . .*, Dublin, 1897, 365.

[18] See note 13, and J. J. Digges La Touche (Ed.), 'Registers of the French Confirmed Churches of St Patrick and St Mary', Dublin, *Huguenot Society*, 1893, VII, 33.

DODDINGTON, or DODINGTON, Sir EDWARD (fl. 1602). He is first noted in Ireland in 1602 as Captain of Foot active in Munster during the Tyrone war.[1] His name is not mentioned in the contemporary records of engineering works undertaken during the war. Afterwards he became Constable of Dungiven Castle, Co. Derry, and Killybegs Castle, Co. Donegal. He received royal funds for the repair or rebuilding of Dungiven Castle in 1611.[2] Later he stated that he had invested the greater part of his estate in this castle, but was forced to surrender it to the Skinners' Company of London as part of its new plantation but stayed as its tenant.[3] As a servitor he does not seem to have benefited from the grants of lands in Ulster. He was discharged in October 1611 and was rewarded with a pension two years later. In 1612 he is mentioned as one of the burgesses of the newly incorporated town of Limavady, Co. Derry.[4] Later he became agent for the Ironmongers' Company but apparently didn't hold this post for long.[5] Evidence is lacking that he designed Lizard Castle, Co. Derry, which was erected soon afterwards on the Company's land. However, the builder of Lizard Castle was Peter Benson (q.v.),[6] who later successfully tendered for the building of the town walls of Derry. Doddington has been credited with the design of the town walls,[7] but Capt. Panton has also been mentioned in this respect, while Capt. John Vaughan rather than Doddington oversaw the erection. In 1611, Doddington adapted his residence,

Dodson

Dungiven Castle, the main seat of the Skinner's Company, to plantation standards. It became a 'strong castle' of two and a half storeys high with a large bawn. He also built the Skinner's other residence at Crossalt, Co. Derry, a building 80 by 34 feet with a bawn and two turrets. Drawings of both buildings show them to have been conventional for their time.[8] Doddington and Theophilus Buckworth, Bishop of Dromore obtained a lease from the Archbishop of Armagh of an area of the town of Armagh, with the aim of 'replanting and re-edifying of the decayed cyttie.' They undertook to lay out and divide the area into plots, and started to lease to tenants who were obliged to build. By 1622 less than half of the tenants had built; ultimately the scheme was not very successful.[9] Doddington himself had covenanted to build a 'fair house' in Armagh and two 'English' houses on the lands which he leased from the See in Co. Tyrone.[10] In an inscription on the 'classical' monument to his first wife Elizabeth who died in 1610, he states that he was the first to build in Coleraine in the English style.[11] He was knighted, but the year is unknown. He died before 1619.[12] His widow Anne, daughter of Tristem Beresford,[13] continued to reside at Dungiven together with twenty-four relatives as was reported in 1618–9. She married secondly Sir Francis Cooke.

[1] S. O'Grady (Ed.), *Sir Thomas Stafford. Pacata Hibernica*, 1896, II, 155.

[2] PRO, A.O. 1/290/1088; *Carew*, 1603–24, 221; *CSPI*. 1608–10, 291.

[3] *CSPI*, 1611–14, 34–5.

[4] *Ibid.*, 151, 300; M. C. Griffith, *Irish Patent Rolls of James I*, Dublin, 1964, 256.

[5] J. Nicholl, *Some Account of the Worshipful Company of Ironmongers*, London, 1851, 415. The other agent of the company was George Hammond.

[6] G. Hill, *An Historical Account of the Plantation of Ulster . . .*, Belfast, 1877, reprinted Shannon, 1970, 442.

[7] *Historic Buildings . . . in the City of Derry*, Belfast, 1970, 15; C. D. Milligan, *The Townwalls of Derry*, Londonderry, 1948, I, 30.

[8] T. W. Moody, *The Londonderry Plantation*, Belfast, 1939, 298–9, 313; *CSPI*, 1615–25, 384; *Carew*, 1603–24, 421; D. A. Chart, *Londonderry and the London Companies . . .*, Belfast, 1928, pl. 31. For a copy of a drawing of Dungiven Castle see also TCD, Ms 1209, f.25.

[9] Armagh Public Library, Ms (stored in oblong box), Dec. 1615, Lease by T. Buckworth, Bishop of Dromore and E. Dodington as trustees for the See of Armagh to J. Hall of a plot in Armagh; R. J. Hunter, 'Towns in the Ulster Plantation', *Studia Hibernica*, 1971, *11*, 40–79.

[10] L. P. Murray, A rent-roll of all the houses and lands belonging to the See of Armagh, *Archivium Hibernicum*, 1941, *8*, 101.

[11] W. D. Girvan, *Historic buildings . . . in Coleraine and Portstewart*, Belfast, 1972, 13.

[12] Griffith, *op.cit.*, 434–5.

[13] *Lodge*, II, 296.

DODSON, WILLIAM (fl. ? 1639–1671), architect, who came from Westminster, London. He may have married Alice Gibson there in 1639.[1] Little is known about his early life. He started his professional career as a farmer of excise (see below), and came over to Ireland prior to 1659, when he was noted in Dublin.[2] From about 1664 onwards Dodson was involved in the construction of additions to Phoenix House, after the departure of Dr John Westley (q.v.). Dodson presented the Lord Lieutenant, the Duke of Ormonde, with several large rebuilding schemes for the house, one of which included a classical portico. The plans were never realized, and Dodson's work on Phoenix House and stables probably was not extensive and seemed to have been interrupted prematurely, possibly due to the problems encountered during the building of the wall around Phoenix Park (see below). The proposed portico at Phoenix House, and the oval St Andrew's Church (the plan of which he may have copied from Serlio's *Tutte l'Opera d'Archittetura*) are indications that Dodson was very aware of Renaissance architecture. He was one of the earliest known architects in Ireland who was involved in landscaping: he

48

planned walks radiating from Phoenix House, together with ponds with islands in them,[3] as well as the laying out of streets towards the park,[4] and towards Ormonde's planned Palace at Oxmantown.[5] At the height of his reputation, Sir George Rawdon considered Dodson 'our great architect here' in Dublin.[6] The last known governmental work by Dodson was the building of a flight of steps in the Privy Council garden, Dublin.[7] The impact of Dodson's work on his contemporaries is hard to assess. He had a deputy (whose name is unknown) for the overseeing of his work, but Dodson was reported to be very often present in person on the building sites.[8] The craftsmanship of his buildings was often of inferior quality.

When Phoenix Park was made into a royal deer park, Dodson presented the Lord Lieutenant, the Duke of Ormonde, with two estimates for building a wall round it.[9] The building of this wall affected Dodson's reputation seriously. In November 1664 he reported to Ormonde that one mile of the new wall was to be pulled down because of its poor condition.[10] Subsequently, the contractor, the mason Henry Gamble, was not paid by Dodson.[11] In March 1665 Dodson left for England to report to Ormonde on the 'proceedings' in the park; the wall at the time was 7 foot high and 9,938 yards long.[12] Shortly after a committee reported on the work by Gamble and Dodson.[13] This was followed by an investigation which showed that the wall was a dry wall without mortar,[14] under the bricklayers James Browne (q.v.), Thomas Browne (q.v.) and the plasterer William Robinson. Dodson's next move was a proposal to keep the deteriorating wall in repair for £100 per annum, for seven years,[15] and ultimately his proposal was accepted.[16] However, in 1667 the Irish Council ordered another investigation,[17] and in the following year it was reported that two-thirds of the wall was insufficiently built, and had to be taken down and rebuilt. This was due to the badness of the stone, and the poor craftsmanship. The expenditure up to date had been £6,080. Col Edward Cooke reported on December 12, 1668, 'the old wall of the [Phoenix] park is as decayed as Dodson is in honesty, but the new work is good'.[18] Even in June 1669 the Duke of Ormonde's steward was of the opinion that Dodson should be glad to escape punishment.[19]

His main profession was the farming of various taxes. The first known contract he made in 1653, together with his long-standing partner Thomas Morrice, was for the farming of the excise in Norfolk, and part of Suffolk for half a year at £2,000.[20] Four years later the two partners contracted for the excise and impost in several towns in Kent and Sussex for three years, at a rent of £120,500.[21] These contracts in England were followed in 1658 by a lease of the custom of tonnage and poundage, and the excise on all native and foreign commodities in Ireland for seven years. For this contract they were joined by John Drury, of London, and together they paid £70,000 a year for the lease.[22] Prior to 1659 Dodson and someone named William Hawkins were also farmers of the excise in the 13 counties of Wales.[23] At the Restoration Dodson's leases for customs and excise were most likely cancelled, but in September 1662 he re-emerged as Revenue Commissioner in Ireland (his patent was renewed in March 1664, and in March 1665). Dodson and Thomas Morrice were granted the farming of the customs and duties in Ireland in October 1663.[24] Dodson in 1664 received approval for taking over the farm of licences for selling ale, beer, etc., in Ireland from Roger Boyle, Earl of Orrery (q.v.) and Lord Kingston.[25] In the meantime, Dodson and Morrice had presented fraudulent accounts of money due to them from the farm of the customs and excise in Ireland during the Commonwealth, which led to the appointment of a committee to inquire into their accounts.[26] A year later Dodson and Morrice petitioned the King to grant them the farming of the customs and excise of Ireland, for eleven years at £70,000 per annum.[27] Up till his death in 1671 Dodson was still involved in the farming of the revenue in Ireland.[28] His activities, both in Ireland and England suggests that he was a man of considerable means. He had estates in Co. Monaghan,[29] and in 1665 was granted a plot on Oxmantown Green.[30] Presumably after his death his widow held several tenements in St Bride's parish, Dublin besides her own house in Aungier St.[31] Dodson died in Ireland, probably in 1671, without making a will, for in January 1672 his son William claimed the administration of his father's goods.[32] His son presumably was the William Dodson (fl. 1665) who as a military engineer and surveyor, worked in the Fens in England under the Dutch engineer Vermuyden.[33] On August 14, 1671 this son petitioned for his father's arrears.[34]

[1] R. M. Glencross (Ed.), *A Calendar of the Marriage License Allegations in the Registry of the Bishop of London*, London, 1937, I, 188.
[2] BL, Add. Ms 21425, f. 65.
[3] *HMC, 6th Rep.*, 771; NLI, Ms 2336, ff. 245–9; Bodl., Carte Ms 33, f. 714.
[4] NLI, Ms 2334, f. 31.
[5] Bodl., Carte Mss 145, f. 190; Ms 141, f. 60.
[6] *CSPI*, 1666–9, 98.
[7] Bodl., Carte Ms 35, ff. 275, 276ᵛ.
[8] NLI, N6268–6271, Pos 7074–7077.
[9] NLI, Ms 2489, ff. 205–6, 249.
[10] Bodl., Carte Ms 33, f. 714.
[11] *HMC, 9th Rep. App. II*, 159–161.
[12] *HMC, Ormonde*, n.s. III, 189.
[13] *HMC, 9th Rep. App. II*, 168.
[14] *HMC, 10th Rep. App. V*, 5.
[15] NLI, Ms 2336, f. 177.
[16] NLI, N6268–6271, Pos 7074–7077.
[17] *HMC, Ormonde*, n.s. III, 291.
[18] Bodl., Carte Ms 215, f. 274.
[19] *HMC, Ormonde*, n.s. III, 293.
[20] *CSPD*, 1652–3, 270.
[21] *CSPD*, 1657–8, 113.
[22] *Ibid.*, 287.
[23] *CTB*, 1660–7, 636.
[24] Bodl., Carte Ms 52, f. 69.
[25] *CSPI*, 1663–5, 401.
[26] *CSPI*, 1666–9, 114, 349.
[27] *HMC, Ormonde*, n.s. III, 278–9; Bodl., Carte Ms 52, f. 69.
[28] NLI, N6268–6271, Pos 7074–7077.
[29] *HMC, 8th Rep. App. I*, 510.
[30] *CARD*, IV, 332.
[31] NLI, Ms 5230, f. 13.
[32] PRO, Prob. 6/46, p. 57.
[33] E. G. R. Taylor, *The Mathematical Practioners of Tudor and Stuart England*, Cambridge, 2nd ed., 1967, 252; H. C. Darby, *The Draining of the Fens*, Cambridge, 2nd ed., 1968, *passim*.
[34] NLI, N6268–6271, Pos 7074–7077.

PHOENIX HOUSE, CO. DUBLIN. Presumably Dodson prepared, in about 1664 or 1665, three estimates for extensive rebuilding of this royal lodge, the highest costing £7,510. In another proposal he planned to erect a classical portico. These schemes were not executed. Instead Dodson made some minor repairs, which, together with the repairs of Chapelizod House, totalled £1,589 13s. 1d. It seems likely that Dodson finished the stables of Phoenix House, which had been started by Dr John Westley (q.v.). (NLI, Mss 2487, ff. 23–4, 53, 113; (2489, 205–6).

LODGES, PHOENIX PARK, CO. DUBLIN. Together with the walls of Phoenix Park (see above) Dodson built several lodges; one of these was erected in 1666 near

Kilmainham gaol, at the cost of about £75 (*HMC, 6th Rep.*, 771; Bodl., Carte Ms 154, f. 71ᵛ). Other lodges rebuilt by Dodson were Ashtown Lodge and Newtown Lodge (*HMC, Ormonde*, n.s. III, 291; *HMC, 6th Rep.*, 771; Bodl., Carte Ms 145, f. 204–5). He built a new lodge at Gallow's Green (NLI, Ms 2489, f. 205–6). None survive.

OXMANTOWN, CO. DUBLIN, ORMONDE'S PALACE. Dodson was from 1664 onwards involved with the surveying of the seven acres granted to James Butler, 1st Duke of Ormonde. He seems to have started planning the palace as well, and in 1666 prepared stone work for the building. Ormonde's worsening finances put a halt to the erection of the Palace (Bodl., Carte Mss 33, f. 714; Ms 144, f. 60; Ms 154, f. 71ᵛ).

SIR GEORGE LANE'S HOUSE. Dr John Westley (q.v.) wrote in 1664 to Sir George Lane (secretary to Ormonde) mentioning Dodson's designs for Lane's house, which he compared unfavourably with his own designs (BL, Add. Ms 45941A, f. 65). This possibly refers to Lane's country house, Rathcline, Co. Longford, which was renovated in 1666–7 (now ruined) or a planned town house in Dublin.

CHAPELIZOD, CO. DUBLIN, CHAPELIZOD HOUSE. In 1666 Dodson presented Ormonde with proposals to increase the height of this royal lodge. Two years later, Dodson claimed expenses of £999 5*s* 10*d*. which were rejected by a commission of inquiry (NLI, Ms 2489, ff. 205–6; Bodl., Carte Ms 154, f. 71ᵛ; NLI, Ms 2339, ff. 285, 289, 293; *HMC, Ormonde*, n.s. III, 291). Dem.

CHAPELIZOD, CO. DUBLIN, BRIDGE. Probably in 1663 Dodson made an estimate of building a new bridge at Chapelizod, over the Liffey, at a cost of £870, and included the King arms placed in a piece of 'Architect or Masons' Worke. . . .' (NLI, Ms 2489, f. 205–6). In the 1668 inquiry Dodson's bridge was found to be 'sufficiently' done for the £195 1*s*. 7*d*. paid to him (*HMC, Ormonde*, n.s. III, 291).

LODGE FOR VISCOUNT CONWAY. In 1666 Sir George Rawdon, agent to Edward, 3rd Viscount Conway, contacted Dodson about the model and plan of a lodge, which was planned at Tunney, near Portmore, Co. Antrim. It seems uncertain whether the lodge was erected (*CSPI*, 1666–9, 98).

DUBLIN, ST ANDREW'S CHURCH. Dodson's oval model was approved on April 18, 1670. The first stone was laid on May 28 following by the Lord Lieutenant Berkeley. The church was built at a cost of £1,887 by the carpenter Abraham Hawksworth (q.v.); the overseer was Dr Miles Symner (q.v.). A drawing of the church was made by Francis Place *c*. 1699. (*CSPI*, 1669–70, 142; TCD, Ms 2026; *JRSAI*, 1932, 7th ser., *62*, pl. 6; H. A. Wheeler & M. J. Craig, *The Dublin Churches*, Dublin, 1948, 9.) The oval dome of the church is also shown on Place's view of Dublin from the South, where its shape is slightly different from that in the close-up drawing by Place (R. Loeber, 'An Unpublished View of Dublin by Francis Place', *IGS*, 1978, *21*, pl. 2).

PORTMORE, CO. ANTRIM, STABLE. In May 1670 Edward, 3rd Viscount Conway sent from England the drawings by William Hurlbutt (q.v.) for this grand stable to his estate agent in Ireland, Sir George Rawdon. Dodson then made various proposals for alterations to the roof structure and probably also to its facade which were not approved by Conway and Hurlbutt (Huntington Library, San Marino, California, Hastings Mss 14485; 14486–7).

E

EDBURY, WILLIAM (fl. 1616), carpenter who agreed in 1616 with Sir Richard Boyle to roof the chapel at Youghal with a 'compaste imbowed Roof'. He was also to roof the vestry, and to complete the carpentry of the almshouse near the church.[1] The compass or barrel roof of St Mary's church is one of the earliest documented for the period. Originally it was painted; it was taken down in 1784. His name occurs as a leaseholder in lands of Castletown, Co. Limerick in 1622.[2]

[1] *Grosart* series 1, I, 129; series 2, II, 119–20.
[2] BL, Add. Ms 4756, f. 92.

F

FARNHAM, HUMPHREY (fl. 1616), builder. He is first noted in 1616 when he and Samuel Molyneux (q.v.) examined repairs done at the Bridewell, just outside the walls of Dublin.[1] The building at this time was transferred to Trinity College for the use of students. In the following year Farnham was paid for the erection of the gate house to Dublin Castle, which was not completed until 1618.[2] He also executed repairs to Phoenix House for which he was paid £224 16s. 4d. sometime between 1619 and 1623.[3] This country house just outside Dublin had been acquired by the Lord Deputy Sir Oliver St John in 1618 as a vice-regal country residence. It seems very likely that he acted in a supervisory capacity rather than as a contractor. For example, his payment for the works at Phoenix House included a salary for four shillings per day eighty days 'for his charges and attendance about the works'.[4] His work at Dublin Castle shows a gatehouse which was medieval in character and devoid of architectural decoration.[5] It no longer exists. Other works by him are not known. In 1623 a Humphrey Farnam was named as commissioner for the escheated lands in Co. Cavan, but it is not clear whether this was the same person.[6]

[1] TCD, Ms MUN/P/25, f. 7.
[2] *CSPI*, 1615–25, 196, 202.
[3] PRO, A.O.1/291/1092.
[4] *Ibid.*
[5] R. Loeber, The rebuilding of Dublin Castle; thirty critical years 1660–1689, *Studies*, 1980, *69*, pl. 6.
[6] *CSPI*, 1615–25, 439.

G

GALILEI, ALESSANDRO (1691–1737), architect from Florence, who came to England in 1714 and visited Ireland in the summer of 1718. He came to the British Isles upon the invitation of John Molesworth, who was the British envoy to the Tuscan court from 1710 to 1714. Colvin and Kieven[1] have described Galilei's commissions in England, or rather his near lack of work there. John Molesworth, his father Robert (created Viscount Molesworth in 1716), Sir Thomas Hewett, and Sir George Markham had formed, what they called 'the new Junta for Architecture'. As Colvin relates, Galilei was the chosen disciple of this movement to give British architecture a more classical idiom.

Viscount Molesworth's estate was situated not far from Dublin at Breckdenstown, which he improved at least from 1709 onwards.[2] In a letter, written *c.*1716–17, probably from London, Viscount Molesworth mentioned the laying out of canals and other improvements, and referred to the advice given by Galilei. Evidence, however, that Galilei had come over to Ireland at this time, is lacking.[3] As a committee member, Molesworth had recommended Galilei for the designing of St Werburgh's Church in Dublin in October 1716.[4] However, its foundations had already been laid in July of that year. The Irish Surveyor-General Thomas Burgh (q.v.) supervised its construction. The Italian appearance of the church does not mask Galilei's skills: it was copied from da Volterra's Santa Chiara in Rome (see Burgh q.v.)

In England, Galilei had prepared drawings for some of the fifty new churches in London. Dublin also saw the building of new churches, but on a very much smaller scale. One of these, St Ann's Church was started on the Molesworth estate after April 1719.[5] Again, an Italian design was chosen, as is known from an engraving on Brooking's map of Dublin (1728).[6] It seems practically certain that Galilei was not its author, for the design was copied from the facade of S. Giacomo degli Incurabili in Rome, built after the design of the architects de Volterra and Maderno. According to Craig the architect of the Dublin St Ann's Church was Isaac Wills, who worked closely with Thomas Burgh[7] (q.v.).

Plans for Galilei's employment in Ireland were made at least as early as 1717, when John Molesworth mentioned Galilei, who he thought 'the best Architect in Europe', in connection with his future patron William Conolly, Speaker of the Irish House of Commons. Finally in the summer of 1718 Galilei crossed over to Ireland. Little direct evidence has come to light about his actual stay in the country. His most important commission was the designing of the exterior of Castletown House, Co. Kildare, for Speaker Conolly. This very Italianate 13-bay front with colonades attached to pavilions was not started until 1722, long after Galilei had left Ireland. Much of its interior was the responsibility of the Irish architect Edward Lovett Pearce.[8]

It is not known whether Galilei was asked by the Molesworths to design a new country seat, possibly at Breckdenstown, Co. Dublin. Plans for this structure fell through due to shortage of money. The garden temple at Drumcondra, Co. Dublin, built for Marmaduke Coghill, has been ascribed to Galilei. His design for a mausoleum, possibly for William Stanus of Carlingford, Co. Louth, was never executed. As Galilei made 'different designs for several gentlemen',[9] it is possible that other unidentified Irish patrons made use of his skills.

After his return to England, he failed to receive sufficient commissions, and left for Italy. In 1721 he was still in contact with John Molesworth.[10] A few years later he corresponded with Edward Lovett Pearce, who was then travelling in Italy.[11] They had already met in England in 1719. Their continued contact led to the finalizing of the designs for Castletown House, the building of which was started in 1722. Few other houses in Ireland have such a pivotal place in Irish architectural history. The house marked the end of a period in Irish architecture which was provincial in nature and the beginning of more than a century in which classical architecture matured. Otherwise, Galilei's influence on Irish architecture is hard to trace. His most important design in Italy was the facade of St John Lateran in Rome (1734). He died three years later.

[1] *Colvin*, 324–5; E. Kieven, 'Galilei in England', *Country Life*, Jan. 25, 1973, 210–12. John Molesworth also brought the singer Sarpetini, mentioned in Sir John Perceval's correspondence of 1716, from Italy to England. (BL, Add. Ms 46967, ff. 55, 69v.)
[2] E. Malins & The Knight of Glin, *Lost Demesnes, Irish Landscape Gardening 1600–1845*, London, 1976, 15. Molesworth planned the replanting of his estate, which had been devastated by the war, as early as 1692 (Bodl., Carte Ms 243, f. 94v).
[3] Malins & The Knight of Glin, *op.cit.*, 15; *HMC, Various Coll.*, VIII, 273.
[4] *HMC, Various Coll.*, VIII, 270; see also R. Loeber, 'Classicism in Ireland before the Georgian Era' *Architectural History*, 1979, *22*, 59–60, pl. 12a–126.
[5] An advertisement for sub-contractors for the building appeared in the *Dublin Post-man* of April 8, 1719 (copy in the Gilbert Collection in the Public Library, Pearse St, Dublin).
[6] See *Loeber, op.cit.*
[7] *Craig*, 113.
[8] M. Craig, The Knight of Glin, & J. Cornforth, 'Castletown Co. Kildare', *Country Life*, March 27, 1969.
[9] Kieven, *op.cit.*, 210.
[10] *HMC, Various Coll.*, VIII, 307, 315.
[11] The Knight of Glin, 'New light on Castletown, Co. Kildare', *Quarterly Bulletin of the Irish Georgian Society*, Jan.–June 1965, *13*, 8.

GAWEN, TRISTAM (fl. 1612), appointed on March 16, 1612, together with Samuel Molyneux (q.v.) Clerk of the Works in Ireland.[1] This seems to have been an honorary position, for Gawen is not known to have been involved with building. Sometime prior to 1622 his name ceased to occur on the Irish Establishment.[2]

[1] J. L. J. Hughes, *Patentee Officers in Ireland*, Dublin, 1960, 56.
[2] Kent County Library, Sackville Ms ON 8541.

GRAVES, THOMAS (fl. 1682). From 1682 onwards he supervised the building of the Tholsel in Dublin, which was started in 1676 and took nine years to be completed. He very likely was a master builder, whose salary and that of his servant amounted to 10s. per week.[1] At the Tholsel he oversaw the work of the masons John Rothery, and John Whinrey (q.v.), the joiners Joseph Taylor and Thomas Howell, the carver Peter Delalis, the carpenters Paul Young and Edward Brock, the plasterer William Wallis, and the painter-plasterer-gilder Isaac Chalk. The Dutch sculptor Hendrik de Keyser (q.v.) carved the statues of Charles I and Charles II.[2] Graves' late arrival as overseer makes it unlikely that he designed the Tholsel, which was built in the artisan mannerist style, and was demolished in 1806. Graves received several payments for other Dublin City works: in 1682 £18 for work at Bridge Gate and Essex Gate, and £20 8s. 2d. for work at the Main Guard.[3] He petitioned the City Council in 1687 for the payment of £6 11s. 4d. for several disbursements made for the new guard house under Newgate.[4] He held the office of bearer of the mace, and possibly can be identified with the Thomas Graves who was mentioned in 1680 as adjutant of the militia in the County and City of Dublin.[5] In the early 1660s a Thomas Graves owned a residence with 12 hearths in St Catherine's parish,[6] and he is probably the person who is mentioned several times in the vestry book of St Catherine's Church.[7]

[1] *CARD*, V, 289–90, 380.
[2] *CARD*, V, 46*ff*; *Craig*, 47; *IGS*, 1970, Apr.–Sept., *13*, 43, pp. 20–21.
[3] *CARD*, V, 208, 231.
[4] *CARD*, V, 433.
[5] *Craig*, 47; *CARD*, V, 196.
[6] *57th Report of the Deputy Keeper of the Public Records in Ireland*, 1936, 562.
[7] PROI, M 5122.

GREENE, JOHN (fl. 1663), a carpenter, from outside Dublin, who was admitted to the City as a freeman in 1664. The year before that he had been paid £83 1*s*. for erecting a new gallery in Christ Church Cathedral.[1] From 1669 until 1676 he is mentioned numerous times in the account books of the new Blue Coat Hospital for a variety of carpentry, including the turret of the Hospital, which was his free contribution.[2] In 1674 he took down a castle near the town wall, and erected Essex Gate in its place. He may have built at Oxmantown Green where he was granted two lots in 1665.[3] The date of his death is not known. A carpenter by the name of John Green is mentioned in connection with the building of St Paul's Church in 1708,[4] and he possibly is the person named as city surveyor in 1679,[5] and may have been a relative of John Greene whose work is discussed above.

[1] Bodl., Carte Ms 52, f. 260ᵛ.
[2] C. Lucas, *A Narrative and an Accompt Concerning the hospital on Oxmantown-Green, Dublin . . .*, Dublin, 1749, 22, 30.
[3] *CARD*, V, 44–5, 144–5; IV, 330.
[4] King's Hospital, Palmerstown, Co. Dublin, Blue Coat School Account Book, p. 334.
[5] *CARD*, V, 184.

H

HALLAM, JOHN (fl. 1659–1673). John Hallam is first mentioned in the 'census' of about 1659 as of Co. Offaly. On February 6, 1661 he received the office of Director, Overseer and Surveyor-General of Fortifications in Ireland, a post in which he was joined a number of days later by Capt. John Paine (q.v.). Hallam possibly was related to Sir Francis Shaen, who, at the time, claimed to have obtained the position for 'his brother' Hallam, recommending him from London to the Earl of Orrery (q.v.).[1] Orrery in turn had already recommended him to Secretary of State Nicholas at the end of 1660, saying that Hallam was well-known to the Marquis of Ormonde. Elsewhere Hallam recalled that he had been 'a faithful subiect'. In April 1661 he is mentioned as having received pardon for his activities during the Commonwealth,[2] in which he was 'a great sufferer for his Majesty'. Together with Capt. John Paine he requested, in October 1662, a raise in salary,[3] which was refused. It seems likely that Hallam's patent as Director, Overseer and Surveyor-General never became operative. In a petition to Ormonde dated July 1663, he requested 'for want of the present posessing' of this position, to be granted employment either as Lieutenant or Cornet of Horse.[4] This request was agreed upon by Ormonde, but delay forced Hallam to petition again in order to be put on the army list.[5] Under the Acts of Settlement and Explanation Hallam was granted estates in the counties of Offaly and Westmeath. He had his residence at Hallam Hill, Co. Offaly; in 1663 he was Justice of the Peace and Sheriff of the same county. He made his will on September 4, 1671, naming as the only beneficiary Thomas L'Estrange, son and heir of William L'Estrange, of Castle Bennett, Co. Offaly. The will was proved June 20, 1673.[6] No designs or buildings of Hallam have been identified.

[1] E. MacLysaght (Ed.), *Calendar of Orrery Papers*, Dublin, 1941, 8.
[2] *CSPI*, 1660–2, 138, 318; Bodl., Carte Ms 32, f. 706.
[3] *CSPI*, 1660–2, 604.
[4] Bodl., Carte Ms 32, f. 706.
[5] NLI, Ms 2495, f. 461.
[6] Geneal. Off., Ms 424, p. 170.

HAMOND, JOHN (fl. 1611), mason, who was admitted as freeman to the town of Youghal on January 8, 1611.[1] In the following March he and his father Richard Hamond (q.v.) agreed with Sir Richard Boyle (later Earl of Cork) for the mannerist decoration of polychrome marble of the outside gate of the College at Youghal, and for the erection of a classical, double-storied marble chimney piece in the parlour of the house – which remained unfinished until 1615 – and another in the dining room. In 1612 the two Hamonds were paid for polishing the 'black' window in the gallery, and a year later they were presumably responsible for the erection of a double chimney piece in the 'new' study, 'answerable' to the one in the dining room.[2] None of these works survive.

[1] R. Caulfield (Ed.), *The Council Book of the Corporation of Youghal*, Guildford, 1878, 16.
[2] *Grosart*, series 1, I, 8, 22, 76; Chatsworth, Lismore Ms 3, f. 131.

HAMOND, RICHARD (fl. 1611), mason, who was employed by Sir Richard Boyle (see under John Hamond). Richard Hamond's son John signed the receipts in 1612

Hand

for work executed jointly, which might indicate that by then Richard Hamond had left Youghal or had died.

HAND, THOMAS (fl. 1720–1729), appointed as first Clerk to the Works at Dr Steevens' Hospital Dublin, January 27, 1720, presumably upon recommendation of the architect Thomas Burgh (q.v.). Little is known about Hand's work. He died in 1729, after which his post was given to Charles Lyndon (q.v.).[1]

[1] T. P. Kirkpatrick, *The History of Doctor Steevens' Hospital, Dublin, 1720–1920*, Dublin, 1924, 33, 359.

HANSARD, Sir RICHARD (fl. 1600–1619), military engineer and builder of English extraction. He was the third son of Richard Hansard of Biscathorpe, Lincolnshire, and Elizabeth, coheir of Robert Blount, son of Thomas, Baron Mountjoy. Through his wife Richard Jr was related to Lord Mountjoy, who as Lord Deputy of Ireland was influential in steering Richard Hansard's career. He is first noted in 1600 among the horsemen who arrived in Ireland from England. Shortly afterwards he was employed as Lieutenant of the Ordnance by the Earl of Ormonde in the journey into Munster against the Earl of Tyrone. Subsequently he became a Quarter-Master of the army during the Lord Deputy Mountjoy's campaign in the North of Ireland,[1] where he was also employed as a trenchmaster for fortifications.[2] Aside from a short trip to England,[3] Hansard, who carried the rank of Captain, was employed in the North. In November 1600 he was ordered by Lord Mountjoy to draw plans for the building of a fort near Newry (later called Mount Norris Fort, Co. Armagh, but Hansard's plans were rejected in favour of one possibly made by Levan De Rose.[4] Shortly afterwards Hansard with his troop of 100 Foot went to Carlingford, where he was shot in the back, which made him lame.[5] He was sent to England in 1601, being recommended by Lord Mountjoy to Sir Robert Cecil for his 'valour, industry, and understanding in his profession ...'.[6] At this time Sir Geoffrey Fenton, Clerk-General of the Works, thought that Hansard had 'a very good insight in fortifications ...'.[7] His troop is mentioned as being stationed at Moyry, Co. Armagh in June 1601,[8] where a new fort was being raised under the direction of the engineer Levan De Rose. Later in the year he was directed to move to Munster to combat the Spaniards. As a Lieutenant of the Ordnance he attended the siege of Kinsale.[9] Evidence is lacking that he erected fortifications there, but he may have come in contact with Paul Ive and Josias Bodley (q.v.) who were the active engineers at the siege. His company returned to the North, and was stationed at Loughfoyle in 1603.[10] The next year Hansard was knighted.[11] In 1607 he was allowed to move his Company to Lifford, Co. Donegal,[12] which town had been granted to him in 1610.[13] There he designed and built a new fort, which was described in 1611 as 'A good and strong fort built of lime and stone with bulwarks, a parapet, and a large ditch of good depth ... with a storehouse for victuals and munition, a gatehouse with a drawbridge'. The survey of 1622 mentions a 'faire' stone house within the fort, probably the storehouse mentioned above, which measured 112 by 21 foot, and had two storeys with four dormers. He also improved the adjoining town, where he built 21 out of the 58 houses.[14] At the nearby plantation estate Monester (also called Manister) Hansard bought an interest before 1613. For a share of £100 he bound himself to 'perform ye stone-building' required by the conditions of the plantation. The 1622 survey confirms that Hansard built 'a Bawne of lyme and stone, 80 foot square, and 12 foot high, with 4 Flankers; on the fore part whereof he hath built a house of stone and

58

lyme, slated, 40 foot long, and 20 foot broad, being a storie & a half high, with 2 Returnes, 12 foot a peece.'[15] These buildings no longer survive.

Considering the many plantation buildings which were started in the 1610s, it seems quite probable that Hansard volunteered for other commissions. As a servitor he obtained a grant of 1,000 acres elsewhere in Co. Donegal, which he passed shortly afterwards to Capt. William Stewart.[16] Little is known about the last years of Hansard's life, which he probably spent at Lifford. His will was proved in 1620, and he was buried at Lifford, where a monument to him is still extant.[17] His wife was Anne Morbury, who predeceased him by one year.[18] Sir Richard Hansard had stipulated in his will that out of his estate £400 a year was to be settled for the building of a church and a free school at Lifford, with a reversion to his relative John Hansard. The trustees of the estate, who included Sir John Vaughan seemed to have conveyed the estate, to themselves, which led to long litigations.[19]

[1] PRO, A.O. 1/287/1081.
[2] *CSPI*, 1600, 430.
[3] *Ibid.*, 278.
[4] *CSPI*, 1600–1, 20. Although De Rose is not specifically mentioned, he was much employed by Lord Mountjoy in the building of fortifications at this time.
[5] *CSPI*, 1600–1, 30, 330.
[6] *Ibid.*, 330.
[7] *Ibid.*, 359; See also *CPSI*, 1606–8, 35 for Sir Arthur Chichester's comments to that effect.
[8] *CSPI*, 1600 1, 447.
[9] PRO, A.O. 1/288/1082; *Carew*, 1601–3, 116, 152.
[10] *Carew*, 1601–3, 397
[11] *Carew*, 1603–24, 384.
[12] *Ibid.*, 221.
[13] G. Hill, *An Historical Account of the Plantation in Ulster . . .*, Belfast, 1877, reprinted Shannon, 1970, 324.
[14] *Carew*, 1603–24, 221; *CSPI*, 1606–8, 35; PRO, A.O. 1/290/1089; BL, Add Ms 4756, f. 115ᵛ.
[15] *HMC, Hastings*, IV, 172; Hill, *op. cit.*, 522; BL. Add. Ms 4756, f. 115ᵛ.
[16] Hill, *op. cit.*, 324, 524; *Carew*, 1603–24, 228.
[17] Sir Arthur Vicars (Ed.), *Index to the Prerogative Wills of Ireland, 1536–1810*, Dublin, 1897, 216.
[18] A family tree of Sir Richard Hansard is in NLI, Ms 16003, p. 47–8.
[19] *CSPI*, 1625–32, 282, 389, 604; *CSPI*, 1633–47, 197.

HAWKSWORTH, ABRAHAM (fl. 1664–?1701), carpenter and builder who was admitted as non-resident or foreigner to the freedom of the City of Dublin in 1664 (as Abraham Hawkesworth). Hawksworth in the meantime had started building St Andrew's Church, Dublin, after the designs of William Dodson (q.v.). Originally he had contracted to build the church for £1,500, but expected in 1674 to exceed the estimate by £387 15s. 9d.[1] In 1681–2 Hawksworth acted as 'undertaker' for the Surveyor-General William Robinson (q.v.) for the rebuilding of a house for Sir John Perceval,[2] which was located on Merchant Quay, in St Audoen's parish.[3] Hawksworth probably was on good terms with Robinson, and might have put up more buildings for him. After Hawksworth's death, his wife, whom he had married in 1671[4] and whose maiden name was Elizabeth Sims is mentioned in Robinson's will to receive £25.[5] Abraham Hawksworth prepared his will in 1701,[6] and probably died shortly afterwards.

[1] TCD, Ms 2062, p. 2.
[2] BL, Add. Mss 46958A, ff. 110, 164, 174; 46960A, f. 29.
[3] PROI, Ms 1A/30/29, f. 14.
[4] *Appendix 26th Report of the Deputy Keeper of the Public Records in Ireland*, 1895, 400.
[5] PRO, Prob. 10/1512.
[6] F. S. Marsh, 'Additions to . . . Vicar's index to the prerogative wills of Ireland', 1914, typescript in the reading-room, TCD.

Herne

HERNE, JOHN, also HEARNE (fl. 1670), bricklayer, native of Dorchester in Dorset, England, who was naturalized in 1670.[1] In that year he was admitted as Freeman to the City of Dublin. He built a house of 'three storeys high besides the garrets and cellars' at the corner of Aungier and York Streets.[2] He probably lived at Dame Street, for a person of the same name living there made his will in 1706, leaving his wife Elizabeth the 'goods in the house'.[3] He is not to be confused with John Herne Jr (fl. 1670–1685) who was a mathematical practitioner, diallist and surveyor in Dublin.[4]

[1] W. A. Shaw (Ed.), 'Letters of Denization and Acts of Naturalization for Aliens in England and Ireland, 1603–1700', *Huguenot Society*, 1911, *18*, 343.
[2] N. T. Burke, 'An early modern Dublin: the estate of Francis Aungier', *Irish Geography*, 1972, *6*, 374.
[3] PROI, Prerogative Wills.
[4] E. G. R. Taylor, *The Mathematical Practitioners of Tudor & Stuart England*, Cambridge, 1954, reprinted 1967, 263.

HILLIARD, JOHN HARRISON (fl. 1660). He was employed for the purpose of keeping Dublin Castle, its stables, and Phoenix House, Co. Dublin, in repair for the government. Payments to him are only known from accounts in 1660,[1] when he had presumably been working under Randall Beckett (q.v.), Overseer of the Public Works. He was probably superseded by Capt. John Paine (q.v.), who became Director-General and Overseer of the King's Fortifications early in the next year.

[1] NLI, Ms 2700, f. 444, under date 25 Dec. 1660.

HOLENUS, THADEUS (fl. 1626), a Franciscan monk who, according to a latin inscription at Muckross Abbey, Co. Kerry, supervised the rebuilding of the abbey in 1626[1]. The community left the abbey three years later. Nothing is known about Brother Thadeus' earlier or later career, or how he became skilled enough to supervise the rebuilding.

[1] T. J. Barrington, *Discovering Kerry*, Dublin, 1976, 85, where the full inscription is quoted.

HURLBUTT or HULBERT, WILLIAM ·(fl. 1670), a master carpenter and architect of Stareton, near Coventry. He was a craftsman-architect whose skills transcended those of his colleagues. In the correspondence of the Earl of Conway he is first noted early in 1670 when his 'modell' for a grand stable at Portmore in Co. Antrim had been sent to the estate agent Sir George Rawdon.[1] Conway, who also had designed a 'plot' of the stable, mentions Hurlbutt as 'my Architect'.[2] The stable was very closely modelled on Hugh May's stable at Cornbury in Oxfordshire, drawings of which were also sent to Ireland.[3] These probably had been made by Hurlbutt, who is known to have copied some interiors of Roger Pratt's Kingston Lacy for the new rooms in Warwick Castle.[4] Hurlbutt's design for the Portmore stable has not been found but the correspondence shows his great concern for the proportions of the elevations and the correct placement of the 'leads'. He did not approve of the alterations to his designs which the Irish architect William Dodson (q.v.) made at this time. The preliminary work was probably done by an English contractor Mr Stubbs, who came to Ireland in June 1670.[5] His relationship to Hurlbutt is unclear. Hurlbutt was planning in February of that year to send over his brother (probably Roger Hurlbutt) and five other carpenters,[6] and he himself followed about a year later. In Dublin he discussed with Sir George Rawdon the plans and foundations of the stable. Hurlbutt had brought two bricklayers and one carpenter with him, who all went to Portmore. There he probably directed the laying out of the building and supervised the first stages of its construction. Although it was hoped that he would drink of 'St Patrick's well' and stay in Ireland, he left in August of that year, taking with him a plan of the second storey of the stables, and a plan and prospect of Portmore House, to show to Conway in England.[7] Shortly afterwards, Conway wrote to Sir George 'Mr Hurlebut shewed me the Drafts of Portmore and the Stable, which I thinke are well sett out, only I dislike the Ovall Figure and have altered it to Sex Angular as the more defensible ...'[8] Hurlbutt's oval lay-out for the complex was without precedent in the British Isles, and gives an indication of his architectural sophistication. Conway mentioned in November 1671 that he planned to bring Hurlbutt over next spring,[9] but evidence is lacking that he came a second time. The masonry on the site was carried out by John Darley (q.v.). The stable, which measured 140 by 35 by 40 feet, had two returns at the ends not unlike the Cornbury stable; its roof was completed in June 1672.[10] It is not known whether Hurlbutt's overall layout was built. The stable was pulled down in 1763.

In 1679 Hurlbutt prepared a 'model' for Conway's seat, Ragley Hall in Warwickshire. He built the house, but with major alterations by the architect Robert Hooke.[11] Aside from various private and public structures mentioned by *Colvin*, Hurlbutt built at Toddington in Gloucestershire. In one of Conway's letters, dated July 1, 1670, he mentioned that his architect [Hurlbutt] was leaving Warwick for 'my Lord Tracy at Tuddington [who was related to Conway][12] where he is upon a great peece of worke'.[13]

---

[1] Huntington Library, San Marino, California, Hastings Ms 14485 (referred to below as HA).

[2] Hurlbutt is not directly mentioned by name as the designer of the Portmore stable. However, the architect, who is frequently mentioned in Conway's letters 'drew the plotts, [and] did offer himselfe to me to doe it [i.e., execute the building], as soone as his Worke at Warwick is over ...' (HA 14483; 14489). There is little doubt that this refers to Hurlbutt who was then engaged on two projects in Warwick (see *Colvin*, 440).

[3] HA 14483; 14485–6; 14489; PRO, SP 63/327, f. 120.

[4] *Colvin*, 440.

[5] HA 14489–90; *CSPI*, 1669–70, 143, 156. The identity of this Mr Stubbs is unclear; he is not mentioned in *Colvin*.

[6] HA 14500; For Roger Hurlbutt see *Colvin*, 440.

[7] PRO SP 63/330, ff. 172, 204; SP 63/343, f. 134.

[8] HA 14506.

[9] HA 14510.

[10] S. Lewis, *A Topographical Dictionary of Ireland*, London, 1837, I, 112; PRO SP 63/331, f. 80.

[11] *Colvin*, 440.

[12] Lord Conway's grandfather Edward, 1st Viscount Conway, had married Dorothy, daughter of Sir John Tracy of Toddington.

[13] The Lord Tracy referred to was John Tracy, Viscount Tracy of Rathcool. Toddington was rebuilt in 1819; its early appearance is known from a painting (which I have not been able to examine) and from a description in J. B. Burke, *A Visitation of the Seats and Arms ...*, London, 1853, 205–6.

J

JARMAN, (?) (fl. 1612), master carpenter of the city of London, who supervised the carpenters building the houses for the city's plantation at Londonderry. Details of his life are noted under his colleague Peter Cobb (q.v.).

JOHNSON, JOHN (fl. 1618–1641), cleric and engineer. He was educated at Trinity College, Dublin, where he obtained his B.A. (1618), and his M.A. (1621) and became a Fellow in 1622.[1] In that year he is first noted in the Regal Visitation of the Diocese of Kilmore as 'minister and a preacher' for the vicarages Inchonarra, Dromlease, and Conclare, all in Co. Leitrim. His residence, however, was in another parish of the same county, Killenry, of which he was incumbent, and where had built 'a Tymber house ... with convenient houses of office ...'.[2] Around this time, the plantation of Co. Leitrim was finalized, and Johnson probably took care of the religious needs of the new settlers. Close to his parish, the estate of Dromahaire had been assigned to a brother of the Duke of Buckingham, Sir William Villiers. The unusual castle at Dromahaire on a U-plan with stairs on the inside corners was built after 1628. It is unclear whether at this time Johnson's architectural interest had manifested itself, and whether he was involved in the building of this castle or any other of the plantation residences. In fact, nothing is known about Johnson's activities between 1622 and 1636. At the end of that period Lord Wentworth, Lord Deputy of Ireland, made him engineer over his palatial building at Jigginstown, Co. Kildare. Here he probably acted in a supervisory capacity, leaving the actual building to the bricklayer John Allen (q.v.).[3] Other commissions from Lord Wentworth included building at Carnew (possibly Carnew Castle, leased by Calcott Chambre),[4] and at Cosha, both in Co. Wicklow.[5] At the latter place Lord Wentworth started the erection in 1637 of a 'Frame of Wood', which became a hunting lodge for Fairwood Park at the cost of £1,200.[6] In the following year Lord Wentworth obtained permission to put up a rectangular fort at Cosha, with bulwarks on its corners, and a horn work and a ravelin.[7] Unfortunately, the extent of Johnson's involvement in the design and execution of these works is obscure. He had been a non-resident of his parishes for some time; in 1639 he became vicar of Athenry. In a deposition of Johnson's wife, named Juliana, it becomes clear what happened to the Johnson family during the Rebellion. She related that due to various robberies they lost goods to the value of £2,656. At Christmas 1641 her husband and her eldest son were killed 'in a skirmish by the sept of the O'Molloys' at Inch, in Co. Offaly. She and her nine small children survived, and after much misery reached Dublin.[8] It seems very likely that many of Johnson's private papers were lost during this period.

Among his intellectual achievements was the development of a 'universal character' which could be used in all languages and nations.[9] He composed this with the encouragement of William Bedell, who, as Bishop of Kilmore from 1629 onwards, was his superior. The 'universal character' was later sponsored by a fellow-clergyman and engineer Miles Symner (q.v.), who took on the role of its 'midwife, nurse and adopting father'. Symner entrusted sheets of Johnson's work to Major Anthony Morgan, a member of the Samuel Hartlib circle in Ireland. Unfortunately, several attempts, supported by Hartlib, to have the 'universal character' printed, failed.[10] No copy of it seems to have survived. Johnson through

Symner, Morgan and Hartlib must have been in close contact with the emergence of the New Learning in Ireland. His skills as engineer were matched by those as a surveyor, for he was to survey Idough, Co. Kilkenny for Sir Christopher Wandesford and Lord Mountgarret in 1636.[11] More importantly, two years later he served as Clerk 'for diverse and necessary services for the plantation in Connaught'.[12] He is noticed in August 1638 at Loughreagh where, as a member of the Galway commission, he and the Surveyor-General Sir William Parsons checked the book of the measurers.[13] According to William Petty, the organizer of the Strafford Survey was the surveyor William Gilbert,[14] who together with Capt. Nicholas Pynnar (q.v.) supervised the surveyors. Johnson's relatively high salary of £100 per annum could suggest a coordinating role, but it is unclear what his relationship was to Gilbert and Pynnar.

[1] G. D. Burtchaell & T. U. Sadleir, *Alumni Dublinenses*, Dublin, 1935, 441.

[2] TCD, Ms 1785, pp. 211, 216.

[3] A. Vicars, 'Jigginstown Castle', *KASJ*, 1891–95, *1*, 19. The earliest reference to building activity at Jigginstown occurs in the Earl of Cork's diary under the date March 22, 1635–6 (*Grosart*, series I, IV, 170).

[4] The castle at Carnew is noted in 1635 by Sir William Brereton as a 'neat, rough-cast, and well-contrived, convenient house' (E. Hawkins (Ed.), *Sir William Brereton. Travels in Holland, The United Provinces, England, Scotland, and Ireland*, London, 1844, reprinted 1968, 146).

[5] A. Clogy, *Memoirs of the Life and Episcopate of Dr William Bedell, Lord Bishop of Kilmore*, London, 1862, 60.

[6] W. Knowler (Ed.), *The Earl of Strafford's Letters and Dispatches*, London, 1739, II, 105.

[7] *CSPI, 1633–47*, 199; Sheffield City Library: Strafford Ms 10, f, 192–3 & Ms 11, ff. 123–7.

[8] M. Hickson (Ed.), *Ireland in the Seventeenth Century*, London, 1884, II, 14–15, where the deposition is printed, dated February 8, 1643. The slaying is also mentioned in another deposition, printed in P. Dwyer, *The Diocese of Killaloe*, Dublin, 1878, 236.

[9] Clogy, *op.cit.*, 60.

[10] T. C. Barnard, 'Miles Symner and the New Learning in Seventeenth-Century Ireland', *JRSAI*, 1972, *102*, 137, 141–2. Later John Keogh and John Wilkins worked on a universal language (K. T. Hoppen, *The Common Scientist*, London, 1970, 154–5).

[11] *HMC, Ormonde*, n.s. I, 36–7, 38; NLI, Wandesford Ms.

[12] Longleat, Ms 95.

[13] *HMC, Egmont*, I, 105.

[14] I am indebted to Dr John Andrews for this information from Petty's *Political Anatomy* (p. 58). For Gilbert see also *HMC, 12th Rep. App. I*, 285, 312; II, 81, 246–7; *CSPI, 1633–47*, 279, 353, 365; Knowler *op.cit.*, I, 107.

JONES, RICHARD, 3rd Viscount and 1st Earl of Ranelagh (?1638–1712), gentleman-architect of Irish birth who is known for his works in England but may have practised in Ireland. For the first thirty years or more that he lived in Ireland there is little known about his life. He was the son of Arthur, 2nd Viscount Ranelagh, and Catherine, daughter of Richard Boyle, 1st Earl of Cork. It seems likely that he went on a grand tour for he is known to have visited Basle in 1658.[1] However, the extent of his travels is unclear as is the nature of any architectural experience he may have gained in the process. At the Restoration, his family regained prominence probably through the connection with Roger Boyle, 1st Earl of Orrery (q.v.), who became Lord Justice, and was also a gentleman-architect. Richard Jones was soon awarded several important offices such as Chancellor of the Exchequer (1668 onwards) and manager of the Irish revenue. He probably lived in Dublin, where his father had a large residence with 16 hearths in Dame Street[2]. In 1670 Richard, then Viscount Ranelagh, inspected the partly finished royal lodge, Phoenix House, outside Dublin in the company of the Lord Lieutenant Berkeley[3]. The outcome of this possibly architecturally inspired visit remains unclear. Ranelagh's relatives and professional colleagues may have enabled him to design buildings in Ireland, but evidence to that effect has not yet come to light. With his known taste for luxury, it seems unlikely that Ranelagh would not have beautified or improved his residences in Ireland. Two of these were old-fashioned fortified strongholds: Roscommon Castle and Athlone Castle of which he became governor in 1661 and 1672 respectively.[4] It is not known whether Ranelagh executed any repairs to these residences, which as official garrisons fell under the care of the Surveyor-General William Robinson [q.v.][5]. Over the years, Robinson and Ranelagh probably developed a friendship, and Robinson assigned £500 to Ranelagh in one of his last wills[6]. It seems likely that the two architects were exposed to each other's work. Ranelagh was appointed in 1680 as one of the commissioners for the building of the Royal Hospital in Kilmainham,[7] which was designed by Robinson. When a few years later a similar soldiers' hospital was built outside London at Chelsea, Ranelagh was closely involved in its construction, although the designs came from the hand of Christopher Wren.[8] In 1700 Ranelagh was awarded with a similar (but smaller) position in England held by Robinson in Ireland, namely 'Sur-intendent generall of oure Buildings & of our works in our parks', which he held until William III's death in 1702. Ranelagh and Robinson's careers ran parallel in other respects. By 1691 Ranelagh had become Paymaster General in England. Robinson at this period had been given the post of Deputy Paymaster of the Forces in Ireland.

Ranelagh's architectural career was well under way before 1680, the year in which he is said to have left Ireland for good.[9] However, his known architectural works are all situated in England. When in 1677 his mother the Dowager Lady Ranelagh decided to rebuild the house where she and her brother Robert Boyle lived in Pall Mall, London, she mainly used the architect-scientist Robert Hooke to make drawings of the alterations. However, Hooke's diary reveals that he had 'much Discourse [with Lord Ranelagh] about his buildings'. In May of 1678 they visited Chiswick near London, the seat of Ranelagh's uncle Richard Boyle, 1st Earl of Burlington, where they viewed the 'temple'. Stronger evidence of Ranelagh's concern with building projects dates from this period when Ranelagh advised Lord Conway on William Hurlbutt's [q.v.] drawings for Conway's country house Ragley.[10] Over the next six years he continued to act as an advisor to Lord Conway on this project and on a house built for Lord Conway at Newmarket.[11] He also supervised the enlargement in 1704 of the residence of the 2nd Duke of Ormonde at Richmond, who was then Lord Lieutenant of Ireland.

Ranelagh is mostly known for the building of his own house near the Royal Hospital at Chelsea. According to Mackey he 'spent more money, built more fine houses, and laid out more on house-hold furniture and gardening, than any other Nobleman in England'.[12] This is not immediately evident from the appearance of Ranelagh House at Chelsea (dem. 1805). A contemporary, Edward Southwell, compared the Dutch country seat De Voorst with Ranelagh House. As both buildings were very different in outer appearance, the interior of Ranelagh House may have resembled the exuberant decoration of Daniel Marot's interior of De Voorst.[13] A second house of Ranelagh formerly stood adjoining the Horse Guard in Whitehall, which according to Le Neve 'created him some Envy'.[14] In 1700 he acquired a third residence near the Royal Court, called Cranbourn Lodge in Windsor Park, which he is known to have improved.

Practically nothing is known about how Ranelagh acquired the skill of designing buildings. His uncle, Roger Boyle, 1st Earl of Orrery [q.v.] was also a gentleman-architect. Ranelagh had contacts with professional architects in England, but it is unclear what he learned from such individuals as Robert Hooke and Christopher Wren. Aside from his early trip to Switzerland, and perhaps Italy, Ranelagh visited Holland after April 1692.[15] In Irish history he is ill remembered as a farmer of the revenue who defrauded it of large sums. At the end of his life he wrote a will in which he left sums of money to his friends and to a number of craftsmen who had worked under him. He also arranged in 1708 the founding of a trust for the erection of two free schools in Athlone, of which William Robinson was one of the trustees.[16] Ranelagh died on January 5, 1712 in England. His eventful life has been described in more detail in the *Dictionary of National Biography* and by H. M. Colvin in his *A Biographical Dictionary of British Architects*.

[1] This entry has been largely based on *DNB* and *Colvin*.

[2] *57th Report of the Deputy Keeper of the Public Records of Ireland*, 1936, 562.

[3] *CSPI*, 1669–70, 115. By 1679 he seemed either to have let this house, or to have sold it (*CSPD*, 1678–80, 221).

[4] *CSPI*, 1660–2, 440, and Bodl., Rawl. Ms C686 (12530); *CSPD*, 1672, 360–1, and BL, Add. Ms 28937, f. 234.

[5] Robinson made an estimate for the repair of Athlone Castle in 1677; work at this location has been ascribed to him (see William Robinson, q.v.).

[6] PRO, Del. 1/357/809, dated 1709.

[7] N. Burton, *The Royal Hospital, Kilmainham*, Dublin, 1843, 15. Presently known records of the hospital only date back to 1684, and do not reveal whether Ranelagh played an important role in the early phase of the building.

[8] *Colvin*, 474. In 1690 Ranelagh, who was Treasurer of the Royal Hospital at Chelsea from 1685 onwards, petitioned for land near the hospital, claiming that 'he had had the care of overseeing the building of Chelsea Hospital' for the last four years (*CSPD*, 1689–90. 454).

[9] C. G. T. Dean, *The Royal Hospital, Chelsea*, London, 1950, 95. He left for Ireland, however, from England in August 1679 (Bodl., Carte Ms 243, f. 377).

[10] *CSPD*, 1677–8, 201, 399.

[11] *Colvin*, 474; H. W. Robinson & W. Adams (Eds.), *The Diary of Robert Hooke, 1672–1680*, London, 1935, 415, 457; *CSPD*, 1678–80, 623; Bodl., Carte Ms 243, f. 377.

[12] Cited in *Colvin*, 474.

[13] K. Fremantle, 'A visit to the United Provinces and Cleves in the time of William III', described in Edward Southwell's Journal, *Nederlands Kunsthistorisch Jaarboek*, 1970, *21*, 54.

[14] J. Le Neve, *The Lives and Characters of the most illustrious Persons British and Foreign, who died in the year 1712*, London, 1714, 205–12, contains a biographical sketch of Ranelagh.

[15] Le Neve, *op.cit.*

[16] M. Quane, Ranelagh Endowed School, *Old Athlone Society*, 1969, *1*, 24.

K

KELLY, THOMAS (fl. 1641), an architect in the service of the Earl of Cork. While in England, Kelly borrowed on May 20, 1641 £6 from the Earl, after having drawn the plan for either the new works at Lismore Castle or Askeaton Castle.[1] He subsequently came over to Ireland, where he supervised building activity on both sites and at Castlelyons, Co. Cork. His last recorded payment was on December 27, 1641. He perhaps can be identified with the surveyor Thomas Kelly. He is first noted as a candidate for a survey of Idough in 1636,[2] and later made a survey of the estate of Castlewarden, Co. Kildare, for Sir Philip Perceval in 1638.[3] The house at Castlewarden was subsequently rebuilt, but it is unclear whether Kelly oversaw this work. His architectural skills are hard to evaluate as none of his work survives.

[1] NLI, Ms 6246.   [2] *HMC, Ormonde*, n.s. I, 34.   [3] *HMC, Egmont*, I, 110, 121.

CASTLELYONS CASTLE, CO. CORK. In 1639 Kelly's plan for the rebuilding of this castle is mentioned by the overseer Edward Morley (q.v.). Financed by the Earl of Cork, it was built for his son-in-law the Earl of Barrymore. Altered (Chatsworth, Lismore Ms 20, f. 122).

ASKEATON CASTLE, CO. LIMERICK. In November and December 1641 Kelly was paid for overseeing the building of new defences (Chatsworth, Lismore Ms 22, f. 85). Ruined.

LISMORE CASTLE, CO. WATERFORD. In December 1641 he was paid for several, presumably, defensive works (NLI, Ms 6900). Altered.

KENN, BENJAMIN (fl. 1671). He was the son of the architect Capt. William Kenn (q.v.), who possibly employed him on Burton House, Co. Cork, which he built for Sir John Perceval. It is certain that Benjamin Kenn completed Burton House, after his father's death, from November 25, 1671 onwards, partly to the contract his father had made, partly on work not included in the contract. He is frequently mentioned as overseeing the work and as borrowing substantial sums of money from Perceval's agent in order to proceed with the building. While Kenn's accounts were judged to be honest,[1] less favourable comments were made about his brother-in-law the mason [Simon?] Cowell[2] who was also employed on Burton House. Benjamin Kenn was probably heavily in debt after the completion of Burton House, for he had to give bonds of his land of Cahernarry, Co. Limerick, as security. This property he had presumably inherited from his father, as he was the oldest son. Nothing is known of him subsequent to 1672 or 1673. Perhaps the Francis Kenn, mentioned in 1686 as a tenant on the Burton Estate, was a relative of his.[3]

[1] BL, Add. MSS 46948, f. 150; 46949, f. 67.   2 BL, Add. MS 46948, f. 29.
[3] BL, Add. MS 47038, f. 32.

KENN, JOHN (fl. 1627), mason from Bristol. The Corporation records of Bristol mention on a number of occasions mason's work done by John Kenn and his two 'boys'.[1] By 1640 Kenn was in Ireland and had executed the stone windows at Gill

Abbey, Co. Cork for the Earl of Cork, at a cost of £310.[2] Possible descendants of John Kenn are William Kenn (q.v.) and the latter's son Benjamin (q.v.).

[1] D. M. Livock (Ed.), *City Chamberlains' Accounts . . .*, Bristol, 1966, 101 *ff.*   [2] *Grosart*, series 1, V, 143.

KENN, WILLIAM (fl. 1653–?1671), architect and probably engineer. He possibly came from Bristol, for he had an intimate knowledge of building materials which could be purchased there.[1] Furthermore, a possible relative, the freemason John Kenn (q.v.) came from that city and had worked for the 1st Earl of Cork earlier in the century.[2] Little is known about William Kenn's training as a soldier and architect, although he reached the rank of captain. He was aware of London architecture for he mentions, in 1665, balconies there cut in 'leaves and antics'.[3] In 1653 he was in Ireland, for he was then ordered by the Commissioner for Ireland to set out the platform of a citadel at Londonderry, for which he was allowed £20.[4] He had probably come over to Ireland as a soldier, for the 'census' of 1659 mentions his estate at Cahernarry, Co. Limerick (probably granted to him for his services), which he shared with John Ouzell. After the Restoration he oversaw the building of Charleville Castle for the Earl of Orrery (q.v.), but it is unclear for what period of time.[5] In 1665 Kenn wrote from Liscarrol, Co. Cork, to Sir John Perceval about the building of a country house for Sir John at Burton, Co. Cork, plans for which were interrupted by the death of Sir John in the same year. In May 1669, Kenn, as architect, presented designs and estimates for this house to the guardian Robert Southwell, and, on September 27, 1670, these led to a contract for building the house, Kenn's designs were complemented by others of Thomas Smith for laying out the outbuildings and defence works around the house. From the accounts in the *Egmont Papers* it appears that Kenn oversaw the early stages of the house, and made contracts with masons and carpenters.[6] He was probably involved about this time in other buildings, for he wrote to Southwell that he was 'induced ... by several' to build.[7] On February 24, 1671 Southwell congratulated Kenn on the latter's recovery from a sickness, and reveals Kenn's intimacy with the Southwell family by ending his letter with 'My wife and daughter present their love and service unto you. Your veri affectionate frend & servant Robert Southwell'.[8] It seems likely that Kenn also built, prior to 1669, a house for a relative of Southwell's son Sir Robert Southwell, namely Sir Thomas Southwell. This house is mentioned in some detail in one of Kenn's letters,[9] and it was probably the wing attached to Castlematrix, Co. Limerick, rebuilt in the 19th century. His death presumably occurred before November 25 of that year, when the first loan was made to Kenn's son Benjamin (q.v.), who completed Burton House. No drawings by William Kenn seem to have survived. A conjectural reconstruction of Burton House, based on Kenn's contract,[10] shows the typical late Caroline style of his building. He was said to have been honest with his accounts for Burton House,[11] and he may have employed his son Benjamin and his son-in-law, the mason [?Simon] Cowell there.

[1] *HMC, Egmont*, II, 15.
[2] *Grosart*, series 1, V, 143.
[3] *HMC, Egmont*, II, 15.
[4] *Analecta Hibernica*, 1944, *15*, 238.
[5] NLI, Ms 13233 (2).
[6] *HMC, Egmont*, II, 14–15; BL, Add. Mss 46946A; 46947B, f. 734c; 46948 *ff*; B. de Breffny & R. ffoliott,

The Houses of Ireland, London, 1975, 66, 69.
[7] BL, Add. Ms 46948, f. 24.
[8] BL, Add. Ms 46948, f. 29.
[9] BL, Add. Ms 46946A.
[10] *IGS*, Jan.–June 1973, *16*, 26.
[11] BL, Add. Ms 46948, f. 150.

KEYSER, WILLIAM DE see DE KEYSER, WILLIAM

L

LANGREDG, NICHOLAS also **LANGREDY** (fl. 1609), carpenter, who contracted for a number of buildings for Sir Richard Boyle, later Earl of Cork. He presumably can be identified with the 'Mr langries' who supplied in 1609 a moulding for a garret window to the Waterford mason John Walshe.[1] Two years later he is noted as one of the inhabitants of Sir Richard Boyle's plantation.[2] His first documented contact with Boyle occurred in 1613 when he made alterations to the latter's house in Youghal.[3] Other works undertaken by 'Mr. Langredg' at this house included building a new kitchen, a new stable, a slaughter house and a coach house (1615) as well as garden steps and a kitchen terrace (1616).[4] In 1614 he agreed with Sir Richard to finish the carpentry of the school house and the alms house in Youghal,[5] the latter of which still survives. Another project, in 1616, again for his patron, was the building of a gallery at the church in Tallow, Co. Waterford,[6] which must make this one of the earliest galleried churches in Ireland. His last known involvement in building occurred at Lismore Castle where he acted as contractor in 1622 for a new stable and a new building between the gate house and the upper turret. A year later it was he who presumably raised the gate house by one storey.[7] Langredg must have had some skill in designing buildings, and certainly was able to co-ordinate their erection, and the fact that he was employed by his patron over a great number of years indicates his success as a master-craftsman. The accounts often mention him as *Mr* Langredg, which may indicate a social rank higher than that of a common craftsman. He worked in Youghal for a number of years prior to becoming a freeman of the town in 1618.[8] He had the lease of a house in Church Lane,[9] from where he also traded in woven materials.[10] The date of his death is unknown. A possible descendant is James 'Letgeredge', who was employed as a joiner at Lismore Castle for the 2nd Earl of Cork in 1663.[11]

[1] *Grosart*, series 2, I, 133.
[2] *Carew*, 1603–24, 89.
[3] *Grosart*, series 1, I, 22.
[4] *Ibid.*, 64, 73, 108.
[5] *Ibid.*, 50, 67.
[6] *Ibid.*, 139.
[7] *Ibid.*, II, 45, 49, 70.
[8] R. Caulfield (Ed.), *The Council Book of the Corporation of Youghal . . .*, Guildford, 1878, 54.
[9] *Grosart*, series 1, I, 227.
[10] *Ibid.*, 216, 222.
[11] NLI, Ms 6901.

LEUVENTHEN, (?) (fl. 1706), a Dutchman who built Uniacke House in Youghal from 1706–15[1] in a pleasant but rather provincial style. Nothing else is known of him.

[1] Lord Killanin & M. V. Duignan, *The Shell Guide to Ireland*, London, 1967, 2nd ed., 463.

LODDEN, JOHN (fl. 1622), mason, was employed in a number of engineering works undertaken by the Earl of Cork over a period of fifteen years. He seems to have specialized in the building of town walls and bridges. He was a reasonably successful builder. However, when in 1637 his bridge at Castleconner was destroyed by a flood, the Earl thought that Lodden had deceived him with poor workmanship, though, curiously, in the Earl's will, made in 1642, Lodden is mentioned as 'the fittest man' to rebuild it.[1] A probable descendant of Lodden is Walter Lodden, who in 1694 was employed to keep a causeway near Youghal in repair.[2]

[1] *Grosart*, series 1, V, 26.
[2] R. Caulfield (Ed.), *The Council Book of the Corporation of Youghal*, Guildford, Surrey, 1878, 392.

BANDON, CO. CORK, TOWN WALLS. In 1622 Lodden in place of Richard Crofte (q.v.) became the chief contractor for the building of the walls, castle, and flankers of the Earl of Cork's town of Bandon. Unsigned drawings of one of the gates may be associated with either Lodden's or Richard Crofte's (q.v.) work (TCD, Ms 1209, f. 40, published in *Loeber*, pl. 11; NLI, Ms 16 L 9). When in 1623 the mason Francis Wharton offered to complete the work for £6 10s. a perch, Lodden was preferred despite his rate of £7 a perch. Robert Belcher contracted for the carpentry at the gates in 1627 (*Grosart*, series 1, II, 63, 66, 73, 141, 152, 211).

LISMORE CASTLE, CO. WATERFORD. In 1628 Lodden erected a new building at this Castle for the Earl of Cork (NLI, Ms 6897).

BANDON, CO. CORK, BRIDGE. A three-arched stone bridge erected in 1636 for the Earl of Cork near the school and almshouses (*Grosart*, series 1, IV, 204; NLI, Ms 6899).

BANDON, CO. CORK, IRISH BRIDGE. Lodden was paid £5 by the Corporation in 1636 for a two-arched bridge connecting the south gate with Irish-town (G. Bennett, *The History of Bandon*, Cork, 1869, 96–7).

CLONMEL, CASTLECONNAGH, BRIDGE, across the river Suir. In February 1637 the Earl of Cork commissioned Lodden, for £100, to build this bridge which was swept away by a flood in August of that year due to poor workmanship. Lodden was to rebuild the bridge as appears from the Earl's will, dated 1642, but it is unclear whether he actually did (NLI, Ms 6899; *Grosart*, series 1, V, 26; D. Townshend, *The Life and Letters of the Great Earl of Cork*, London, 1904, 494).

LUCAS, THOMAS (fl. 1632), architect and probably a carpenter. He was admitted as Freeman of the City of Dublin in 1632 after serving his apprenticeship as architect. Nothing is known about his early career. He may be identified with the carpenter Thomas Lucas, who agreed in 1668 with the Dean and Chapter of St Patrick's Cathedral, Dublin, for the repair of the east side of the cathedral and of the chapter house. In December of that year he took down the decayed roof of the cathedral. He repaired the chancel of St Kevin's Church, and designed a 'Portall' at the west end of the choir of St Patrick's in the following year. Finally, he signed articles for roofing the nave and the south aisle of the Cathedral in 1671.[1] The next year his name is mentioned as the designer of Sir Hierome Alexander's buildings (i.e. the front) of Trinity College, Dublin,[2] which were built by Richard Mills (q.v.) in the artisan mannerist style. In the Chapter Minutes of St Patrick's he is mentioned as late as 1674, but his subsequent career remains obscure.

[1] St Patrick's Cathedral, Dublin, Chapter Minutes, 1660–70, *ff.*; 1671–7 *ff.*
[2] TCD, MUN/P/2/1, f. 27; *IGS*, Jan.–June 1973, *16*, 10–11.

M

McMORRIS, JOHN (fl. 1639), mason who was paid on various occasions for stone windows and a water table for Askeaton Castle, Co. Limerick, then the property of the Earl of Cork. The stonework was carved at Thomond presumably in partnership with the mason Edmond O'Cloghur. Other similar stonework was carved by a William O'Corkus. The accounts suggest that McMorris may have been employed in some supervisory capacity during the works at Askeaton. The last recorded payment to him occurred in June 1641.[1]

[1] NLI, Ms 6897.

MASON, (?) (fl. 1683), builder who agreed in 1683 to build a market-house at Castle Island, Co. Kerry, for Lord Herbert of Cherbury, who was to be sent the 'draught' of the structure.[1] He may be identified with the 'Mr Mason', who, on Lord Herbert's orders, was to repair the town hall and other houses of Montgomery in Wales about 1688.[2] None of these works survive.

[1] W. J. Smith (Ed.), *Herbert Correspondence*, Cardiff and Dublin, 1968, 280.
[2] *Ibid.*, 341.

MAXWELL, (?) (fl. 1670), carpenter and builder, possibly from Belfast. He is mentioned by Sir George Rawdon in relation to the proposed flat part of the roof of the stable at Portmore, Co. Antrim. In Sir George's words 'Mr Maxwell and several in Belfast cover with deal [flat roofs], pitched and so ordered that they are staunch and light and the up-atop rooms as good as the middle storey'.[1] Perhaps he can be identified with the unnamed 'ingenious' carpenter who was to build a windmill at Clanconnell for Sir George in that year. Maxwell also gave advice on Hurlbutt's (q.v.) designs of the stable at Portmore.[2] His absence there is noted by Rawdon in February 1671,[3] which might indicate that Maxwell was employed in the preparations for the building of the stable. His name does not reoccur afterwards in the Conway correspondence.

[1] *CSPI*, 1669–70, 140.
[2] *Ibid.*, 246.
[3] PRO, SP 63/330, f. 22.

MAY, HUGH (1621–1684), Comptroller of the Royal Works in England. His English career has been dealt with in *Colvin*. Although he probably never visited Ireland, he had some involvement with works there. When the Lord Lieutenant, the Earl of Essex, repaired Dublin Castle after 1674, he possible followed the designs of Hugh May, who was his kinsman, for on January 5, 1675 he wrote to him, mentioning a present given to May, adding 'I have received many kindnesses from you since my being here [i.e. Ireland] ...'.[1] Essex was also responsible for the employment in Ireland of a kinsman of May, Edward May.[2] None of May's presumed work at Dublin Castle survived a fire in 1684.

In England May twice acted as arbiter for contracts of sculpture for Anglo-Irish patrons. On March 12, 1681 he is mentioned as having mediated between Sir Robert Southwell (who also acted for Sir John Perceval) and the sculptor Francis

Quellin concerning the contract for a tomb,[3] presumably to commemorate Robert Southwell and his wife Helena, which was later erected in St Multose Church, Kinsale, Co. Cork. On December 23, of that year May became arbiter in the agreement between Francis Aungier, Earl of Longford (who acted for the Duke of Ormonde), and John Bonnier or Bennier for the casting of 4 large and 16 smaller statues after those in the King's Privy garden,[4] which most likely were for Kilkenny Castle. Four days later, the Earl of Longford records in a letter to the Duke of Ormonde that he went to May to consult him about the proportions of piers to frame a doorway at Kilkenny Castle. Prior to this May had sent Ormonde an unidentified design, which the Duke returned.[5] Although the piers might have related to one of the outer doorways of the Castle, it seems likely that they were for the round waterhouse in the gardens of the Castle. This, long since gone, was one of the earliest classical structures in Ireland with giant pilasters on the outside, and it might have been after Hugh May's design. May's influence on Irish architecture is difficult to trace. In common with William Robinson (q.v.) he had a preference for round-headed windows as can be seen at Windsor Castle and at the Royal Hospital, Kilmainham. At least one of May's designs was directly copied for an Irish building by another architect. When the Earl of Conway started building the large stable at Portmore, Co. Antrim, designs of May's classically inspired stable at Cornbury in Oxfordshire were sent over to Ireland. It seems likely that these were drafts made by the English architect William Hurlbutt (q.v.), rather than May's original designs. The Portmore stable was very closely based on May's example.[6]

[1] R. Loeber, 'The Rebuilding of Dublin Castle: thirty critical years, 1661–1690' *Studies*, 1980, *69*, 60.
[2] *Letters written by . . . Earl of Essex . . . in the year 1675*, Dublin, 1770, 1–2, 106.
[3] BL, Add. Ms 46958A, f. 36. See also R. Loeber 'Arnold Quellin's and Grinling Gibbons' monuments for Anglo-Irish patrons' (submitted to *IGS*).
[4] *HMC, 7th Rep.*, 752.
[5] NLI, Ms 2417, f. 237. This document is partially misquoted in *HMC, Ormonde*, n.s. VI, 279–80. See also *IGS*, Jan.–June 1973, *16*, 35.
[6] Huntington Library, San Marino, California, HA 14483; 14485–6; 14489; PRO, SP 63/327, f. 120.

MILLER, EDWARD (fl. 1692), carpenter, was admitted as Freeman of the City of Dublin in 1692, presumably as an immigrant from England.[1] Late in 1700 he is mentioned in connection with an addition to the Infirmary of the Royal Hospital, Kilmainham, after the design of William Robinson (q.v.).[2] On June 20, 1702 Robinson recommended Miller as overseer of the works of the hospital, and the governors accepted him at an annual salary of £10. The accounts of the hospital mention Miller's name subsequently, usually in relation to alterations and maintenance of the buildings.[3] During this period he may have continued his private building practice, but no details have come to light. The Surveyor-General Thomas Burgh (q.v.) employed him at various Royal Works, such as the Houses of Parliament (also called Chichester House) from 1703 to 1708,[4] and at Dublin Castle in 1705.[5] His employment at the Royal Hospital ended abruptly in 1707 when he was sacked after renewed complaints of negligence.[6] His subsequent career remains obscure. His office at the Royal Hospital was taken over by Thomas Burgh (q.v.).

[1] Geneal. Off., Ms, G. Thrift, 'Roll of Freemen of the City of Dublin'.
[2] PROI, RHK 1/1/1, f. 162.
[3] PROI, RHK 1/1/1, f. 199, and *passim*.
[4] *Commons Jour.*, 1703–13, 666.
[5] PRO, W.O. 55/1984.
[6] PROI, RHK 1/1/2. f. 14ᵛ.

Mills

MILLS (or **MYLLS**), JOHN (fl. ?1638–?1673), Master Carpenter of Ireland. In 1638 a joiner John Mylls, who was either a foreigner or non-resident, was admitted as Freeman of the City of Dublin. He is mentioned as Master Carpenter and Petarder of the train of artillery, probably about 1648, together with the engineers William Webb, Miles Symner (q.v.) as being under the command of Lord Broghill (later Earl of Orrery, (q.v.)).[1] During 1655–6 he was employed together with Randall Beckett (q.v.) on the Royal Works in and around Dublin, and is mentioned as a member of the Corporation of Carpenters in 1656. Shortly after the Restoration he was paid £51 4s.,[2] by the Treasury for unspecified works and on September 13, 1661 he received the patent as Master Carpenter in Ireland. Soon afterwards, the Lord Chancellor of Ireland, Sir Maurice Eustace, wrote that, aside from Dr John Westley (q.v.), [John] 'mylls' and Capt. John Paine (q.v.) were the only experts on building in Ireland.[3] John Mills may be identified with the Mr Mills who was appointed in 1663 to oversee the rebuilding of the Hall of the Vicars Choral of St Patrick's Cathedral, Dublin. The work was not completed until 1666.[4] John Mills died, probably intestate, in 1673.[5]

[1] *HMC, Ormonde*, II, 244.
[2] PROI, Corporation Records, Beseeches XIII; NLI, Ms 2700, f. 441.
[3] Bodl., Carte Ms 31, f. 373.
[4] St Patrick's Cathedral, Dublin, Chapter Minutes, 1660–70, 300, 342.
[5] *Appendix 26th Report of the Deputy Keeper of the Public Records in Ireland*, 1895, 601.

DUBLIN, CUSTOM HOUSE. This building had been erected in 1638–40. In 1656 Mills and Randall Beckett were paid more than £200 to make the building suitable for housing the Privy Council, Court of Exchequer, Treasury, and Pells Office (*Analecta Hibernica*, 1944, 13, *ff.*), which may have entailed the building of an addition to it. Burned in 1711.

PHOENIX HOUSE, CO. DUBLIN. Henry Cromwell had a wing added to this former Royal lodge, presumably for which Randall Beckett and John Mills were paid in 1656 (*Ibid.*, pp. 292, 294). Dem.

DUBLIN CASTLE. Randall Beckett and Mills were paid for repairs on one of the towers of the Castle, and the 'burnt' stores, probably in the Castle, in May and June 1656 (*Ibid.*, pp. 292, 294). Between Dec. 14 1661 and March 19 1663 Mills again worked in the Castle, under the Surveyor-General Capt. John Paine (q.v.), for £43 16s. 6d. then became due to him (*HMC, 8th Rep. App. I*, 526). Rebuilt.

MILLS, RICHARD (fl. 1671–1719), bricklayer, who as a native of Frampton, Gloucestershire, was naturalized and admitted as Freeman of the City of Dublin in 1671.[1] He must have had an early reputation there, for in the next year he obtained a contract as mason and bricklayer for Sir Hierome Alexander's buildings at Trinity College, Dublin,[2] the front of which had been designed by Thomas Lucas (q.v.). Subsequent work by Mills is mostly found in Dublin, where he must have lived the remainder of his life. He became a member of the guild of bricklayers,[3] and later represented the carpenters.[4] Whether he designed buildings, is not known: in many instances he is mentioned in contemporary records as the overseer of structures. A number of these were buildings put up for the Dublin Corporation. This side-line became, after his appointment as Assistant to the Masters of the City Works in 1702, his main business.[5] This is reflected by the increase of his salary, which started in 1702 at £20 per year and rose to £50 by 1709.[6] A document describing his duties mentions overseeing the city's public buildings and the craftsmen working on them, and keeping account of the building materials used.[7] Most likely he was overseer of the building of the Workhouse, later called the Foundling Hospital (1701–4),[8] and certainly of the erection of the Tailors' Hall (1704),[9] Molyneux House (1706),[10] the tower of St Mathew's, Irishtown, Ringsend (1713),[11] St Werburgh's Church (fl. 1716),[12] and the Marshalsea (1717).[13] He may be identified with the 'Mr Mills' who was sent by the governers of the Blue Coat School in Dublin to repair the chancel of the church in Mullingar in 1715.[14] In the year of his death, 1719, he is reported as one of the benefactors of the school.[15] His will was dated April 9, and was proved on May 2 of that year. His wife was Bridget (whose family name is unknown) and he left a daughter Mary.[16] Little is known about the extent of his estate, other than that he had been granted a lot in the new development north of the Liffey in 1717,[17] and that he had a house in Turnstile Ally near College Green. His office of Assistant to the Masters of the City Works passed after his death to James Nelson (q.v.).

[1] W. A. Shaw (Ed.), 'Letters of Denization and Acts of Naturalization for Aliens in England and Ireland, 1603–1700', *Huguenot Society*, 1911, *18*, 344.
[2] TCD, Ms MUN/P/2/1, f. 27–9.
[3] Marsh Lib., Ms Z.2.2.7 (40).
[4] *CARD*, VII, 574–5.
[5] *CARD*, VI, 260–1.
[6] *Ibid.*, 278, 345, 532. Some references to minor works executed by Mills occur on pp. 269, 467.
[7] PROI, M 2549.
[8] *Craig*, 75, who suggests that Mills may have been the architect of both the Workhouse and Molyneux House.
[9] *JRSAI*, 1918, *8*, 42.
[10] *Craig*, 78.
[11] *Craig*, 112; *CARD*, VI, 476. The stonework was executed by the mason Henry Lee.
[12] TCD, Ms 2063; BL, Eg. 1772, p. 112; S. C. Hughes, *The Church of St Werburgh*, Dublin, 1889, 27.
[13] *CARD*, VII, 23.
[14] King's Hospital, Blue Coat School, Account Book, p. 370.
[15] Gilbert Ms 69, p. 288.
[16] Geneal. Off., Ms 240, p. 243.
[17] National Gallery of Ireland, Dublin, Ms 11881.

MOLYNEUX, SAMUEL (fl. 1594–1625), Clerk of the Royal Works in Ireland.[1] He was the elder son of Sir Thomas Molyneux, Kt. of Dublin, (Chancellor of the Exchequer in the reign of Queen Elizabeth), and Catharine, daughter of Ludovic Slobert of Bruges in Flanders. Samuel, presumably, was born in Bruges for he and his brother Daniel were made free 'denizens' of Ireland on August 16, 1594, being at that time citizens of Bruges.[2] From 1594 Samuel worked as an agent for Robert Newcomen, Victualler of the Army in Ireland who was married to Samuel's sister Catharine. During the next years he was much taken up by his trade in provisions, travelling several times between England and Ireland, which brought him in contact with important English officials such as Lord Burghley.[3] His satisfactory service may have led to his appointment as Marshal of the Court of Castle Chamber in 1597 which he held until 1615. On June 9, 1600 he succeeded Sir Geoffrey Fenton as Clerk-General of the Queen's Works in Ireland at an annual salary of £10.[4] It is not known what prior experience Molyneux had in building and engineering. He got actively involved in the Tyrone war and probably served near Loughfoyle where in 1600–1 he supplied victuals for carpenters and masons, who presumably were building the forts of Derry and Culmore. By warrants in 1600 he was paid over £3,500, but it is unknown for what purpose.[5] About a year later numerous other sums paid to him occur in the state accounts and these included payments for works and fortifications at Carrickfergus.[6] In the North he was assisted by Thomas

Molyneux

Rookewood (q.v.), who acted as Deputy Surveyor of the Works at Loughfoyle. In August 1601 Molyneaux made a report on the repairs needed at forts in the centre of the country at Maryborough, Philipstown, and Athlone.[7] Evidence is lacking, however, that he executed these. In the South of Ireland he had another deputy, Richard Hawett, whose duties Molyneux took over early in 1603 when Hawett was murdered. Subsequently, he oversaw the completion of the forts of Halebolin and Castle Park which had been designed by the engineer Paul Ive. Molyneux also at this time was involved with alterations to the fortifications at Galway, and probably also at Limerick.[8] He seems to have had a limited reputation for his skill in engineering as he is not mentioned among engineers of the period.[9] In 1610, although he had the Lord Deputy Chichester's recommendation, Molyneux unsuccessfully opposed his replacement by Sir Josiah Bodley (q.v.) for the finishing of the forts.[10] By this time, Molyneux's reputation must already have been tarnished. The family biographer, Sir Capel Molyneux relates that 'he seems to be a man careless of his temporal concerns, and the business of the world; by his employment much of the King's money passed through his hands, for which he was accountable to the Exchequer, upon all his accounts, he was found indebted to the King . . .'. Samuel's brother Daniel, who stood as security, was subsequently forced to sell part of his estate. Molyneux's poor budgeting most likely led in 1606 to the creation of the position of Comptroller of the Royal Works (filled by Francis Annesley, later Viscount Valentia). It seems beyond any doubt that Molyneux was excluded from the construction of fortifications, which became the sole responsibility of the Director-General of the Fortifications and Buildings, first Sir Josias Bodley (q.v.) and later Nicholas Pynnar (q.v.) and Thomas Rothcram (q.v.). From 1613 onwards Samuel, as Clerk of the Royal Works, was formally responsible to the Director-General. Before the fire at the Public Record Office in Dublin there was extensive documentation of Molyneux's supervision of the Royal Works, in particular at Dublin Castle. However, even there Molyneux had to compete with amateurs like Sir Edward Brabazon (q.v.) and Sir John Bourchier. However, it seems likely that Molyneux can be credited with building the gallery in Dublin Castle for Lord Deputy Falkland.

In 1613 he surrendered his patent of Clerk, and was regranted the position on March 16 of the same year,[11] but he now had to share it with Tristam Gawen. In the absence of any architectural evidence, it seems likely that Gawen's appointment was honorary only, and that Molyneux remained as independent as before. His architectural works, as far as they have been identified, have all been altered, so that one can but speculate about his skill as an architect, which may have reflected the mannerist style of his native Flanders. He held a few official positions such as the Marshal of the Court of Castle Chamber, already mentioned, and of Seneschal of the King's Manors in Co. Dublin from 1607 onwards, and he also served in Parliament in 1613 for Mallow, Co. Cork. He died unmarried in 1625 at Newlands, near Clondalkin, Co. Dublin, where he lived with his brother Daniel, who became his heir. Little is known about his estate. Together with Daniel he had inherited an estate at Ballyfermot, Co. Dublin,[12] and in 1610 he had been mentioned as a possible lessee for the new plantation in Ulster,[13] but he did not participate in the settlement. It seems likely that some part of Molyneux's library descended via Daniel to the Surveyor-General and scientist William Molyneux (q.v.). With Molyneux's death the post of Clerk of the Royal Works ceased to exist. Its functions were amalgamated with the position of the Director-General and Overseer of the Fortifications and Buildings held then by Nicholas Pynnar and Thomas Rotheram (q.v.). Samuel Molyneux is not to be confused with his nephew

Samuel, (1616–95), son of Daniel Molyneux, and father of William Molyneux (q.v.).

[1] Original documents by Samuel Molyneux's are rare, while his drawings are not known to have survived. His account book from 1610–16 was formerly in the Public Record Office, Dublin (*C. L. Falkiner, Illustrations of Irish History*, London, 1904, 22*n*. 1), while another of his books 'A Book of Disbursements for repairs of the Castle, Courts of Justice, &c. 1622' was formerly in the Auditor General's Office, Lower Yard, Dublin Castle (*Supplement to 8th Report of the Commissioners on the Public Records of Ireland*, Dublin, 1819–20, p. 318). Two of his letters to Lord Burghley are mentioned in *CSPI*, 1592–6, 313, 515. Two secondary sources on Samuel Molyneux are not always reliable in the data used: [Sir Capel Molyneux], *An Account of the Family ... of Sir Thomas Molyneux kt*, Evesham, 1820, and N. Z. R. Molyneux, *History ... of the Molyneux Families*, Syracuse, N.Y., 1904. The first source is used especially for the compilation of this entry.
[2] M. C. Griffith, *Irish Patent Rolls of James I ...*, Dublin, 1966, 349; *Lodge*, VI, 86*n*.
[3] *CSPI*, 1592–6; 1596–7, 1598–9; *HMC, Salisbury*, II, 384.
[4] J. L. J. Hughes, *Patentee Officers in Ireland*, Dublin, 1960, 91.
[5] PRO, A.O. 1/287/1081.
[6] PRO, A.O. 1/288/1082.
[7] PRO, SP 63/209 Pt I, f. 142.
[8] *Carew*, 1601–3, 415; Bodl., Laud Ms 612, f. 136.
[9] *Carew*, 1601–3, 250.
[10] *CSPI*, 1608–10, 374.
[11] Note that this appointment almost coincides with the grant to Inigo Jones of the office of Surveyor of the Works in England, in reversion of Simon Basil.
[12] NLI, D 17856.
[13] *CSPI*, 1608–10, 367.

CORK, HALBOLIN FORT. Build by Molyneux between 1601 and 1604 after the design of Paul Ive at a cost of £1,772 8*s*. 7*d*. (*CSPI*, 1603–6, 202; R. Caulfield (Ed.), *The Council Book of the Corporation of Kinsale*, Guildford, 1879, xxxi; Bodl. Laud Ms 612, f. 136).

KINSALE, CO. CORK, CASTLE PARK FORT. Completed by Molyneux between 1602 and 1604 after the design of Paul Ive at a cost of £2,050 14*s*. 4*d*. (*CSPI*, 1603–6, 202; Caulfield, *op.cit.*, xxxi; Bodl., Laud Ms 612, f. 136).

GALWAY, ST AUGUSTINE FORT. Repaired between 1602 and 1604 at a cost of £2,404 12*s*. 4*d*. (*CSPI*, 1603–6, 202; Caulfield, *op.cit.*, xxxi).

DUBLIN, FOUR COURTS. The removal of the Four Courts from the old King's Inns necessitated the building of other quarters. In 1608 Molyneux was paid £21 10*s*. 4*d*. for building the Four Courts next to Christ Church Cathedral, on a cross-plan. Part of its roof was blown down in 1610. The Courts were moved back to Dublin Castle in 1622 (see below); the old building is no longer extant (Gilbert Ms 62, p. 12; *HMC, Hastings*, IV, 5; E. M. Hinton, *Ireland Through Tudor Eyes*, Philadelphia, 1935, 7; *CARD*, II, 478, 501).

DUBLIN CASTLE. In 1613 Molyneux fitted up the great Hall of the Castle for the meeting of the two Houses, and in 1616 repaired the bedroom of Lady Chichester (Falkiner, *op.cit.*, 22 *n*. 1). He made extensive repairs in 1622–3 costing £464 16*s*. 16*d*., and these included the building of the Long Gallery in the Castle for the Lord Deputy Falkland (Kent County Library, Sackville Ms ON 8541; R. Loeber, 'The Rebuilding of Dublin Castle: Thirty Critical Years, 1661–1690', *Studies*, 1980, *69*, 45–69) and bringing back the Four Courts from the site near Christ Church Cathedral to Dublin Castle. On December 8, 1624 he presented to the Lord Deputy Falkland a proposal for the rebuilding of the north-west tower, which had fallen down in the preceding May (BL. Sloane Ms 3827, f. 46). Altered.

MOLYNEUX, WILLIAM (1656–1696), Surveyor-General of the Fortifications and Buildings. Born in 1656 in Dublin, the son of Margret Dowdall and Samuel

Molyneux

Molyneux[1] (Master Gunner in Ireland, and nephew of Samuel Molyneux, Clerk of the Royal Works in Ireland, q.v.). There are a number of sources that deal with Molyneux's life: however, it is mainly his architectural career that will be dealt with here. In 1678 he married Lucy, daughter of William Domville. Through other family connections he was related to prominent Irish families, such as the Usshers and the Newcomens. In 1675 he was sent to London to study law, and returned to Ireland three years later. On 1679 and again in 1680, he went to London with his wife to try to find a cure for her blindness and 'dreadful' headaches. He was much troubled by her illness and as he later wrote, counteracted this by 'The diversions I took . . . was chiefly in books, and especially in studying the mathematicks. This was the grand pacificum I used; these were the opiates that lulled my troublesome thoughts to sleep.' In 1682, following the traditional interest of his ancestors, he made a model of his design to test current theories regarding the flight of projectiles. In the same year he was sending out queries in relation to a geographical atlas of Ireland, as part of a scheme started in 1676 by the London bookseller Moses Pitt, assisted, amongst others, by the scientist-architect Dr Robert Hooke. Molyneux knew Hooke probably through their mutual friendship with Flamstead, the Astronomer Royal. In 1683 Molyneux and Sir William Petty founded the Dublin Philosophical Society, in emulation of The Royal Society in England. Petty became first president, and Molyneux first secretary. Presumably in the following year Molyneux, as he himself records, proposed to William Robinson, the Irish Surveyor-General (q.v.) a 'present' of £250 if Robinson would surrender his patent and take out a new one for both of them to go to the longest-lived of the two. Molyneux agreed that he 'would not intermeddle with the salary without his [Robinson's] consent, and unless by his consent I acted in the place'. The Lord Lieutenant, the Duke of Ormonde, consented 'immediately' to this plan, and a joint patent for the Surveyor-Generalship in Ireland was issued on October 31, 1684 for the salary of £300 per annum.[2] Molyneux and Robinson's superior, William Stewart, first Viscount Mountjoy, Master of the Ordnance, had written to Ormonde five months earlier asking him to send Molyneux on a foreign journey. Mountjoy held Molyneux in high esteem, saying that he 'is as well qualifyed to make observations in what relates to an engineer as any in this kingdom or perhaps in any other . . .'. For security reasons Molyneux had to memorize his instructions,[3] which strongly suggests that he was secretly to inspect fortifications abroad. From the government Molyneux received £100 for his travels, and he left Dublin on May 13, 1684, passed through England, met Lord Mountjoy on June 6 in Calais, and travelled with him to the Netherlands, to parts of Germany, and to Paris. It seems likely that he had been instructed to sketch the fortifications in these areas, but, if any such drawings ever existed, they have not been identified. He returned to Dublin at the end of September 1685 or 1686. In February 1687 Robinson, upon the arrival of the Duke of Tyrconnell as Lord Deputy, fled to England, and left Molyneux in charge of the Surveyor-General's office to finish the south-east range of Dublin Castle. This incident seems to exemplify Molyneux's involvement in the office of the Surveyor-General. As stipulated in the original agreement, Molyneux only acted as Surveyor-General with the explicit consent of Robinson. Such an occasion seems never to have arisen again. One and a half years after Robinson's departure, Molyneux was deprived of his position by Tyrconnell, and he subsequently moved to Chester. With the Williamites Molyneux returned to Ireland, and held several offices. Although his position as Surveyor-General seems not to have been cancelled, Robinson's return to Ireland in 1690 most likely spoiled his chances of future involvement with the Royal Works or fortifications in Ireland.

In 1693 the governors' minutes of the Royal Hospital, Kilmainham, mention an order that 'Mr Molineux, one of the Survey[rs] of the Kings Buildings' should view the repairs done at the Hospital by [William] Spike,[4] but no evidence has been found that Molyneux actually practised as Surveyor-General after 1688. However, it seems very likely that he was extremely interested in architecture. When in 1730 the library of his son Samuel was auctioned,[5] it contained thirty-two architectural books (Palladio, Serlio, Vitruvius, Scamozzi, Le Muet, etc.) and four books on fortifications, most of which could have been in the possession of William Molyneux as only four of them were published after his death.[6] In an autobiographical account Molyneux does not mention that he ever designed a building for one of his numerous relatives in Ireland; in fact, drawings by him are not known. Robinson seems to have been nothing more than a business partner of Molyneux as he was excluded from Molyneux's list of intimate friends, which was headed by Bartholomew Vanhomrigh. Shortly after Molyneux's famous *The Case of Ireland Stated* was published in 1698, he died at the age of 42. For most of his life he lived in Dublin in his father's house near Ormonde (also Gorman) Gate, and inherited from his father an estate at Castle Dillon, Co. Armagh,[7] where he does not seem to have been active in building.

[1] See for example, the *DNB*; K.T. Hoppen, *The Common Scientist* ..., London, 1970; and, [Sir C. Molyneux], *An Account of the Family ... of Sir Thomas Molyneux*, Kt., Evesham, 1820, which contains an autobiographical tract by William Molyneux.
[2] *CSPI*, 1700–2, 218.
[3] Bodl., Carte Ms 217, f. 156.
[4] PROI, RHK 1/1/1, f. 62[v].
[5] The auction catalogue is now in TCD, vvi, 45.
[6] However, if I am well informed, Molyneux left part, if not all, of his books to Trinity College, Dublin.
[7] Armagh Diocesan Library, Ms H.II.20, f. 1.

DUBLIN CASTLE. Between 1687 and 1688 Molyneux erected the south-east range with the terrace walk behind it, presumably to the designs of William Robinson (R. Loeber, 'The Rebuilding of Dublin Castle: Thirty Critical Years.' *Studies*, 1980, *69*, 66).

DUBLIN, MOLYNEUX'S HOUSE, near Ormonde Gate. Samuel Molyneux finished this house in 1666; after 1692 his son William made 'considerable Improvements and Ornaments about it ...', erected a new entrance into the court, railed in the front of the house, added to it 'a handsome Portall', pulled down the old stables and coach house, and rebuilt them larger and more conveniently. In addition he was at considerable expense in altering and adorning his garden (Armagh Diocesan Lib., Ms H.II.19, f. 10).

MOORE, WILLIAM (fl. 1667), builder. Writing from Rathcline, Co. Longford, on February 26, 1667 to Sir George Lane, Moore described the progress on the wainscotting of the dining room at Lane's country house Rathcline, and the difficulty of hiring two men to speed up the work. He was probably a builder, for he mentions that the articles of his contract had not been sealed, for his partner, an unnamed soldier, had been called to his troop.[1] Evidence as to whether Moore was working to the designs of John Westley (q.v.) or William Dodson (q.v.) for Sir George Lane's house has not come to light.

[1] NLI, Ms 2341, f. 427.

MORLEY, EDWARD (fl. 1639), builder, who oversaw the rebuilding of Castlelyons, Co. Cork, after the designs of Thomas Kelly (q.v.), which he was forced to alter.[1] The building was largely financed by the Earl of Cork for his son-in-law, the Earl of Barrymore.[2] Morely is last mentioned in March 1640,[3] but the building was still unfinished a year later.[4] Rebuilt at a later date.

[1] Chatsworth, Lismore Ms 20, f. 122.
[2] *Grosart*, series 2, IV, 35, 212.
[3] *Grosart*, series 1, V, 129.
[4] Lady F. P. Verney & M.M. (Eds.), *Memoirs of the Verney Family*, London, 1892–1904, I, 210.

MORTON, JOHN (fl. 1662–1668), a contractor and possibly an architect. He was a Captain in the army, whose company of Foot is mentioned in 1662 or 1663 as 'late, Capt. Moreton's'.[1] However, he seems to have regained the company, for it was stationed in Kilkenny in 1668 under his name.[2] From 1663 until shortly before his death in 1668 he supervised, if he did not design, the rebuilding of Dunmore House and Kilkenny Castle for the Duke and Duchess of Ormonde. His work for the Ormondes included sending Kilkenny marble for a chimney piece to the English Lord Chancellor, the Earl of Clarendon in 1664.[3] He also gave advice about the laying out of the Dunmore gardens.[4] His yearly salary, paid by the Ormondes, was £100, which he collected for the last time in Whitehall in 1668. The Duke felt relieved by Morton's discharge because of his 'Chargeable Reckings' (i.e. his heavy expenditure). Two months later, on November 9, 1669, Lady Ormonde reported that Morton had died of a fever the previous week.[5] Morton's architectural work is hard to evaluate due to a lack of surviving evidence, and his work at Kilkenny Castle was later altered. He may have been familiar with classical architecture.

[1] *HMC, 14th Rep. App. VII*, 356.
[2] *HMC, Ormonde*, II, 195. See also *HMC, 10th Rep. V.*, 105.
[3] Bodl., Carte Ms 145, f. 86; Clarendon was then building Clarendon House, Piccadilly, London after the design of Sir Roger Pratt. Dem. 1683.
[4] *HMC, Ormonde*, n.s. III, 282–3.
[5] NLI, Ms 2503, ff. 4, 21, 24.

DUNMORE HOUSE, CO. KILKENNY. Rebuilding of the older structure, from Feb. 1663 till Oct. 1664, cost £3,308. Work, however, continued and in the following year a carved staircase was erected, wainscotting inserted and a front of a classical portico with pillars set up. At Morton's death, the debt to the workmen at Dunmore House and Kilkenny Castle (see below) amounted to £1,585. Ruins dem. early 19th century. (Bodl., Carte Ms 33, f. 352; NLI, Ms 2503, ff. 4, 6; *HMC, Ormonde*, n.s. III, 201).

KILKENNY CASTLE. Morton supervised alterations at a total cost of £799 between Feb. 1663 and Oct. 1664. Subsequent work included the erection of a coach house, and other changes in the castle, which most likely took place up till 1668 (see above). Rebuilt in 1826. (Bodl., Carte Ms 33, f. 352; NLI, Ms 2503, ff. 4, 6, 23; *HMC, Ormonde*, n.s. III, 200–1).

KILKENNY COLLEGE. In 1665 Morton surveyed for the Duke of Ormonde an existing house, which formerly had belonged to Robert Shee, and gave him three estimates for repairing the building (*HMC, Ormonde*, n.s. III, 200). This was possibly altered in 1666 into a school (described in *JRSAI*, 1934, *64*, 48–9) on which Morton was reported to have worked (NLI, Ms 2503). In 1679 Ormonde claimed that he expended on rent and building of the school at least £2,000 (T. Carte, *The Life of James, Duke of Ormonde*, Oxford, 1851, V, 137). Replaced in 1782. (*Transactions of the Kilkenny Archaeological Society*, 1849–51, *1*, 221–9).

N

NELSON, JAMES (fl. 1701), carpenter, who became Assistant to the Masters of the City Works in Dublin. He was admitted as a Freeman of the city in 1701.[1] Of his work there for the ensuing 18 years nothing is known. He represented the guild of carpenters in 1714.[2] In 1719 he succeeded Richard Mills (q.v.) in the office of Assistant to the Masters of the City Works.[3] He continued to attend to his private business despite the increasing demands of the city,[4] but by 1723 was forced to concentrate solely on the latter. This included overseeing the erection of the pedestal for Van Nost's statue of King George I, making a leaden water-main from the city bason,[5] building an infirmary at the Blue Coat Hospital and repairing its chapel (1725).[6] His last known work was superintending the building of the steeple of St Werburgh's Church in 1729.[7] Evidence is too scanty to say whether Nelson designed buildings. It is not known whether he ever built on the lot granted to him in the new development north of the Liffey.[8]

[1] Geneal. Office, Ms G. Thrift, Roll of Freeman of the City of Dublin.
[2] *CARD*, VII, 574.
[3] *Ibid.*, 94.
[4] *Ibid.*, 167, 236.
[5] *Ibid.*, 204; R. Gunnis, *Dictionary of British Sculptors, 1660–1851*, London, 1951, 281.
[6] King's Hospital, Blue Coat School Accounts, pp. 430, 436.
[7] S. C. Hughes, *The Church of St Werburgh*, Dublin, 1889, 27. The actual building was in the hands of the mason William Borrodale.
[8] National Gallery of Ireland, Dublin, Ms 11881.

NEVILL, FRANCIS (*c.* 1648–1727), civil engineer. He was born about 1648, but little is known of his early life. He is noted in December 1688 as one of the committee members who were to regulate the concerns of the City of Derry. Early in the next year he confirmed his adherence to the Williamite cause by signing the Declaration of Union. Subsequently he participated in the war, acted as engineer to the Corporation of Derry, and on return from an official mission outside the city, was refused re-entry. Soon afterwards he was taken prisoner and was sent to Dublin, where he managed to escape. Consequently his services were not available during the siege of Derry. He returned to the city when the enemy had retreated, and prepared a map of the siege,[1] which was published subsequently as part of a tract with the title 'A Description of Londonderry as it was closely besieged by ye Army in April, 1689. A Description of the Towne and Workes about it. A Description of the Enemy's Camp'.[2]

He was chosen and sworn a burgess of the City of Derry on December 5, 1689.[3] Three years later he built for the Corporation its second Town House, which he designed in the artisan mannerist style, and which is only known from an engraving.[4] Apart from some correspondence with the scientist William Molyneux (q.v.) concerning the latter's Castle Dillon estate,[5] little is known of Nevill's contacts in Irish society. He became Collector of the Revenue, but it is not known at what date.

He was also paid in 1705 for the repair of Charlemont Fort when he was under the supervision of Capt. Thomas Burgh[6] (q.v.). The scarcity of known architects in

Ulster about 1700 suggests that Nevill's services could have easily been used by private patrons, but no evidence of this has come to light so far.

Nevill's reputation was largely based on his surveys to improve waterways in Ulster. In 1703 he surveyed the Glan Bog between counties Down and Armagh, and the course of the 'Upper Band' and Newry River, with the intention of creating a canal between Lough Neagh and Newry. He estimated its cost at £20,000. Heads of a bill for this purpose were presented to the Irish House of Commons in 1703, who awarded Nevill, then with the rank of Captain, £200 for 'his extraordinary pains and service'.[7] Two years later the House of Commons decided that it could not forward the project.[8] More than twenty years afterwards Capt. Thomas Burgh (q.v.) attempted to realize the same plan.

Nevill was the author of 'Some Observation of Lough Neagh' in 1713.[9] He is known to have surveyed the estate of Waringstown in Co. Down.[10] Nothing is known about his work between that date and 1726, the year in which he made his will. He resided then at Belturbet, Co. Cavan. His only son Charles had died in 1718. In his will he mentioned that he was 78 years old. He left his property to his four surviving daughters and their husbands. The will was proved on August 18, 1727.[11]

[1] C. D. Milligan, *History of the Siege of Londonderry, 1689*, Belfast, 1951, 50, 122, 171; C. D. Milligan, *The Walls of Derry*, Londonderry 1950, pt. II, 24.

[2] A copy of this tract is in TCD.

[3] Milligan, *op.cit.*, 1950, 24 *n*. 2.

[4] W. S. Ferguson, A. J. Rowan, J. J. Tracey, *List of Historic Buildings ... in and near the City of Derry*, [Belfast], 1969–70, 7.

[5] Armagh Diocesan Library, Ms H.II.20, f. 179. Another letter by Nevill is in BL, Sloane Ms 4065, f. 138, which I have not examined.

[6] PRO, W.O. 55/1984.

[7] W. A. McCutcheon, *The Canals of the North of Ireland*, London, 1965, 17; *Commons Jour.*, 1703–13, 100, 158, 161. His survey is now in PRONI, D695/M.

[8] T. Thorpe, *Catalogue of Southwell Manuscripts*, London, 1834, 246.

[9] Information kindly provided by Dr John Andrews. I have not seen this tract.

[10] E. D. Atkinson, *An Ulster Parish: Being a History of Donaghcloney (Waringstown)*, Dublin, 1898, opp.p. 86.

[11] His will is in PROI, Preg. Wills, under date May 6, 1727; his descendants are also named in Geneal. Office, Ms 241, p. 303.

O

O'BRIEN, JOHN (fl. 1709), mason who built, and possibly designed Shannongrove, Co. Limerick for John Bury from 1709 onwards.[1]

[1] M. Craig & The Knight of Glin, *Ireland Observed*, Cork, 1970, 97.

ORRERY, 1st Earl of, see Boyle, Roger.

P

PAINE (or **PAYNE**), JOHN (fl. 1642–?1670), Director-General and Overseer of the King's Fortifications. Nothing is known about his parentage and training. In 1642 he is mentioned heading a new company of 200 pioneers, quartered at Naas, Co. Kildare.[1] By order of the Earl of Ormonde he is said to have succeeded Nicholas Pynnar (q.v.) temporarily in 1644 as Director-General and Overseer of the Fortifications and Buildings in Ireland.[2] In that year he and a John Bartlett proposed to erect a blockhouse in Dublin Harbour, which probably was never executed.[3] He remained in the service of the Royalists during the troubles following. He was stationed in Dublin in 1648. It is not known whether he advised on the repair and strengthening of the walls of the city which took place at that time.[4] Subsequently he served under the Commonwealth, but in all probability lost his function as Director-General, for after the Restoration he was pardoned for accepting £100 'in the usurper's time', and was granted his arrears for his services in Ireland before 1649.[5] On August 14, 1660 he received a payment as Quartermaster-General of the Army.[6] When in that year the post of Director-General and Overseer of the King's Fortifications and Plantations in Ireland had to be refilled, Paine was preferred not only before Col. John Rosworme but also before Capt. John Boulton who was nominated by Charles II.[7] On February 22, 1661 Paine received the patent for this post for life.[8] This position he initially shared with Capt. John Hallam (q.v.), whose patent probably never became effective. In 1662 Paine and Hallam petitioned to have their salary of 5s. per day raised to 15s. per day,[9] which it seems was not allowed, for Paine's salary in 1666 was 6s. per day.[10] Three years later his yearly salary was 'increased' [sic] to £91 5s., which in fact was about 5s. per day![11] The last known references to him are disbursements for his work at Chapelizod House, Co. Dublin,[12] in 1666, and in 1667 at the Parliament (also Chichester) House, Dublin.[13] Paine petitioned for the approval of his accounts. A commission was instituted in June 1666 to examine these.[14] Paine probably died in 1670, for he was succeeded in that year by William Robinson (q.v.). Paine presumably had his residence in Swan Alley, St Andrew's parish, Dublin, in 1659,[15] but in 1665 is mentioned as being of Dame Street.[16] At the time of the Restoration he held a pew in St Werburgh's Church, Dublin.[17] Under the Acts of Settlement and Explanation he was granted houses in the cities of Dublin and Waterford. In 1661 he was M.P. for Clogher, Co. Tyrone. No drawings by Paine have been identified. A great part of work on the Royal residences was supervised not by him, but by Dr John Westley (q.v.) and by William Dodson (q.v.). As an engineer his prominent position was shared by others. The engineers William Webb and John Rosworme both worked under him, but seem to have been fairly independent. It seems to have been exceptional for Col. William Legge to come to Ireland and, in his position as Lieutenant-General of the English Ordnance, survey the fortifications in the North of Ireland,[18] of which Paine was in fact in charge. Paine was not involved in the repair of Rincurran Fort and Castle Park Fort, both near Kinsale, undertaken by the Earl of Orrery (q.v.) and Paine's superior, the Master of the Ordnance, Sir Robert Byron.

---

[1] *HMC, 14th Rep. App. VII*, 141, 185; *CSPI*, 1633–47, 778.
[2] *Royal Engineers' Journal*, 1926, 40, 666.

[3] *HMC, Ormonde*, n.s. I, 88–9.
[4] *HMC, 8th Rep. App. I*, 597; *HMC, Ormonde*, n.s. I, 113–4; *CARD*, III, 480.
[5] *Irish Statutes*, 17 &'18 C.2.c.2 § 164; PRO, SP 44/18/160.
[6] Bodl., Rawl. Ms A237, f. 95.
[7] *CSPI*, 1660–2, 393.
[8] Bodl., Carte Ms 61, f. 662; *CSPI*, 1660–2, 214, 508, 529.
[9] *CSPI*, 1660–2, 604.
[10] *CSPI*, 1666–9, 70.
[11] *CSPI*, 1669–70, 8.
[12] NLI, Ms 8642 (10).
[13] Bodl., Carte Ms 52, f. 276ᵛ.
[14] *HMC, 10th Rep. App. V*, 1.
[15] *CARD*, IV, 560.
[16] *57th Report of the Deputy Keeper of the Public Records in Ireland*, 1936, 540.
[17] S. C. Hughes, *The Church of St Werburgh*, Dublin, 1889, 19.
[18] County Record Office, Stafford, Dartmouth Ms, (?1662), Report by Col. William Legge on the fortifications in the North of Ireland.

DUBLIN CASTLE. Paine made extensive alterations to the Castle for the 1st Duke of Ormonde from 1662–7. Master Carpenter on the site was John Mills (R. Loeber, 'The Rebuilding of Dublin Castle: Thirty critical years, 1661–1690?, *Studies*, 1980, *69*, 45–69.

DUBLIN, FORTIFICATIONS. Before August 28, 1662. Detailed estimate for the repair of the fortifications around Dublin for a total cost of £2,708 16s. (*HMC, Ormonde*, n.s. III, 25–6; NLI, Ms 2326, ff. 395–6). Unexecuted.

DUBLIN, HORSE GUARD, near Essex St, consisting of stables and a guard house, built by Paine near the site of the Old Council Chamber in 1663–5 (Carte Ms 52, ff. 261ᵛ, 291; Ms 165, f. 241), Dem.

KILMAINHAM, DOG KENNELS, Co. Dublin. Undated, detailed estimate for dog kennels at Kilmainham Lock (near Phoenix House) for the 1st Duke of Ormonde, costing £181 7s. 6d. (NLI, Ms 2326, f. 389). Probably never built.

POWDER STORE. Undated estimate for small powder store and shed for a total cost of £38 8s. (NLI, Ms 2488, p. 447).

PAPS, NICHOLAS (fl. 1614), mason who was commissioned by Sir Arthur Chichester to rebuild the ruined church of St Nicholas in Carrickfergus. The alterations included the construction of the Donegal aisle,[1] which was to house a large monument to the Chichester family (not by Paps). It is not known whether Chichester employed Paps again at the building of Joymount House, his residence within the walls of Carrickfergus. This large house, according to a datestone, had been erected in 1616. It was demolished in the 18th century.

[1] G. Campbell & S. Crowther, *Historic buildings ... in the Town of Carrickfergus*, Belfast, 1978, 14.

PARROTT, or PARRAT, WILLIAM (fl. 1627), builder. His name occurs first in 1627 in a letter from the Earl of Antrim, who requested the Secretary of State, Lord Conway, to give Parrott a pass in order to free him from the dangers of being pressed into military service in England.[1] In the same year Parrott contracted for the building of St Columb's Cathedral in Londonderry at a cost of £3,400. The building was completed in 1633 in the late gothic style and the general supervision of the work was in the hands of Sir John Vaughan.[2] Little is known about Parrott's subsequent career. He may be identified with the 'Mr Parret' mentioned in the MacDonnell papers among the Irish debts of the Earl of Antrim and his wife the Duchess of Buckingham. According to this document, in 1638 'Parret' was to be

Petty

paid £1,800 (at a bond of £3,500),[3] which may refer to the restoration of the chapel at Dunluce Castle, Co. Antrim, undertaken by the Duchess of Buckingham between 1637 and 1640.[4] A William Parratt [sic] was Mayor of Coleraine in 1642.[5]

[1] *CSPI*, 1625–32, 284.
[2] D. A. Chart (Ed.), *Londonderry and the London Companies*, Belfast, 1928, 109; W. S. Ferguson, A. J. Rowan, J. J. Tracey, *List of Historic Buildings ... in and near the City of Derry*, [Belfast], 1969–70, 7, 16.
[3] G. Hill (Ed.), *An Historical Account of the MacDonnells of Antrim*, Belfast, 1873, 476.
[4] C. L. Adams, *Castles of Ireland*, London, 1904, 158.
[5] J. Hogan (Ed.), *Letters and Papers relating to the Irish Rebellion*, Dublin, 1936, 7, 12.

PETTY, Sir **WILLIAM** (1623–1687), political economist, who possibly also was a gentleman-architect. His eventful career as a physician, organizer of the first national survey of Ireland, inventor and economist has been described in the *Dictionary of National Biography*. His activity as a designer of buildings is less clear than his other specialities. When staying in a house in Dublin in 1677, which probably was in St George's Lane, he wrote a number of letters to his wife about building projects at his residence. He planned to make 'a small but elegant building for your [i.e. his wife's] reception and the reception of our friends'. He added that he had also 'designed another fabric upon that ground'.[1] Because of the shortness of his lease and the state of his affairs he was then postponing the building of 'a great house', but, as he wrote, 'I do elude my melancholy sometimes by contriving many noble palaces on paper'.[2] In a list of projects written by Petty, there is mention of 'Building a new Palace for the Chief Governor £20,000', which probably refers to the major rebuilding of Dublin Castle, which took place after the disastrous fire there in 1684.[3] However, it is unclear whether Petty ever built a 'palace' for himself;[4] his project for Dublin Castle was not realized. On his estate in Co. Kerry, he saw to the building of a principal residence and fortification at Killowen near Kenmare.

[1] I am greatly indebted to Dr T. Barnard for passing on to me the following references of Petty's letters to his wife from Osler Ms 7612, p. 65, now at McGill University, Montreal, Quebec, Canada, and from the Lansdowne Mss at Bowood Ms 5, items 17, 39, 122.
[2] Osler Ms 7612, p. 65.
[3] R. Loeber, 'The Rebuilding of Dublin Castle: Thirty critical years 1661–1690', *Studies*, 1980, *69*, 62.
[4] Perhaps Kerry House in Dublin, pulled down in 1815, refers to Petty's residence there (his daughter Anne had married Thomas Maurice, 1st Earl of Kerry; their son inherited the Petty estate). The house was described by Austin Cooper in 1795 as an 'old fashioned style – great staircase etc. of oak' (A. Cooper, *An Eighteenth-Century Antiquary ...*, Dublin, 1942, 144, 120).

PORTALL, ?**FRANCIS** (fl. 1722). He is mentioned as a Captain who made several drafts of a dome to be erected over the belfry of St Canice's Cathedral, Kilkenny in 1722,[1] none of which seems to have been executed. The identity of Capt. Portall is rather obscure and he may be the Francis Portall, who served in the English army in Brig. Farrington's Regiment of Foot in 1704.[2]

[1] J. Graves & J. G. A. Prim, *The History, Architecture, and Antiquities of the Cathedral Church of St Canice, Kilkenny*, Dublin, 1857, 55.
[2] *Dalton*, V, 98.

PRANKER, also **PRANKLIN,** THOMAS (fl. 1636), stonemason who is only known from the work for his patron, the 1st Earl of Cork. He is first noted in 1636 when he was paid for 62 freestone lights for the new dining room at Lismore Castle, where he also tiled over the 'compass window', and provided water-tables.[1] Other tiling work followed in the next year, again for the dining room, and also for the porch of the chapel, and for the summer house on the bowling green. In 1638 he was paid for making and setting up 'one lardge fayre dorecase' of stone at the west end of St Carthage Cathedral at Lismore (altered later by Sir William Robinson (q.v.)). In that year he also took down the great window and ten smaller ones in the North Abbey at Youghal for insertion in St Carthage Cathedral. Another great window was taken down by Pranker in the Abbey of Castlelyons, Co. Cork, presumably for the same purpose. All this was part of the Earl of Cork's effort to rebuild the Cathedral, which he had partially pulled down in 1634.[2] How far the restoration proceeded remains unclear. It was still in progress in February 1640.

[1] NLI, Ms 6899.
[2] *Grosart*, series 1, IV, 6; V, 46, 124.

PYNNAR, (also **PINNAR**), NICHOLAS (fl. 1600–1644), Director-General of the Fortifications in Ireland. He came to Ireland from the Low Countries in May 1600 as a Captain of Foot in Sir Henry Docwra's army which was sent to Lough Foyle.[1] He does not seem to have been involved in the building of any of the numerous forts erected during the period. Pynnar, according to the Earl of Tyrconnell, treated the Irish with extreme harshness during the campaign in the North, but an official inquiry was not instigated. In 1604 Pynnar's company was disbanded and he received a pension of four shillings a day. Shortly after, he presumably left Ireland and was in London in May 1606. In the following September he and his colleague Edmund Yorke[2] were in Venice, where both were introduced by the English ambassador Sir Henry Wotton to the Doge. Their request for service with the Venetians, in anticipation of a conflict with the Pope over the interdiction he had put on Venice because of objections to the temporal prerogatives of the papacy there, while met with reservations did not prevent them each being given a golden collar to the value of 150 ducats. Pynnar stayed in Italy for more than a year, where he was employed as engineer. In December 1607 Sir Henry Wotton dispatched Pynnar to London on a secret mission and gave him a portrait of padre Paolo Scarpi for King James I, and a New-Year's gift for Prince Henry. Pynnar should also have carried Italian architectural drawings for the Earl of Salisbury (then building Hatfield House), but Wotton did not have them ready when Pynnar left.[3] Unfortunately, this is the only reference to Pynnar's contact with Italian architecture, his interest in which may have been stimulated by the connoisseur Wotton. Being unemployed for a while, before May 1609, Pynnar left London for Sweden with Irish troops to join the Swedish King Charles IX in his fight to prevent Polish control of Russia.[4] He may have returned to Ireland the next year, for he offered himself as a servitor in the plantation of Ulster. After his discharge in 1611 he was granted 1,000 acres in Co. Cavan to be known as the 'manor of Pynnar'.[5] However, he did not proceed with the enterprise, and is found the same year among the 'tenants and inhabitants' of Sir Richard Boyle's estate in the south of the country.[6] In about 1620 he was granted 700 acres in the new plantation of Co. Leitrim, but evidence is lacking about his compliance to the conditions of the plantation.[7] Between 1611 and 1612 he sat on a committee which decided on controversies in the plantation of Cavan. He left Ireland in the latter year and travelled, probably in the company of Cromwell, to France,[8] and most likely went once more to Venice, since he is reported to have met the new English ambassador Sir Dudley Carleton.[9] The purpose of his second tour remains unknown. Sometime prior to March 1617 he returned to Ireland to view the forts in Ulster and Connaught. On the death of Sir Josias Bodley (q.v.), Pynnar and Sir Thomas Rotheram (q.v.) received a joint patent for life as 'Directors-General and Overseers of the Fortifications and Buildings', dated February 27, 1618, at a fee of 10 shillings per day.

Initially Pynnar was required to survey land and fortifications, and early in 1618 he viewed the fortifications in Ulster and Connaught. Together with Sir Thomas Rotheram and William Parsons he reported in that year on the acreage in Co. Longford and the territory of Ely O'Carroll.[10] From December 1, 1618 to March 28, 1619 he also surveyed the six escheated counties of Armagh, Tyrone, Donegal, Cavan, Fermanagh, and Londonderry.[11] In 1618 he was appointed as Muster Master of the undertakers or settlers in Munster and Connaught.[12] Three years later his name occurs among the burgesses of Londonderry incorporated by charter,[13] but there is no evidence that he had his residence there. In the same year he made a survey of repairs necessary to the castle of Limerick, the forts of Galway, Duncannon, Halebolin, Castle Park, and Banagher, also known as Fort Falkland. By 1623 Pynnar estimated that the repairs of the forts would cost £3,000. A year later he made another survey of necessary repairs, which he illustrated with drawings of the forts.[14] Finally, in 1625 Sir Thomas Rotheram (q.v.) and Pynnar received £1,000 for building three new citadels at Waterford, Cork (Elizabeth Fort), and Galway, which were all built to Pynnar's design. Shortly afterwards Rotheram and Pynnar went to England to present to the Council of War plans for the continuation of this work (in which Frederick Nanson, (q.v.) assisted). Already in 1623 Pynnar's arrears were considerable.[15] Four years later he was strictly forbidden to sell materials from the Waterford Citadel.[16] In 1630 his name lapsed from the Irish Establishment, which caused him to go to England to further his cause. Four years later arrears (for ten-and-a-half years!) due to Pynnar and Rotheram amounted to almost £2,000, half of which the government offered to pay in return for a renewal of the patent, but to Nicholas Pynnar only, at half of his initial salary. This he accepted. Subsequently he took part in the surveys of Connaught, and Co. Wicklow between 1637 and 1640,[17] and surveyed the condition of Castle Park Fort near Kinsale in 1638. After this date little is known about his engineering, which seems strange as, after the Rebellion of 1641, many strongholds in Ireland were improved. His role in the rebuilding of the Royal Works in Ireland remains obscure. Following the death of Samuel Molyneux (q.v.) he was the sole head of the Royal Works, but there is no evidence that he assisted the Lord Deputy Wentworth in the alterations at Dublin Castle. As a draughtsman Pynnar lacked skill in perspective. In 1643 he was appointed as Surveyor-General of the Lands, Plantations, and Mines, a position he combined with that of Director-General of the Fortifications.[18] He died presumably in 1644 when his office was granted provisionally to Capt. John Paine (q.v.). While a number of Pynnar's drawings survive, some contemporary copies are also extant in a different hand.[19] A manuscript reported to have been by Pynnar, dealing with plantation houses in 1630[20] probably never existed.

[1] F. Moryson, *An Itinerary*, Glasgow, 1907–8, II, 218. Much of the following account is based on W. P. Pakenham-Walsh, 'Captains Sir Thomas Rotheram Kt. and Nicholas Pinnar, Directors-General of Fortifications in Ireland, 1617–1644', *Royal Engineers' Journal*, 1909, *10*, 125–34; 1926, *40*, 664–8, and the *DNB*.

[2] The same individual as Avery Yorke who created some fortifications in Ireland in 1590, served in the Tyrone War, and probably left Ireland subsequently.

[3] *HMC, Salisbury*, XX, 120; PRO, SP 99/4 pt. 2, f. 201; SP 99/5 pt. 1, f. 8; *CSP Venice*, 1603–7, *ff*;

1607–10, *ff*; L. P. Smith (Ed.), *The Life and Letters of Sir Henry Wotton*, Oxford, 1907, reprinted 1966, I, 363, 407, 409, 419; *HMC, Downshire*, II, 79, 435–6. Wotton's designs may be associated with the south front of Hatfield House, which was erected in this period.

[4] *CSP Venice*, 1607–10, 273; *HMC, Salisbury*, XX, 120.

[5] G. Hill (Ed.), *An Historical Account of the Plantation of Ulster*, Belfast, 1877, 338.

[6] *Carew*, 1603–24, 91.

[7] BL, Add. Ms 4756, p. 129ᵛ.

[8] *HMC, Hastings*, IV, 165; *Analecta Hibernica*, 1938, *8*, 42.

[9] *CSPI*, 1625–32, 531, where it is mentioned that Pynnar had met Sir Dudley Carleton (later Lord Dorchester) as ambassador at Venice.

[10] BL, Add. Ms 4756.

[11] NLI, Harris Ms 15, f. 97 *ff*; TCD, Ms 864. First printed in W. Harris, *Hibernica*, 1747, later published in Hill, *op.cit.*, 445 *ff.* and in *Carew*, 1603–24, 392 *ff.*

[12] For full text of the patent see J. Lodge (Ed.) *Desiderate Curiosa Hibernica*, Dublin, 1772, II, 46–52.

[13] M. C. Griffith, *Irish Patent Rolls of James I*, Dublin, 1966, 538.

[14] BL, Add. Ms 24200; BL, Cotton Ms Aug. I, II, f. 36; part of the text was published in *JWAS*, 1899, *5*, 151–3.

[15] NLI, Ms 8013 (1).

[16] RIA, Stowe Ms A/1/1, f. 221.

[17] *Proceedings of the Royal Irish Academy*, 1861–4, VIII, 54; Longleat, Ms 95.

[18] *Royal Engineers' Journal*, 1926, *40*, 666.

[19] BL. Cotton Ms Aug. I, vol. II, 31, 33, 34, 35.

[20] *Irish Builder and Engineer*, 1946, *88*, 532. None of the other sources mentioned in this paper have come to light.

GALWAY, WEST CITADEL. In May 1625 Pynnar sent the plan for this fort (then in construction) to the Lord Deputy Falkland; its completion was delayed until 1638 (BL, Sloane Ms 3827, f. 52; *33rd Report Dep. Keeper PROI*, 1901, 56; *CSPI, passim*; M. D. O'Sullivan, 'The Fortifications of Galway', *Journal of the Galway Archaeological Society*, 1934, *16*, 34–7).

WATERFORD, CITADEL, also called ST PATRICK'S FORT. Pynnar and Sir Thomas Rotheram (q.v.) with the assistance of the engineer Nanson (also named Noon), selected its location in 1625 on the site of an unfinished fort (started by Capt. Edmund Yorke, in 1590), after which Pynnar drew the plan (TCD, Ms 1209, f. 66; BL, Add. Ms 24200; TCD, Ms 1209, f. 72 may be contemporary). Shortage of money delayed the completion, but in September 1626 it was 'fairly tenable' thanks to a contribution made by the Earl of Cork (*CSPI, passim*; B. Jennings (Ed.), *Wadding Papers*, Dublin, 1953, 102–3; *JRSAI*, 1934, *64*, 53; G. A. Hayes-McCoy, *Ulster and Other Irish Maps*, Dublin, 1964, 28 and pl. XVII).

CORK, CITADEL also called ELIZABETH FORT. The partially rebuilt remains of the older fort were renovated from 1625 onwards by Pynnar, with financial support of the Earl of Cork. This plan of the fort is now in the TCD (Ms 1209, f. 50). (*CSPI, passim*; M. Mulcahy, 'Elizabeth Fort, Co. Cork', *The Irish Sword*, 1959–60, *4*, 127–34).

KINSALE, CASTLE PARKE FORT. Pynnar reported in 1621, 1624, presumably also in 1625 and finally in 1638 on the necessary repairs (*CSPI, passim*; Hayes-McCoy, *op.cit.*, 33, and pl. 22).

DUBLIN CASTLE. In 1624 Pynnar surveyed the 'ruins', and together with the masons Thomas Graye and Thomas Pynnock recommended the pulling down of the north-west tower, repair of walls, and building of two platforms for artillery (C. L. Falkiner, *Illustrations of Irish History*, London, 1904, 38–40).

R

RANELAGH, VISCOUNT, see JONES, ROGER, VISCOUNT RANELAGH.

ROBB, JAMES. 'Chief mason', supposedly of the King's works in Ireland at the end of the 17th century, and said to have been an apprentice assistant to Inigo Jones. In the *Irish Builder and Engineer* of November 17, 1945,[1] it was suggested that Robb had built Portmore Castle, and had carried out renovations at Killyleagh Castle, Waringstown House and Church and at other places, but no evidence whatsoever has been found to confirm this. Contemporary documents fail to mention the office of Chief Mason in Ireland, and the Conway papers have no record of Robb's suggested work at Portmore.[2] A presumed book written by James Robb, entitled *An Account of the Many Fortifications and the Seats of the Nobility and Gentry of Ireland*, published in 1688,[3] has not been identified or located in main libraries in Ireland, England, the United States, or Canada. James Robb's name originally was only mentioned in the *Irish Builder*, but has now appeared in other secondary sources, including *Burke's Landed Gentry of Ireland* (1958), and *An Archaeological Survey of County Down*, (1966). The only Robb whose existence in Ireland in 1668 has been confirmed is the mason Thomas Robb who worked at Charleville Castle, Co. Cork.[4]

[1] pp. 599–600.
[2] *CSPI, passim.*
[3] Mentioned in *The Irish Builder*, 1946, *88*, 532.
[4] NLI, N 6268–6271, Pos 7074–7077.

ROBINSON, SIR WILLIAM (fl. c. 1643–1712), Engineer and Surveyor-General of the Fortifications and Buildings. He was descended from an 'ancient' family in Yorkshire, but the background of his parentage remains mysterious.[1] He was born in about 1643. Nothing is known about his youth, other than that he stipulated in 1686 that his executors should burn those of his writings 'that may in anyway reflect upon me as vain and idle essays of youth . . .'.[2] The papers in question do not seem to have survived. Nothing is known about Robinson's training, but considering the few opportunities in Ireland prior to 1670, he might well have been trained in England. By 1674 he had obtained such competence that the Lord Lieutenant, the Earl of Essex, recommended him to the English Master of the Ordnance as 'a very ingenious man & well skilled in some parts of ye Mathematicks . . .'.[3] Possibly Robinson had come to Ireland under the patronage of the Lord Lieutenant, the 1st Duke of Ormonde, for in 1670 a William Robinson acted as Clerk to the Council of Trade which had been set up by the Duke. During the Lord Lieutenantship of Lord Berkeley, Robinson, who had no prior military rank, became 'Engineer and Surveyor-General of all fortifications, buildings, etc., in Ireland' on January 11, 1671 succeeding Capt. John Paine (q.v.). Not long afterwards he obtained the position of Clerk of the Ordnance,[4] which probably made him one of the more influential individuals in that department. In the latter position he surveyed (together with Jonas Moore) the stores of the Ordnance in 1674. Robinson obtained a licence to go to England for six months in that year,[5] presumably on government business. Before 1675 he had executed building and repairs for the

Royal Works, at Chapelizod House and Phoenix House, and Dublin Castle. At the latter, the then Lord Lieutenant, the Earl of Essex, may also have employed his kinsman, the architect and Comptroller of the English Royal Works, Hugh May (see below). It is perhaps not accidental that in Ireland Robinson used round-headed windows with tracery very similar to those of Hugh May in England. Each architect may have been familiar with the other's work.

Robinson returned to England in 1677, where he married (see below). In the same year he was sent abroad in the King's service and, judging from some of his later works, may have gone to France to view the Hôtel des Invalides in Paris which had just been inaugurated. Nothing is known about the extent of his travels. He probably returned to Ireland prior to October 1677, when he prepared estimates for the repair of the fortifications there. This report led to the assignment of £19,840 in 1681 for the repair of the fortifications, the supply of stores, etc. These works were superintended by Robinson and Francis Cuffe (deputy of the Master of the Ordnance, the Earl of Longford). Both travelled considerable distances within Ireland for this purpose.[6]

Although the Duke of Ormonde thought Robinson to be 'very knowing' in engineering, it was not Robinson but engineers employed under him, with some from the English Ordnance, who planned or carried out major works. At Rincurran (later Charles Fort) plans for improvements were in the hands initially of Paulus Storff and later of James Archer (q.v.). Sir Bernard de Gomme planned a gigantic citadel near Dublin in 1673. Thomas Phillips made an extensive survey of Irish fortifications, and prepared plans for major improvements to most of these. Much later, in 1693, the engineer Rudolph Corneille (q.v.) and not Robinson, designed large outworks for Charles Fort.

Robinson visited England again in 1679, where he showed plans (probably those of the Royal Hospital, Kilmainham) to the King. Upon the recommendation of the Duke of Ormonde, Robinson's salary was increased at the same time from £150 to £300 per year. 1679 must have been one of the busiest years in his architectural career, for his largest projects, the fort at Rincurran and the Royal Hospital, coincided with smaller ones such as Lismore Cathedral, Co. Waterford, the erection of a Presence Chamber probably in Dublin Castle[7] and designs for a quay for Lord Conway probably at Glanavy, Co. Antrim.

Robinson played a pivotal role in the re-designing of Dublin Castle in 1684 after a disastrous fire. Although Robinson started its rebuilding, he did not see the completion of his plans which was achieved by his successor Thomas Burgh (q.v.). In 1684 Robinson surrendered his patent as Surveyor-General, and was granted a new patent in the same year which he from then onwards shared with William Molyneux (q.v.). The latter seems to have taken a less active role than Robinson in the Royal Works. After James II's accession, Robinson's position became less and less tenable, and on the arrival of the Duke of Tyrconnell he 'thought fit to retire to England'. There, warrants were issued to apprehend him, but presumably thanks to the protection of the former Lord Lieutenant, the 2nd Earl of Clarendon, he avoided imprisonment. There is some evidence that the Earl employed Robinson in 1688 for a bridge at his Cornbury estate in Oxfordshire.[8]

In 1689 Robinson obtained a number of posts dealing with the provisions of the Williamite Army (see below). He landed in the North of Ireland on March 4, 1690, and from then onwards was solely involved with this task. Contemporary sources fail to indicate that Robinson was considered for siege or defence building during the Williamite War. It may very well have been that his skills as engineer compared poorly with those of the many foreign and English engineers who came over to

Ireland in this period. However, he was allowed to make some improvements at Dublin Castle and Chapelizod House at this time. Robinson resumed his post as Surveyor-General after the war. This position was unsuccessfully challenged in 1695 by Brigadier-General William Wolseley, who as Master of the Ordnance was Robinson's immediate superior.[9] Robinson resigned as Surveyor-General on April 19, 1700 on the grounds of infirmity, for he suffered a great part of his life from gout. In that same year he was appointed Trustee and Overseer of the Barracks in Ireland. Very little is known about Robinson's involvement with the actual designing of the Irish barracks which had been built from the early 1690s onwards. Probably Robinson and Rudolph Corneille (q.v.) can be credited with the creation of the Barracks Department within the Department of the Irish Ordnance. Two maps of Ireland,[10] drawn by William Robinson in 1700, show the location of the barracks in the country. At Robinson's death £289 9s. 5½d. was still due to him for the barracks built by him.[11] None of these have been positively identified so far: the one at Ballyshannon is attributed to him, although its rich rustication may also represent the French background of Rudolph Corneille (q.v.).

As an architect, Robinson played a major role in the development of classicism in Ireland. In his designs for the Royal Hospital, and for the east window of St Mary's Church, Dublin, he introduced baroque features of a very high quality. Few of Robinson's pupils are known. He seems to have had a Deputy Surveyor-General, William Spike and after the Williamite War he was assisted by two engineers, Thomas Burgh (q.v.), and Rudolph Corneille (q.v.). One of Robinson's associates seems to have been the carpenter Abraham Hawksworth (q.v.). Robinson was known as a 'merchant and trader in foreign parts', and imported timber from Scandinavia.[12] Near his house at Islandbridge (see below) he had a timber-yard.[13] Very few of Robinson's drawings survive. His intellectual achievements are hard to assess. Probably he was not very involved in the progress of the New Learning which was sponsored in Dublin by his colleague William Molyneux (q.v.), and he is not known to have been a member of the Dublin Philosophical Society. By a will made in 1709 he planned to bequeath the remainder of his estate for the 'erecting and endowing some public works edifice for the advancement of learning and other good works ...', which Francis Gwyn took to mean the turning of Colleges into Halls in Oxford.

Robinson amassed such a considerable number of positions that his function of Surveyor-General must be seen as one among many posts. Before the Williamite War Robinson held the following appointments: Keeper of the Parliament House (1677); he became Auditor and Registrar (1684), Attorney and Agent (1686) and acting Governor from 1697–1707 of the Royal Hospital, Kilmainham; Receiver-General of the Revenue (from c. 1682); First Storekeeper of the Port of Dublin (1683). At the outbreak of the Williamite War he became Comptroller-General of the Provisions for the Forces and Commissionary-General of Pay and Provisions (both of which, in 1689, he shared respectively with Israel Fielding and Bartholomew Vanhomrigh). After the war he was rewarded with the positions of Commissioner for the stating of the Accounts of the Army in Ireland (1690), Commissioner for Forfeited Estates (1690), Commissioner for the Debt of the Army (1691), held jointly with William Molyneux (q.v.)), and a Freeman of the Company of the Royal Fishery of Ireland (1692). For his services as Deputy-Paymaster of the Forces in Ireland, he was given a yearly pension of £600 in 1692. He was a charter member of the Company of Joiners in Dublin (1700). In 1701 or 1702 he was created a knight, not a baronet as stated elsewhere.[14] In the latter year he was admitted to the Irish Privy Council, and became a Trustee for the development and preservation of Linen Manufacture in Ireland. He served as a Commissioner for the Vaudois in Ireland. He represented Trinity College in the Irish Parliament from 1703 to his death, having been M.P. for Knocktopher, Co. Kilkenny in 1692–3, and for the borough of Wicklow in 1695–9. Trinity College awarded him a LL.D. in 1703.

As Deputy Receiver-General he submitted to the Irish Parliament in 1703 a national debt of £103,368 8s. 4d., which was taken as a misrepresentation; a motion in the House to expel him was dismissed, but another declaring him 'unfit for any public Employment in this Kingdom' was accepted on October 16, 1703, and he was ordered to be imprisoned in Dublin Castle 'during the Pleasure' of the House. In prison Robinson wrote a vindication: 'The Case of Sir William Robinson . . .'. The Secretary of State, Edward Southwell, and the Vice-Treasurer, Lord Coningsby, deplored his dismissal, but when the Lord Lieutenant, the 2nd Duke of Ormonde, was told by the Earl of Godolphin 'to do as he thinks fit', he seems not to have re-employed Robinson, even when pressed by the Lord Chancellor Sir Richard Cox. On November 27, 1703 the House of Commons ordered the release of Robinson to allow him to go to England to prepare the account of the Treasury. On June 20, 1704 Robinson was in London, and early in 1705 he was short of cash, though, as he wrote, 'the devills reported that I carryed from Dublin 40 thousand pounds'. At the same time he tried via Joshua Dawson to regain his lost position. He returned to Ireland, but planned to leave for England again on August 24, 1706, probably because of an impending lawsuit arising out of allegations that Robinson and his cashier, Thomas Putland, had falsified the accounts for clothing the army in Ireland. This lawsuit claiming compensation for clothes supplied to the army dragged on well into the 1720s and, long after Robinson's death, the allegations were proven true, and an Act of the Privy Council was passed in 1724 to relieve the creditors.[15] After 1709 Robinson seems never to have returned to Ireland, although at some time he was reinstated as Deputy Vice-Treasurer, a post which he lost in 1710 in return for a pension of £600. In the same year he became trustee of the Duke of Ormonde's estate. Although he wrote many letters from London in subsequent years[16] they seem to have been devoted to political matters, including the sale of Viscountcies to Irishmen, and to have had no architectural interest. A map of Ireland dedicated to him by Charles Price, I. Senex and I. Maxwell, was published in London in 1710. Prior to 1712, the year of his death, he was visited frequently by Jonathan Swift.

Robinson had married in London on January 18, 1677, Margery Tooke, eldest daughter of John Tooke, of Hertfordshire, and Elizabeth, daughter of Sir Thomas Dacres. Robinson was then thirty years old, and she twenty-two. She probably did not inherit much from her father who had died in 1658, being 'much in debt and leaving all his estate entangled and encumbered'.[17] Robinson left no children. His wife was buried on July 7, 1708 in St Martin-in-the-Fields, London. Rumours in Ireland in 1709 that Robinson was newly married to Mrs Vanhomrigh, the widow of his former colleague, were countered by Robinson, who said that he was as indifferent to matrimony as 'Seignor Nichseny or any of the opera fine voices'. He died on October 27, 1712, and was buried at St Martin-in-the-Fields four days later.[18]

During his last years he was plagued by individuals who tried to succeed to his estate. During his lifetime Robinson made a total of five wills, datd respectively 1686, 1689, 1701, 1709 and 1712.[19] At his death he was reported to be worth more than £50,000.[20] He had appointed in his 1709 will three executors, Francis Annesley, Luke King, and Thomas Putland. Annesley alleged that King and

Robinson

Putland, during Robinson's last illness, took possession of his papers which were in his houses in St Martin-in-the-Fields and Chelsea (where he had rented Sir Jacob Bankes's house). King tore off the seal of the 1709 will to cancel it, and, by keeping Robinson in 'a hot suffocating Roome', forced on him a new will, in which only King and Putland were named as executors. They offered Annesley £600 if he would not give them any trouble. Annesley's allegations were countered by allegations made by King and Putland. Robinson's cousin, Sarah Bonsey, claimed the residuary estate, as she stated that she was the daughter and heir to Robert Wren and his wife Martha, aunt of William Robinson.[21] The Prerogative Court proved the 1712 will but the probate was revoked later. Putland and King appealed to the Court of Delegates who confirmed the cancellation. The Crown also claimed the estate due to the fact that Robinson had died 'intestate' and without leaving any relations.[22] Ultimately, Robinson's disputed will of 1711 was probated July 10, 1724, with King and Putland as executors.[23] In 1723 the Irish House of Commons passed a bill for relief from Robinson's Irish estate.[24] A copy of Robinson's will, proved in 1725 in Ireland, may very well relate to this.[25]

Robinson's estate in Ireland had been extensive. In his function as Ranger of Sherwood Park, Co. Carlow, he had leased the property, and later purchased it, from the Earl of Arran. The lease required him to build a house and offices,[26] but it is unclear whether he actually did so. Part of this estate descended via his cousin Sarah to the Palmer family, later of Kilbride, Co. Carlow, who also inherited part of Robinson's real estate in England (see below). Robinson had built a fairly large residence at Islandbridge, near Kilmainham (see below), from where he had a view of his largest work, the Royal Hospital. In 1702 he is mentioned as having a house at 'Ormond Key', Dublin. Having bought forfeited estates in 1703 in Co. Carlow and Co. Louth, he disposed of estates in these counties and in Meath and Offaly from 1708 to 1712. In England, he owned the manor of Walton-on-Thames in Surrey, which he had purchased in 1698 and where he lived for some time, and Fleetwood Hall, in Lancashire.[27] The house at Walton-on-Thames was later altered considerably, but it did not have obvious stylistic characteristics to link it with Robinson's architectural work. It passed via his cousin Sarah into the Palmer family. In London, Robinson lived in a house between Albemarle and Old Bond Streets, the site of which he had purchased in 1710. Whether the house still standing was his is uncertain for the present building resembles more a house a decade or so later.[28]

When living in London, Robinson kept an account in August, 1709 at the bank of Hoare & Co.,[29] which is relatively short and unrevealing. A likely portrait of Robinson was in the estate of Lord Coningsby at Hampton Court. Herefordshire, now in the Huntington Art Gallery, San Marino, California.[30] Robinson left £15 in his 1689 will to James Hayes for a portrait of himself to be hung at Hayes's house at Bedgebury in Kent.[31]

---

[1] Grant of augmentation to his coat of arms, dated 1694, 'Vert a Cheveron Ermine between three Staggs tripping Or on a Canton dester Argent, a Castle Gules. Crest a stag's head erased or' (BL, Stowe Ms 677, f. 77). I acknowledge the most helpful assistance I received from Mr B. F. J. Pardoe, who has uncovered a mass of new information on Robinson, which he very kindly made available to me. Mr Pardoe pointed out to me that the Lancashire family of Lever bore arms of a chevron between three stags trippant.

[2] Will of William Robinson, dated August 21, 1686 (PRO, Original Wills, Prob. 10/1512). Much of the following information on Robinson is based on a description of his life which appeared in *IGS*, Jan.–June, 1974, 3–9. Sources mentioned in that text are deleted here. Newly found sources are only mentioned in the present biographical account.

[3] BL, Stowe Ms 214, f. 259.

[4] BL, Add. Ms 4760, f. 224ᵛ, where this position is mentioned under the date May 21, 1675. When the

patent for the position was drawn is not known.

[5] BL, Add. Ms 4760, f. 143ᵛ; BL, Stowe Ms 214, f. 259.

[6] Bodl., Ms Rawlinson A 237, ff. 55–60; *HMC, Ormonde*, n.s. VII, 186. Their allowance for travel expenses was £250.

[7] The location of the Presence Chamber is unclear but in the light of present evidence was probably in Dublin Castle rather than in Kilkenny Castle as I suggested in *IGS*, Jan.–June 1974, *17*, 4.

[8] S. W. Singer (Ed.), *The Correspondence of Henry Hyde, Earl of Clarendon*, London, 1828, I, 186–7.

[9] Note that the source here is PRONI, De Ross Ms 18, f. 47 and not Ms 14 as stated in *IGS*, Jan.–June 1974, *17*, 5.

[10] BL, King's Maps, 52, ff. 15–16.

[11] PRO, Prob. 10/1512.

[12] NLI, Ms 3137, f. 37, 45 *ff.*

[13] Reg. Deeds, 9/436/4139.

[14] *IGS*, Jan.–June, 1974, *17*, 5.

[15] PRO, SP 63/382/847A.

[16] Note that this source is PROI, Ms 1A 52.142 and not 1A 452/142 as stated in *IGS*, Jan.–June, 1974, *17*, 6.

[17] For the following information regarding the Tooke family and their connection with Robinson, I am greatly indebted to Mr H. W. Gray, whose researches were drawn to my attention by Mr B. F. J. Pardoe.

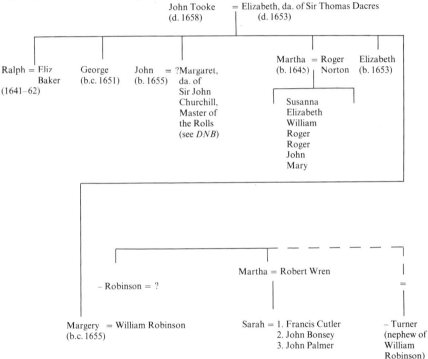

[18] PROI, 1A 52.142. The monument no longer exists; its inscription is recorded in J. Le Neve, *Monumenta Anglicana*, 1717–19, IV, 253.

[19] PRO, Prob. 10/1512; PRO. Del. 1/357/809, which were kindly drawn to my attention by Mr B. F. J. Pardoe, from which most of the following information is drawn. The latter I have only been able to examine in part. A schedule of payments made after Robinson's death by the executors is in PRO, C5/352/14.

[20] PRO, C 5/352/14.

[21] PRO, C 5/352/7, where Robert Wren is mentioned as of St Miles (?St Michael), Cornhill, London. Sarah Wren's mother Martha was Robinson's aunt as can be inferred from this source.

[22] PRO, C 5/352/14.

[23] PRO, PPC 255 Barnes.

Robinson

[24] *Commons Jour.*, 1712–21, 712, 815, 819; 1723–30, 98, 134, 217. See also *Analecta Hibernia*, 1966, *23*, 250–1, for two court cases possibly related to this, dated 1724 and 1729.

[25] *PROI*, Betham Ms I, 57, p. 149.

[26] A survey of Sherwood Park, dated 1682, is in NLI, Ms 11050. See also *HMC, Ormonde*, n.s. VIII, 5; VII, 345; BL, Add. Ms 28878, ff. 42, 137. PRO, F.E.C. 1/0.99. He sold part of the property later (PRO, Prob. 10/1512).

[27] *Victorian History of the Counties of England, A history of Surrey*, III, 470; PRO, C 5/352/14; BL, Add. Ms 28893, f. 340.

[28] Greater London Record Office, Middlesex Land Register, 1709/2/182, conveyance, dated May 13, 1710, from Thomas Highmore, the King's sergeant-painter to Robinson of a plot of ground, which coincides with the present 6–7 Albemarle Saint and 34–39 old Bond Street (mentioned in a letter by Mr A. F. Kelsall to Mr B. F. J. Pardoe, who passed the information on to me).

[29] Hoare & Co., London, Ledger 12, ff. 43, 66.

[30] Published in R. Loeber, 'A Portrait of the Irish Surveyor-General, Sir William Robinson, *IGS*, 1980, *23*, 44–46.

[31] PRO, Prob. 10/1512. As Mr B. F. J. Pardoe has pointed out to me, this may have been Sir James Hayes, Knight, cadet of the Hays, Earls of Errol.

FORTIFICATIONS & MILITARY STRUCTURES

CHARLEMONT FORT, CO. ARMAGH. This fort was repaired for Lord Conway in 1673; the contractor was a Mr Johnson. Robinson's works probably included the pedimented gate which still survives (Bodl., Add. Ms 30222, f. 114ᵛ; *The Irish Sword*, 1958, *3*, 186; J. J. Marshall, *History of Charlemont and Mountjoy Fort*, Dungannon, 1921).

KINSALE, CO. CORK, RINCURRAN FORT, later CHARLES FORT. From 1677 onwards Robinson prepared plans and estimates in co-operation with the Earl of Orrery and the engineer James Archer (q.v.). In 1678 he went to England to obtain the approval for an extension of the fort to secure it from the landward side which was probably unsuccessful. In 1681 the name of the fort was changed to Charles Fort. Plans were prepared in 1693 to finish the fort by Rudolph Corneille (q.v.).

KILMAINHAM, CO. DUBLIN, ROYAL HOSPITAL, 1680–7. The round-arched windows of the N. elevation are similar to the ones used by Hugh May at Windsor Castle. The rich carving in the Chapel is by the Frenchman Jean Tabary (q.v.), who is also probably responsible for the carving in the Hall. In his 1702 will Robinson assigned £100 for a monument to be erected at the Hospital, with an inscription that he had been its 'contriver and builder'.

KILMAINHAM, CO. DUBLIN, POWDER MAGAZINE, ROYAL HOSPITAL, 1684. The N.-E. flanker of the hospital was converted for that purpose.

KILMAINHAM, CO. DUBLIN, INFIRMARY, ROYAL HOSPITAL. Robinson designed aɴ addition in 1701 to this building which he had originally built in 1684 (PROI, RHK 1/1/1, p. 3). This simple building is visible on a drawing made by Francis Place in 1698 (*JRSAI*, 1932, *62*, 7th series, pt. 1, pl. 11).

ROSS CASTLE, CO. KERRY, 1696; repair of the older castle to make it into a garrison.

KILMAINHAM, CO. DUBLIN, STEEPLE, ROYAL HOSPITAL, 1701; although Robinson designed the steeple, Thomas Burgh (q.v.) built it.

ROYAL WORKS & GOVERNMENT BUILDINGS

DUBLIN CASTLE. After the 1684 fire, Robinson prepared plans for the rebuilding. Some surviving designs are probably by his hand (BL, Ms K 53, f. 19 a–i), but only one wing of the State Apartments was built by William Molyneux (q.v.). A proposed extension of the range in 1698 was probably designed by Robinson, but was postponed at the time. The S. range was completed by Thomas Burgh (q.v.) basically following Robinson's plans.

CHAPELIZOD HOUSE, CO. DUBLIN, 1684. Robinson made an addition to the house, probably a chapel and stables.

DUBLIN, THE FOUR COURTS. Rebuilt in 1695 probably on the remains of the early 17th-century structure erected by Samuel Molyneux (q.v.). Robinson's work became ruinous later, and is shown on engravings of the S. side of Christ Church Cathedral; its plan is in NLI, Art Dr. 29. An engraving of its interior was published in the *Gentleman's Magazine*, April 1788, Fig. 3. Robinson's work probably included the cupola or dome in the centre of the cruciform building.

DUBLIN, CHICHESTER HOUSE. Robinson obtained a lease in 1678 for 90 years of the outgrounds and gardens of this which served as the Houses of Parliament. He was not allowed to build there, but in return for the lease was to keep Chichester House in repair. Subsequent repairs were partly charged to government accounts, and its condition was described as very ruinous in 1700 (*Commons Jour.*, 1703–13, 660–2, 664).

CHURCHES

DUBLIN, ST BRIDE'S CHURCH, repaired and added to in 1679.

LISMORE, CO. WATERFORD, ST CARTHAGE'S CATHEDRAL. Rebuilt from 1679 onwards with the exception of the choir. Thomas Gent was carpenter. Robinson's work survives in the N. and S. transepts.

DUBLIN, ST MARY'S CHURCH. Robinson prepared a model for the E. window and probably designed the greater part of the church which was built from 1701 onwards. Contractor was John Whinrey.

DOMESTIC ARCHITECTURE

KILKENNY CASTLE. Rebuilt for the Duke of Ormonde. In 1681 Robinson competed with Grinling Gibbons for a design of an iron gate for the castle or its gardens. Further rebuilding was directed by Robinson in 1682, together with the setting up of a large fountain in the garden, and this was probably carved by the Dutchman William de Keyser (q.v.).

DUBLIN, PERCEVAL'S HOUSE. This old house, on Merchant Key, was totally rebuilt after Aug. 1681 for Sir John Perceval, by the 'undertaker Abraham Hawksworth', who was supervised by Robinson; the latter received 20 guineas.

CARTON, CO. KILDARE, 1692 and 1696, repairs to the house.

ISLANDBRIDGE, CO. DUBLIN, SIR WILLIAM ROBINSON'S HOUSE. Robinson lived here at least as early as 1691. It is certain that he erected an adjoining house which served as offices and servants' lodgings, and it seems likely that he was also responsible for the main house, a large building on a rectangular plan with a hip roof. By 1715 it was in the possession of Robert Curtis, who offered the property for sale in that year. The house is shown in a drawing by Francis Place in 1698 (*Whalley's Newsletter*, April 20, 1715; *The Post Boy*, June 20, 1715; Reg. Deeds, 9/436/4139, 11/118/4140; *JRSAI*, 1932, 7th series, *62*, pt. 1, pl. 11).

CHURCHTOWN, CO. CORK, BURTON HOUSE. Robinson was consulted by Sir John Perceval during the rebuilding of this country house. The supervision of the work was in the hands of Thomas Smith (q.v.). The classical portico, which has been ascribed to Robinson (*IGS*, Jan.–June, *1974*, 17, 9), as recent research indicates was built to an early 18th-century design sent from Italy, and Robinson had no hand in it. Rebuilt.

OTHER STRUCTURES

DUBLIN, ESSEX BRIDGE, 1677–8, sponsored by Humphrey Jervis. Robinson acted as technical adviser, and contractor for the bridge and the two bridge houses (*CARD*, VI, 597; TCD, Hutchison Ms of Rendham Court formerly lodged at TCD).

Robinson

DUBLIN, ORMONDE BRIDGE, 1682, sponsored by Humphrey Jervis. Robinson supervised the building. The stonework was executed by William Rothery (TCD, Hutchinson Ms of Rendham Court formerly lodged at TCD).

CLONMEL, CO. TIPPERARY, PRISON, 1677. Robinson made a model for the Duke of Ormonde. Evidence is lacking that he put up the Main Guard, built in 1674–5. Its provincial design does not suggest Robinson's hand.

GLANAVY, CO. ANTRIM. In 1679 Robinson was to draw a plan for the quay for his patron Viscount Conway; the contractor was to be a Mr Johnson, who also executed Robinson's work at Charlemont Fort (see above) (*CSPI*, 1669–70, 229; PRO, SP 63/339, f. 29).

DUBLIN, MARSH'S LIBRARY. Built for Archbishop Narcissus Marsh in 1703–4. Robinson's work then comprised only a rectangular building with two small projections. The present L-shaped addition, marked on a map in the library was erected after 1707 (Marsh's Library, Ms Z.2.2.3c).

ATTRIBUTIONS

THOMASTOWN HOUSE, CO. TIPPERARY. Built in 1670 by George Mathew. He might have employed Robinson in 1682 (NLI, Ms 2418, f. 479) for the recessed, rusticated portico. Rebuilt in 1820, now ruined.

DUBLIN, WEST FRONT OF TRINITY COLLEGE. Probably originally called Sir Hierome Alexander's Buildings. Richard Mills, in 1672, contracted to build it to the plans of Thomas Lucas. After 1684 the French-looking centre, and the S. wing were added after a design probably by Robinson. Altered in 1755. It seems likely that Robinson carried out other works (see also below) at the College, and is said to have presented it with an 'ornament' at a cost of £189 12s. 10½d. (PRO, Prob. 10/1512).

DUBLIN, SOUTH RANGE OF TRINITY COLLEGE. This range, which adjoined the W. front, was built in 1698. A plan of the building (TCD, Ms MUN/MC/81) is in the same handwriting as that of what is probably Robinson's design for an addition to Dublin Castle (q.v. of the same year. Altered.

BALLYSHANNON, CO. DONEGAL, BARRACKS. According to the date-stone built in 1700; now a public house.

KILKENNY CASTLE, GATE HOUSE. Built probably after 1698 for the 2nd Duke of Ormonde.

ATHLONE CASTLE, CO. WESTMEATH. The main tower as shown on a drawing of 1685 (NLI, Ms 3137, f. 33) is very similar to the S.W. tower of Kilkenny Castle at that time. Dem.

PLATTEN HALL, CO. MEATH. The large square country house originally with three storeys, a very spacious staircase, and a central courtyard, was built after 1691 for the Graham family (see M. Craig, *Classic Irish Houses* . . ., London, 1976, 29–30; NLI, Ms 6486; J. D'Alton, *History of Drogheda*, Dublin, 1844, II, 362, 462–4; *The Irish Georgian Society, Records of Eighteenth-Century Domestic Architecture in Ireland*, London, 1909–13, V, 6, 99). Dem.

ATTRIBUTIONS: CHURCHES

DUBLIN, ST CATHERINE'S CHURCH. In 1678 'Mr Robinson ye Surveyor' was paid four shillings by the churchwardens for the hire of a coach. He might have made designs for the church, which was altered in 1679–80 by the mason Thomas Browne (PROI, M 5122, pp. 167, 179–80). Replaced in 1769.

DUBLIN, ST MICHAN'S. Rebuilt between 1683 and 1686; as with all ecclesiastical work by Robinson it carries the typical round-arched windows with a concave moulding. Altered 1828.

ARMAGH, ST PATRICK'S CATHEDRAL. Its E. end was rebuilt before 1675 for Archbishop Margetson. Reconstructed in the 19th century.

KILDARE, ST BRIGID'S CATHEDRAL. Its choir was erected in 1686 for William Moreton, Bishop of Kildare, who was appointed executor in William Robinson's 1686 will. Rebuilt 1894–5.

DUBLIN, CHRIST CHURCH CATHEDRAL. The St Mary Chapel on the N.E. side of the Cathedral was rebuilt in 1693. Rebuilt 1831 (G. E. Street & E. Seymour, *The Cathedral of the Holy Trinity* . . ., London, 1882, 42).

DUBLIN, ST PATRICK'S CATHEDRAL. An external doorway, formerly in the S. transept resembled Robinson's work.

ROOKEWOOD, THOMAS (fl. 1602), Deputy Surveyor of the Works about Lough Foyle, Co. Derry. He served under Sir Henry Docwra, and between April 1, 1601 and March 31, 1602 was paid over £227 as a reimbursement for money spent on 'works and fortifications' at and about Lough Foyle.[1] He was probably an assistant to Samuel Molyneux (q.v.), Clerk of the Works.

[1] PRO, A.O. 1/288/1082.

ROPER, Sir THOMAS, 1st Viscount Baltinglass, (?–1637), soldier, architect, and entrepreneur. He is one of the few of the early 17th-century British settlers whose life has been described in Thomas Fuller's *The History of the Worthies of England* (1662).[1] He was born in London, but the year is not known. His father Thomas Roper, who was a servant to Queen Elizabeth, was a descendant of the house of Heanour in Derbyshire.[2] Early in life he probably began a military career. He became page to Sir John Norris, and accompanied him to the Low Countries either in 1577 or in 1585 to join the English army there against the Spaniards. He behaved himself 'valiantly and honourably' during the expedition to Portugal in 1589. Three years later he left for France in the army under Sir John Norris, and distinguished himself at Brest. He may have followed Sir John to Ireland in 1594 on his return there to his post of Lord President of Munster, and died in that year. Thomas Roper was in active military service during the six-years' war in Ireland. He possibly saved Sir Henry Harrington from an ambush[3] in 1599, and may have married Sir Henry's daughter Ann around this time. He fought as a captain under Sir Conyers Clifford at the Curlews[4] and later in 1599 joined the Earl of Essex in the campaign in Ulster where he was known for his 'gallant conduct'.[5] His company was stationed first at Kells, then at Armagh. Afterwards he fought at the siege of Kinsale in 1602. In 1603 at the end of the war he was knighted. Two years later, probably as a reward for his service, he was granted the constableship of Castlemagne usually called Castlemaine in Co. Kerry. He repaired the castle between 1611 and 1613 for which he was paid over £265.[6] Sometime before 1610 he had been made governor of this county, where he built up an estate. He had received grants of land there and in the counties of Cork and Tipperary in 1611 and 1612.[7] Perhaps the largest estate which he managed was the seignory of Mount Eagle Loyal and Castle Island in Co. Kerry, covering 13,276 acres. He had leased the lands some time before 1605 from Sir Edward Herbert (later 1st Lord Herbert of Cherbury). The latter ultimately bcame very dissatisfied with Roper's exploitation of the estate. He was reproached for having spoiled the woods, and for neglecting the main residence at Castle Island.[8] Already in 1611 Roper had obtained permission to export 120,000 pipestaves from the south of Munster.[9] An inspection in 1622 revealed that the castle was very ruinous, and that only part of the conditions for the Munster plantation were adhered to.[10]

Sir Thomas was lauded because of his industry in establishing fishing communities in the west of Ireland. He induced some hundreds of families to settle at Crookhaven in Co. Cork,[11] possibly in cooperation with Sir Thomas Crooke of Baltimore in the same county. He built a fort at this location before 1622 to protect its harbour. Although it is not known whether he was responsible for its design, he probably had knowledge of the engineering of defence works. Not far from Crookhaven, Sir Thomas may have founded another fishing village at Bantry in the same county.[12]

In 1620 he expanded his commercial interests by the setting up of a clothing industry near Dublin, where 'in carding, spinning, weaving, working, dressing and dyeing cloth, many poor people are daily set on work ...'.[13] The exact location of this industry is not known; it may have been not far from his residence, Roper's Rest, which is first noted in 1616.[14] Drawings of this house do not seem to have survived. Considering his experience as an architect (see below) he may have designed it, but evidence to that effect has not been found. A carpenter by the name of John Smyth was employed by him sometime before 1637 for the building of the 'new' house adjoining Roper's Rest.[15]

Early in 1631 Roper, who by then had been created Baron of Bantry and Viscount Baltinglass, received his first known commission as an architect. His patron the 1st Earl of Cork, spent £300 for the building of some additional lodging and a gallery 'which the Lo. of Baltinglass was Architect of...' at a house which the Earl had purchased from Lord Caulfeild in Dame Street, Dublin.[16] The work also included three tenements under the gallery and the building of a stable. The buildings were executed in brick; the workmen were the carpenters William Whalley and Edmund Tingham (q.v.).[17] The Earl of Cork found that 'by the default of the workmen & overseers [it had become] a most weake, and deceiptful buylding.' He did not re-employ Roper for his rebuilding of Maynooth Castle, Co. Kildare, but preferred instead Edmund Tingham. Unfortunately, nothing is known about the nature of Roper's skills as an architectural designer. As he had seen contemporary architecture in the Low Countries and France, he might have followed some continental examples. He became a member of the Irish Privy Council, which brought him in contact with the wealthiest Irish landowners, who could have commissioned designs from him. He could have played a role in the Irish Royal Works, but this remains equally obscure.

Roper may have chosen architecture as a sideline to supplement his income. The papers of the Earl of Cork show that Roper borrowed money regularly.[18] He is known to have wanted to sell his lease in Co. Kerry in 1622.[19] He was granted a pension for giving up the grant to license alehouses in Ireland.[20] Little is known about the end of his life. In 1634 he erected a sculptured tomb for his family in St John's Church in Dublin. The monument no longer exists, but is known from a 17th-century drawing,[21] which shows an elaborate but rather conventional Jacobean design. He died on February 18, 1637 and was buried in that church. His wife died three years later. Their son Thomas inherited the estate and the title of Viscount Baltinglass. The Peerage became extinct in 1672.

[1] Nuttall, P. A. (Ed.), *Thomas Fuller, The History of the Worthies of England*, London, 1840, II, 368–70. Thomas Fuller had married Mary a daughter of the 1st or 2nd Viscount Baltinglass.
[2] *Ibid.*, 368; V. Gibbs (Ed.), *The Complete Peerage*, London, 1910, I, 397, doubted the relationship. Nuttall's Fuller is quoted from here onwards unless stated otherwise.
[3] *CSPD*, 1598–1601, 209; He was the son of Sir James Harrington, and brother of John, first Lord

Harrington. Sir Henry Harrington had an extensive estate in Co. Wicklow, where he had his residence at Baltinglass. One of Roper's later titles derived from this location. The estate was granted to Roper Nov. 10 1626.

4 *CSPI*, 1599–1600, 114.

5 *CSPI*, 1600, 527, 529.

6 Griffith, M. C., *Irish Patent Rolls of James I*, Dublin, 1966, 86. He was also granted a pension of 10s. a day for the rest of his life on December 10, 1610 (*Ibid.*, 320); PRO, A.O.1/290/1090.

7 *Ibid.*, 208, 226–7.

8 W. J. Smith (Ed.), *Herbert Correspondence*, Cardiff, 1963, *passim*. Sir Thomas was already tenant there in 1605 (*CSPI*, 1663–5, 593).

9 *CSPI*, 1611–14, 67.

10 BL, Add. Ms 4756, f. 93ᵛ; see also *CSPI*, 1625–32, 132. Roper denied some of the charges (Smith, *op.cit.*, 76).

11 *CSPI*, 1615–25, 361.

12 *Ibid.*, 534–5, 685: *Grosart*, series 2, II, 261.

13 PRO, SP 63/278, f. 271, Calendar of events in Ireland, under 1620, 'Sir Thomas Roper sets up clothing manufacture near Dublin'. This industry, which produced coloured cloth, is mentioned as being not successful in 1624 (*Grosart*, series 2, III, 144). Roper also erected a salt-house, probably in one of his fishing towns in Co. Cork, which yielded a better profit (*CSPI*, 1647–60, 269–70).

14 Griffith, *op.cit.*, 517; the house was situated south of the city outside its walls. Its location is shown on the Dublin map of the Down Survey.

15 Marsh's Library, Dublin, Ms Z. 3.2.6., f. 110.

16 Huntington Library, San Marino, California, HA 13,999, 12 Feb. 1637 [–8] the Earl of Cork to [John Bramhall] Bishop of Derry.

17 *Grosart*, series 1, III, 75, 85, 176; IV, 1. Roper apparently made first a contract with a carpenter called Andrews and then with William Whalley. The latter was sued by the Earl of Cork for payment and imprisoned. His petition for release is mentioned in BL, Harl. Ms 430, f. 91.

18 *Grosart*, series 1, I, II, III, IV, *ff*.

19 W. J. Smith (Ed.), *Calendar of Salusbury Correspondence, 1553–c. 1700*, Cardiff, 1954, 65.

20 BL, Add. Ms 4756, f. 60ᵛ; *CSPI*, 1625–32, 241, 622.

21 Reproduced in R. Loeber, 'Sculptured memorials to the dead in early 17th-century Ireland: a survey from *Monumenta Eblanae* and other sources' (submitted to the Proceedings of the Royal Irish Academy.)

ROTHERAM, Sir THOMAS (fl. 1596–1648), Director-General of the Fortifications in Ireland. He was a native of Bedfordshire in England and second son of George Rotheram, who owned the manor of Luton in that county. As a soldier Thomas Rotheram, with his relative John Rotheram (later Sir John), went to Ireland.[1] Thomas is first noted in 1596 when he was waiting to be embarked.[2] In 1600 he served in the army in Ireland under Sir Conyers Clifford at the Curlews. In that year he accompanied the Lord Deputy Mountjoy on the campaign in the North, was wounded, and was praised by Mountjoy. He served at the siege of Kinsale in 1601, where he defended the west fort, in which he won 'great reputation'.[3] As Rotheram's name is lacking from lists of engineers of the period, it seems unlikely that he was involved in building fortifications during the time. In 1603 he became governor of St Augustine Fort, near Galway (then just finished by Samuel Molyneux, (q.v.)), a position which he held until 1636.[4] He was knighted by Lord Mountjoy in 1605,[5] and may have continued living at his post near Galway. In 1612 he was elected Mayor of that City.[6] Three years later he was a member of a commission for a general visitation of Ireland. In that year he also received a commission for the civil government of Connaught which he shared with Sir John King. In 1616 he became a member of a commission to inquire what lands were chargeable *with composition* (i.e. certain fines) in the counties of Sligo and Mayo. His first known involvement with fortifications occurred in 1617 when he surveyed the castle and forts of Monaghan, Mountjoy, and Charlemont, in the North of Ireland.[7] Before 1618 he, with William Parsons, and Nicholas Pynnar (q.v.) measured the number of acres in Co. Longford and the territory of Ely O'Carroll. Rotheram and Parsons, now Sir William, surveyed Co. Leitrim in 1620 for the intended plantation.[8] On the death of Sir Josias Bodley (q.v.) Rotheram received a joint patent with Nicholas Pynnar as Director-General of the Fortifications in Ireland dated February 27, 1618. This position, however, seems to have been a nominal one, for Rotheram's involvement with the building of fortifications was minimal. Sir Thomas may have been out of Ireland for some years. In 1625 Rotheram and Pynnar received more than £5,200 for the building of citadels at Cork, Waterford, and Galway, but Rotheram supervised only the building of the new citadel on the west side of Galway City, plans of which had been drawn up by Pynnar.[9] In addition he built 'some houses' possibly as lodgings for soldiers, and repaired St Augustine Fort. Here again, Rotheram's skill in fortifications remains obscure: he did not select the site, nor was he able to finish the new fort, in which he invested £200 of his own money.[10] In 1627 the Lord President of Munster, the Earl of Clanricarde appointed Rotheram Deputy Lieutenant-Governor of Galway City and County both for the civil and military government.[11] From 1630 onwards Rotheram seems to have lived in Dublin, where he had a residence in Bride Street.[12] In Wentworth's parliament in 1634 he sat for Tuam. In that year he gave up the patent for the Director-Generalship of the Fortifications, being compensated for only half of his arrears. For unknown reasons the Earl of Clanricarde failed to reappoint Rotheram in 1636 as Deputy-Lieutenant for Co. Galway. When Rotheram became a Privy Councillor is unclear, but from 1641 to at least 1644 he attended the Council meetings very regularly, and signed most of its dispatches. During the preparation of the defence of Dublin, Rotheram's company was situated strategically near his own residence. Little is known about his last years. The date of his prerogative will is 1648, but this document seems to have been lost.[13] He married Margaret, daughter of Sir John Southwell who died December 23, 1640.[14] A contemporary author mentions Sir Thomas' son John Rotheram, who was left 'a very Great fortune' by his father.[15] Sir Thomas had been granted extensive estates, which included the manor of Armagh in Co. Fermanagh, land in the counties of Cavan, Longford, and Leitrim, and 1,000 acres in Co. Offaly, where he presumably built a castle at Raghra,[16] now called Shannonbridge.

[1] Details based on W. P. Pakenham-Walsh, 'Captains Sir Thomas Rotherman Kt and Nicholas Pynnar, Directors-General of Fortifications in Ireland', *Royal Engineers' Journal*, 1909, *10*, 125–34. Information regarding his family is in BL, Add. Ms 4820, p. 271; J. Nichols, *Progresses of James I*, London, 1828, II, 203; N. E. McClure (Ed.), *The Letters of John Chamberlain*, Philadelphia, 1939, I, 113.

[2] *HMC, Salisbury*, VI, 559.

[3] F. Moryson, *An Itinerary*, Glasgow, 1907–8, II, 346, 353; III, 55, 346, 353.

[4] J. Hardiman, *The History of the Town of and County of Galway*, Galway, 1926, 103; *HMC, 10th Rep. App. V*, p. 464*ff.*

[5] *Carew*, 1603–24, 384. Note that Nichols, *op.cit.*, II, 203, states that Rotheram was knighted by James I at Grafton in early August 1608.

[6] Hardiman, *op.cit.*, 103.

[7] *CSPI*, 1615–25, 141, 195.

[8] BL, Add. Ms 4756.

[9] PRO, A.O. 1/291/1093; *CSPI*, 1615–25, 569.

[10] *CSPI*, 1625–32, 102.

[11] Hardiman, *op.cit.*, 108 *n.* 29.

[12] *Grosart*, series 1, III, 14, 93, 196; *HMC, 14th Rep. App. VII*, 153; C. L. Falkiner, *Illustrations of Irish History*, London, 1904, 381. However, as late as 1643 he is mentioned as an alderman in Galway City (*HMC, 10th Rep. App. V*, 493).

[13] Sir Arthur Vicars (Ed.), *Index to the Prerogative Wills of Ireland*, Dublin, 1897, 407.

[14] BL, Add. Ms 4820, p. 271.

[15] *KASJ*, 1906–8, 5, 432.

[16] BL, Add. Ms 4756; G. Hill (Ed.), *An Historical Account of the Plantation of Ulster*, Belfast, 1877, 484; M. C. Griffith, *Irish Patent Rolls of James I*, Dublin, 1966, 313, 360, 551; C. MacNeill (Ed.), *The Tanner Letters*, Dublin, 1943, 63. Ruins on the site of Raghra probably date from the late 17th century.

S

SEAWELL, JOHN (fl. 1671), mason who probably, together with James Chatterton (q.v.), worked on the rebuilding in 1671 of Castle Island, Co. Kerry, the residence of Lord Herbert of Cherbury. In the same year Seawell and Chatterton were said to have erected the steeple of St Fin Barre Cathedral, Cork,[1] which was in fact built by William Armstead (q.v.) and Thomas Smith (q.v.).

[1] W. J. Smith (Ed.), *Herbert Correspondence*, Cardiff & Dublin, 1968, 198–9.

SMITH, THOMAS (fl. 1639), builder and 'contriver', who worked in County Cork. He may be identified with the Thomas Smith of Shaftesbury in Dorset who travelled to the Earl of Cork's estate in Munster in April 1639.[1] Considering that Shaftesbury is not far from the Earl of Cork's Stalbridge Park, which was rebuilt after the design of Isaac De Caux[2] at this time, it is not impossible that Smith had been involved in this building project. Smith's earliest known proposal was the rebuilding for the Earl of Cork of Earl Barry's Castle at Lismore in Co. Waterford, after which he received a good number of other commissions over the following four decades. His background and training is unknown. The only surviving domestic building which is probably his, the Southwell Gift Houses at Kinsale, shows a pleasant but provincial style of architecture, with a porch with classical pilasters and pediment. At Burton in Co. Cork he planned out-buildings with classical symmetry. Together with William Armstead (q.v.), his partner for many years, Smith contracted a number of times for the masonry of Charles Fort. The size of this project suggests that Smith must have had considerable organizing talent, and presumably sufficient funds to work for a government which was usually slow in issuing warrants for payment. He had his residence at Charleville, now Rathluirc in Co. Cork;[3] otherwise very little has come to light about his private life. Sir John Perceval valued his judgement as a builder, and insisted that the Surveyor-General William Robinson (q.v.), who was Smith's superior at Charles Fort, should allow Smith to be consulted on domestic projects.[4] Smith seems to have been serviceable to patrons in three ways. Firstly, as a builder; secondly, as a designer of the defensive courts around a country house, as at Burton, since he was preferred above William Kenn (q.v.); and thirdly as a surveyor.[5] He is last noticed in 1686 when he was to receive a gratuity of £10 left to him by his late patron Sir John Perceval.[6] The date of his death is not known.

[1] *Grosart*, series 1, V, 81.
[2] *Colvin*, 256. Note, however, that Smith's name does not seem to occur in the printed contemporary documents relating to Stalbridge Park (see *Grosart, passim*).
[3] *HMC, Egmont*, III, 369; *CSPI*, 1666–9, 726.
[4] BL, Add. Ms 46 958B, ff. 68, 71.
[5] *Analecta Hibernica*, 1944, *13*, 26.
[6] BL, Add. Ms 47038, f. 61.

WORKS

LISMORE, CO. WATERFORD, EARL BARRY'S CASTLE. In an undated document from *c.* 1639, Thomas Smith made an estimate for rebuilding for the 1st Earl of Cork, 'Earl Barry's Castle', at a total cost of £800 3*s*. It is unclear whether he actually rebuilt the castle (Chatsworth, Lismore Ms 24, f. 80).

Smith

CARNIGGNYGILAGH or GARRIGINGELLAGH CASTLE, CO. WATERFORD. Among the Orrery Papers is an account of the expenditure for the repair of this castle, signed by Thomas Smith or Smithes in 1652 (NLI, Ms 13,192).

RATHLUIRC, formerly CHARLEVILLE, CO. CORK, SCHOOLHOUSE, built by Smith and William Armstead (q.v.) for the 1st Earl of Orrery (q.v.) in 1667 (NLI, Ms 13192).

BURTON HOUSE, CO. CORK. While the house was built by Capt. William Kenn (q.v.) for Sir Robert Southwell, guardian of Sir Philip Perceval, 2nd bart., Thomas Smith laid out the surrounding defense works and outbuildings in 1671 (*IGS*, Jan.–June 1973, *16*. opp. p. 1, 26; BL, Add. Mss 46948, f. 166; 46949, f. 67). He is not to be identified with the Mr [Samuel] Smith who surveyed the house in 1672 after Kenn's death (BL, Add. Mss 46948, ff. 124, 125; 46949, f. 67). From 1681 onwards Thomas Smith rebuilt Burton House for Sir John Perceval, 3rd bart. He probably had assistance from the Surveyor-General William Robinson (q.v.), who was his superior at the nearby Rincurran Fort (see below). Sir John may also have sought the advice of the scientist-architect Dr Robert Hooke for the rebuilding of this house (BL. Add. Mss 46958, ff. 68, 160, 162^v; Ms 46958B, f. 56, 68, 71, 88, 165, 196; Ms 46959A, f. 15, 119). It is unclear whether Thomas or Samuel Smith surveyed the park and demesne in 1686 (BL, Add. Ms 46966, f. 103^v). As late as that year Thomas Smith assisted Sir John in the accounts of the workmen. Shortly afterwards Sir John died, having arranged for a gratuity of £10 to be paid to Thomas Smith, presumably for his useful services (BL, Add. Ms 47038, f. 61). Dem.

KINSALE, CO. CORK, RINCURRAN, later CHARLES FORT. Thomas Smith and William Armstead (q.v.) possibly worked at the nearby Castle Park Fort in 1666. Two years later they presented their first proposal to finish Rincurran Fort, which had been renovated by the 1st Earl of Orrery (q.v.) in 1667 (*HMC, 6th Rep.* 778). Their proposal was not approved. However, in 1672 they executed all the stone work, in the alterations undertaken by Capt. Paulus Storff (NLI, Mss 2355, f. 67–8; N6268–6271, Pos 7074–7077. Later expansion of the fort, after 1678, was also carried out by them. They followed the designs of William Robinson (q.v.), who was assisted by Capt. James Archer (q.v.) and the 1st Earl of Orrery (q.v.) (BL, Add. Ms 28085, f. 196^v). As late as Oct. 1681 Smith was employed at this site (BL, Add. Ms 46958B, f. 88).

CORK ST FINBARRE'S CATHEDRAL. Thomas Smith and William Armstead were given £20 by the Chapter of the Cathedral in 1677 in consideration for their 'laudable care' in building the tower of the Cathedral (R. Caulfield, *Annals of St Fin Barre's Cathedral*, Cork, 1871, 40). Replaced.

KINSALE, CO. CORK, SOUTHWELL GIFT HOUSES, built following 1680 for Sir Robert Southwell, uncle to Sir John Perceval, 3rd Bt. (see above). Sir Robert gave Smith five guineas in Sept. 1631 'for what he has done about ye Alms House' (BL, Add. Ms 46958A, f. 71). This may have been a payment for his design or advice (see also *IGS*, Jan.–March, 1969, 23; *Lodge*, VI, 10 *n.*).

CHURCHTOWN, CO. CORK, INN and STABLES. In 1682 Smith made an estimate of £150 for building an inn and stables for Sir John Perceval, 3rd Bt. (BL, Add., Ms 48958B, f. 235^v). It is unclear whether these were built.

ATTRIBUTION

RATHLUIRC, CO. CORK, CHARLEVILLE CASTLE, built after the design of the 1st Earl of Orrery (q.v.). It seems likely that Smith and William Armstead (q.v.) executed the greater part of this large castle, for which they received more than £4,000 (see under William Armstead). After the death of the Earl of Orrery, Smith in 1683 advised Capt. Henry Boyle about the dormer windows which were 'hurting' the roof (E. MacLysaght, *Calendar of Orrery Papers*, Dublin, 1941, 269).

SMYTH, FRANCIS (fl. 1637), carpenter, who acted in 1637 as 'contractor and cheef worckman' for the building of Richard Boyle, Earl of Cork's almshouses and school at Bandon[1] (Co. Cork). The masonry at these was done by John Webbe.

[1] *Grosart*, series 1, IV, 224; Chatsworth, Lismore Ms 18, f. 153.

SPIKE, WILLIAM (fl. 1691), Deputy Surveyor-General, who worked under William Robinson (q.v.). Spike has been mentioned erroneously as having received payment in 1692 for the repair of Carton House, Co. Kildare.[1] The Surveyor-General William Robinson was paid directly for this work, and, in addition on January 25, 1692, received £72 19s. 4d. which he disbursed to William Spike for the repair of Dublin Castle.[2] Spike was probably acting already as Deputy Surveyor-General of Their Majesties Buildings for he is mentioned as such in his petitions to the Royal Hospital Kilmainham, in 1693 and 1696 for the payment of £74 18s. 2d., which was due to several workmen who had been employed at the Hospital until May 1693.[3] Whether Spike was functioning as a designer or only an overseer is not clear. In 1707 a 'Mr Spike' was paid £21 for the pointing of the new lodgings (? at St Sepulchre's Palace, Dublin) for Archbishop William King,[4] but this could have been the plasterer George Spike,[5] possibly a relative.

[1] *KASJ*, 1903–5, *4*, 11.
[2] PROI, Wyche docs., 2nd ser. f. 63.
[3] PROI, RHK 1/1/1, ff. 61ᵛ, 81.
[4] TCD, Ms 751 (2).
[5] C. P. Curran, *Dublin Decorative Plasterwork*, London, 1967, 105.

STUTEVILLE, THOMAS (fl. 1638–1642), master gunner who executed some defence works to Dublin Castle. He is first noted in 1638 when he was sent to Ireland from Holland by Sir William Boswell, the English Ambassador at The Hague, who recommended him as a qualified man, of 'a very good and ancient Family of Suffolk ...'. The Lord Deputy, the Earl of Wentworth, found him 'a very extraordinary able Man', who was well suited for the office of Master Gunner of Ireland,[1] for which he soon obtained a pension of 20d. per day,[2] and continued in the office subsequently. At the outbreak of the Rebellion Stutevile carried the rank of Captain and headed a company of foot, stationed in Dublin. There he was paid £100 on December 16, 1641 towards the making of outworks for the defence of Dublin Castle.[3] Afterwards he was employed for the relief of Drogheda, during which he defended by means of granadoes a pinnace coming to the town.[4] He probably died in 1642, when his prerogative will was registered.[5]

[1] W. Knowler (Ed.), *Letters and Dispatches of the Earl of Strafford*, London, 1739, II, 163, 199.
[2] Longleat, Ms 95.
[3] *CSPI*, 1633–47, 764–5, 770.
[4] *Ibid.*, 780; Sir Richard Cox, *Hibernia Anglicana*, 1689–90, II, 91.
[5] Sir Arthur Vicars (Ed.), *Index to the Prerogative Wills of Ireland, 1536–1810*, Dublin, 1897, 444.

SYMNER, MILES (fl. 1626–1686), mathematician, astronomer, and military engineer. He entered Trinity College, Dublin, as a scholar in 1626,[1] and started a religious career which brought him the diocese of Elphin in 1633. Little is known about this period of his life, nor about why he later entered military service. By 1648 he had become Chief Engineer in Ireland, presumably filling the post left vacant by the Royalist engineer Capt. John Paine (q.v.). Symner served together with the engineer William Webb in the Train of Artillery headed by Roger Boyle (q.v.), then Lord Broghill. In 1651 Symner was ordered to carry out repairs at Athlone Castle, which was to serve as the headquarters of the Lord Deputy, but lack of money delayed their completion well beyond July 1652.[2] Two years later he and others were detailed to select garrison buildings and castles for demolition in Connaught and Clare, and also those still to be maintained along the Shannon.[3] Subsequently a good number of castles in Connaught were levelled for which Irish masons were contracted; Symner, who carried by then the rank of Major, received funds to purchase tools for the demolition.[4] His advice on the maintenance of castles and forts along the Shannon has not been preserved, though the advice of Capt. William Webb led to the subsequent erection and repair of works undertaken by Daniel Thomas (q.v.). Considering the great number of fortifications which were built or repaired in Ireland from 1651 to 1656, it seems very likely that Symner got involved with engineering works elsewhere, but evidence confirming this has not yet come to light.

By 1652 he already had a reputation as a mathematician, for in that year he was appointed professor of mathematics at Trinity College, Dublin. As has been pointed out by T. C. Barnard,[5] Symner occupied a pivotal role in the Irish component of the Samuel Hartlib circle which had been responsible for founding the Royal Society in England. His acquaintances include the Boate brothers, William Petty, Benjamin Worsley, and Robert Boyle, all of whom propounded the New Learning. In 1648 Symner explained that,

'In all these studyes my scope is for reall and experimentall learning. I abhor all those ventosities, froth and idle speculations of ye schooles ... in such studyes for this 2000 yeares the purest witts have spent theyr golden & precious houres, and yet are as far to seeke, as those were in Aristotles dayes ... If I have profitted but little more than they, the fault lyes in the sterility of my understanding, not the goodnes of my method ...'

At this time he was engaged on astronomical observations, and had made a quadrant of six-foot radius. He was able to fix the latitude of Dublin at 53° 20'. Later, during the Commonwealth, Symner and his friends provided the germ from which, in 1683, the Dublin Philosophical Society sprang. Nothing is known about the contents of Symner's lectures at Trinity College, but they may have included the principles of surveying. He himself was a member of a committee to inquire into the survey of Connaught and Clare in 1653.[6] After the Restoration, Symner's professorship lapsed, and his lack of occupation may have induced him to seek employment with private patrons. He can be identified with the 'Mr Sumner' who in 1662 and 1664 supervised building projects for the 2nd Earl of Cork at Lismore Castle, Co. Waterford, the first of which was the building of a schoolhouse. In 1664 he visited Lismore to oversee the fitting of ashlar stones for the porch, most likely a classical portico, which stood formerly in the courtyard of the castle.[7] In 1669 he was one of a committee to advise the Dean and Chapter of St Patrick's Cathedral, Dublin, on repairs to the structure.[8] In the following year he acted as overseer of St Andrew's Church in the same city,[9] then being built after the designs of the architect William Dodson (q.v.). He regained his position as lecturer of mathematics at Trinity College, Dublin, in 1668.[10] In March 1686, he was being nursed in the College, and he died soon afterwards.[11] He left no publications. Though he sent

Samuel Hartlib some corrections for Gerard Boate's *Irelands Naturall History*, he did not complete his ambitious plan to write the sections for it that Boate had left unwritten.

[1] Most of the pioneering work on Symner has been done by T. C. Barnard in his 'Miles Symner and the New Learning in Seventeenth-Century Ireland' (*JRSAI*, 1972, *102*, pt. 2, 129–42).

[2] R. Dunlop, *Ireland under the Commonwealth*, Manchester, 1913, I, 80, 83–4, 86, 241–3.

[3] *Ibid.*, II, 410.

[4] E. MacLysaght (Ed.), 'Commonwealth State Accounts: Ireland, 1650–1656', *Analecta Hibernica*, 1944, *13*, 241; NLI, Ms 2745, f. 1.

[5] Barnard, *op.cit.*; see also his 'The Hartlib Circle and the Origins of the Dublin Philosophical Society', *Irish Historical Studies*, 1974, *19*, 56–71. I am very much indebted to Dr T. C. Barnard in providing me with some pertinent information regarding Symner's career as an engineer.

[6] King's Inn, Dublin, Prendergast Ms 1, pp. 162, 172. See also NLI, Ms 11959, f. 112.

[7] Chatsworth, Lismore Ms 32, ff. 75, 159.

[8] St Patrick's Cathedral, Dublin, Chapter Minutes, 1660–70, f. 372^v.

[9] TCD, Ms 2062.

[10] Information kindly conveyed to me by Dr T. C. Barnard.

[11] TCD, MUN/P/4, folder 4.6.

T

TABARY, JAMES (also JAQUES) (fl.1655),French carver and designer. He is first noted as a member of the Academy of St Luke in Paris in 1655. He and his brothers John and Louis (see below) may be identified with the brothers Tabouré, carvers, who worked on the choir of Minimes de Tours (chapelle du lycée). He was of Protestant origin, which caused him to flee France, and settle in London. There he is first noted in December 1681, when he lived in Threadneedle Street, and received £2 in charity.[1] Soon afterwards he came over to Ireland, possibly attracted by the prospect of employment in Dublin. He was admitted to the freedom of the city in 1682, where he was joined by his relatives the carvers John and Louis Tabary (who were admitted three years later).[2] It seems probable that James Tabary started working in 1682 on the interior of the chapel of the Royal Hospital, Kilmainham. Work progressed very slowly, and it was not until January 1687 that the chapel was consecrated.[3] The year before, unnamed carvers and joiners, among whom probably were the carvers Tabary,[4] had been paid a total of £809 12s. 1d. In January 1687 James Tabarict [sic] petitioned the Governors that he had not been allowed the full value of his work 'in carveing, frameing and setting up the Alter-peece, Rayle, Pannell and Table in the Chapell ... [and] it did appeare by the Certificate of Mr Robinson his Mats Surveyr that the said Altar-peece as it then was fixt was vallued at £250 ... unlesse [he] should add other workes thereto which was intended'. He was granted the £250, and was to be paid more if any 'other embellishments' were to be added later.[5] This probably suggests that Tabary was working from a composite design which was completed in stages. Although very little is known about William Robinson's interior designs for churches (he was the architect of the Hospital), the baroque characteristics and details of the Kilmainham altar, the entrance to and interior of the chapel derives much more likely from a French source such as Tabary than from Robinson. It is unclear what the relative contribution was of James, John, and Louis Tabary. That the above payment was made to James, suggests that he acted in a supervisory capacity. The Tabarys' work is of exceptional quality, and one cannot but agree with a contemporary letter-writer who stated that the chapel would be 'one of the finest chapels consecrated the King has in his dominions'.[6]

It has been suggested that John and Louis Tabary had been responsible for the ceiling of the chapel.[7] However, with the exclusion of some details, this ceiling is very similar to contemporary English work, and its design was probably by an unidentified craftsman trained in England.

The uncertain economical climate after 1687 during the Lord Deputyship of the Earl of Tyrconnell, may have given little artistic opportunity for the Tabary family. Whether they remained in Ireland is unclear. The chapel was unaltered until about 1850 when the east window was lowered, and this led to the removal of the carving and panelling at the back of the altar. However, the appearance of the altar in its original position is known from a drawing in a private collection.

[1] I am indebted to Ms Anne Crookshank and Mr G. Jackson-Stops for the above information.
[2] *CARD*, V, 259, 373, 367.
[3] *HMC, Ormonde*, n.s. VII, 379, 411, 463.
[4] A 'book of particular payments' prepared by Robinson, which covered the building expenses of the hospital is mentioned in contemporary accounts, but its present whereabouts is unknown (PROI, RHK

1/1/1, f. 35). It was probably still extant about 1805 when George Burston used some of its information (see footnote 5) in his *Charter of the Royal Hospital*, Dublin, 1805, 42–3.
5   PRO, RHK 1/1/1, under date January 27, 1686[–7].
6   *HMC, Ormonde*, n.s. VII, 463.
7   C. P. Curran, *Dublin Decorative Plasterwork*, London, 1967, 15–16.

THOMAS, DANIEL, Senior (fl. 1631–?1657). His father was from Wainfleet, Lincolnshire, England.[1] Daniel Thomas had been, as he reports, with the best undertakers for building in London for twenty years, when he worked at Furnival's Inn, Holborn, Southampton House behind Grey's Inn, the house of Lord Grey of Warwick in the Charterhouse Yard, and the Charterhouse itself.[2] Judging from the 'artisan mannerist' appearance of Furnival's Inn (Dem. 1818) Daniel Thomas was one of the leading architect-builders in London in the reign of Charles I.[3] In 1647 he is mentioned with the rank of Captain among the soldiers who are to be sent over to Ireland.[4] Thomas records that he started building in Ireland in 1655,[5] and this involved both the erection of government forts and fortified private residences, mainly near the Shannon which served as a barrier against the Irish in Connaught. It is unclear whether he also designed these works. In 1657 Thomas, both in Dublin and at Portumna Co. Galway, offered his services to Henry Cromwell, who became Lord Deputy in November of that year. However, Thomas made his will at Ballymoe on June 24, 1657, and may not have lived long enough to work for Henry Cromwell. In the will his sons Daniel, Philip and Thomas are mentioned as are his brother Thomas and the latter's son Thomas.[6]

1   Geneal. Off., Will Abstracts VI, 259.
2   BL, Lansdowne MS 822, f. 218; for these buildings see *Colvin*, 821–2.
3   *Colvin*, 822.
4   C. MacNeill (Ed.), *The Tanner Letters*, Dublin, 1943, 239; BL, Lansdowne MS 821, f. 150.
5   BL, Lansdowne MS 822, f. 218.
6   See note 1.

TERMONBARRY FORT, CO. ROSCOMMON. Started after 1655, this fort on the Shannon was not finished in 1656, as reported by the engineer William Webb. Its cost amounted to £360 (BL, Lansdowne Mss 821, f. 150; 822, f. 218; *HMC, Ormonde*, n.s. III, 156). Dem.

BALLYMOE BRIDGE, also FORT FLEETWOOD, CO. GALWAY. Erected after 1655, this fort on the Shannon was possibly finished in the summer of 1656. Thomas mentions in 1657 that he was employing English sawyers at the site, and in order to start at Portumna Castle (see below) would free himself from his work at Ballymoe Bridge by settling one of his sons on the site. When the fort at Ballymoe Bridge was finished it had become a strong regular fort with four bulwarks, built of lime and stone at a cost of £2,050, which also included the repair of the bridge (*HMC, Ormonde*, n.s. III, 27, 155; BL, Lansdowne Mss 821, f. 150; 822, ff. 212, 218). Altered.

COL RICHARD COOTE'S HOUSE, ?COLLOONEY CASTLE, CO. SLIGO. Thomas mentions only that he built for Col Richard Coote, and that the building was finished in 1657 by one of his sons. In the 'census' of 1659 Richard Coote is mentioned as of Collooney Castle, Co. Sligo, from where he derived later his title Baron Coote of Collooney (subsequently Earl of Bellamont). In a petition of the early 1660s, Coote mentions that he had spent much on buildings and improvements at Collooney, which most likely involved the rebuilding of an older structure, which was ruined in 1647 (BL, Lansdowne Ms 822, ff. 212, 218; *CSPI*, 1633–47, 596; *CSPI*, 1660–2, 177). Dem.

Tingham

CASTLE COOTE, CO. ROSCOMMON. Although Thomas claimed to have built this for Sir Charles Coote (later Earl of Mountrath, brother of Col Richard Coote (see above)), it was probably an older structure rebuilt. The house or castle had been besieged by the Irish under Preston in 1643. In 1662 Castle Coote was a garrison, consisting of a new bawn with flankers (BL, Lansdowne Ms 822, f. 218; *HMC, Ormonde*, n.s. III, 28). It was a ruin in 1791 (F. Grose, *The Antiquities of Ireland, London, I, 82*).

PORTUMNA CASTLE, CO. GALWAY. Henry Cromwell had been granted in 1654 the Portumna estate of the Earl of Clanricarde. In two letters dated 1657 Thomas urged Henry Cromwell to allow him to do small repairs on the castle and its stable and to erect a bridge across the Shannon. He offered to settle with his wife and family at Portumna, and in return for his work he requested some lands nearby and the customs of the bridge (BL, Lansdowne Ms 822, ff. 212, 218). No bridge was built about that time, and no work at Portumna by Thomas is known.

TINGHAM, EDMUND (fl. 1630), sculptor and contractor, who lived at Chapelizod, Co. Dublin.[1] Tingham is first noted on June 3, 1630 when he agreed with the 1st Earl of Cork, to make a large monument to the design of Alban Leverett, Athlone Pursuivant-at-Arms for the Boyle family in St Patrick's Cathedral, Dublin, for which Henry Power, Viscount Valentia stood security. Lord Valentia by then had finished the building of Chapelizod House,[2] on which he may have employed Tingham. Subsequently Tingham was patronized by the Earl of Cork, from whom he received various loans to proceed with projects, and once a sum of money for his release from a debtor's prison. A first commission was the wainscotting of the gallery at Lord Caulfeild's Dublin house in 1631 bought by the Earl. The gallery and additional lodgings, designed by Thomas Roper, Viscount Baltinglass (q.v.), had three chimney pieces and 'a great case of boxes',[3] which in all likelihood were by Tingham. He played a major part in the designing of the rebuilding of Maynooth Castle, Co. Kildare. With the help of the Earl it was modified in a 'uniform' manner. As a sculptor, Tingham produced effigies which are stiff and inelegant; he employed craftsmen for parts of his commissions, and among these were George Nelden and Hugh Jones.[4] His familiarity with different trades, together with the fact that he produced at least one design (for Maynooth Castle) suggests that, although a sculptor, he also acted as an architect and contractor. He seems to have been aware of classical ideas, which, however, as in the case of the Earl of Cork's tomb, were correct only in details and not in over-all design. He travelled at least once to 'Westchester' in England to purchase timber and alabaster, and he may have felt the influence of English architecture. His wife is mentioned often in the Earl of Cork's accounts as the person who was paid the money for the various building projects. In 1632 she received from the Earl a grey hackney and two cows 'to help to encourage them in forwarding the buildings' at Maynooth.

[1] A biographical note on Tingham was written by W. G. Strickland in his *A Dictionary of Irish Artists* (1913, reprinted Shannon, 1968, II, 449–51), which is partially incorrect (see below).
[2] F. E. Ball, *The History of the County of Dublin*, Dublin, 1902, IV, 167.
[3] *Grosart*, series 1, III, 75, 90, 176. Tingham seems to have been a joiner by trade. He probably can be identified with the joiner of Chapelizod who was to be paid by the Earl of Cork for a round table in August 1630 (NLI, Ms 6246). Note that Strickland and others mistakenly thought Tingham's work to have been at Cork House, near Dublin Castle instead of at Lord Caulfeild's house.
[4] NLI, Ms 6246.

WORKS

DUBLIN, MONUMENT FOR THE EARL OF CORK, St Patrick's Cathedral. Erected from 1630 to 1632 after the design of Alban Leverett for the 1st Earl of Cork. Upon completion Tingham received as a bounty from the Earl £32 and £28 worth of iron (*Grosart*, series 1, III, 35, 121–2, 171; NLI, Ms 6246).

DUBLIN, ST JOHN'S CHURCH. In about 1632 Tingham was paid £30 for masonry (S. C. Hughes, *The Church of St John the Evangelist, Dublin*, Dublin, 1889, 20). Dem.

MAYNOOTH, CO. KILDARE, ST MARY'S CHURCH. Restored in 1632 for the Earl of Cork, while rebuilding Maynooth Castle (see below) (*Grosart*, series 1, III, 135; NLI, Ms 6246). Altered.

MAYNOOTH CASTLE, CO. KILDARE. As guardian and father-in-law to George, 16th Earl of Kildare, the Earl of Cork rebuilt three ranges of the square court of the castle from 1632 to 1635 for which Tingham was paid the total sum of £2,074 7s. 6d. (which includes St Mary's Church, see above). Of this amount £524 7s. 6d. was lent to Tingham, who most likely exceeded his estimate (*Grosart*, series 1, III, 135ff; NLI, Ms 6246). A map of Maynooth Castle said to be dated 1630, can be associated with Tingham's work (*KASJ*, 1891–95, *1*, 237). Ruined.

ATTRIBUTIONS

DUBLIN, MONUMENT TO LORD CHANCELLOR THOMAS JONES AND ROGER JONES, VISCOUNT RANELAGH, St Patrick's Cathedral. This tomb has effigies in a style very similar to those on the Earl of Cork's tomb (see above). (Viscount Ranelagh's son Arthur (later 2nd Viscount) married sometime before 1630 the Earl of Cork's daughter Katherine). The original condition of the tomb can be seen on a drawing in NLI, Pos. 7515.

TROTTER, ?ROBERT (fl. 1670), Dutch painter who acted as building overseer to the Countess of Ormonde. He is first noted in 1670 at her seat Dunmore House, outside Kilkenny. This house had been rebuilt by Capt. John Morton (q.v.). Some time after his death, Trotter was employed there. In a letter, dated July 18, 1679, the Countess wrote about him 'I know him to be very abell in his professione and knowinge besides in things of Buildinge',[1] and no other architect or builder is mentioned in the correspondence. Apart from advising about alterations to the house, he busied himself with the painting inside and outside Dunmore House, and Kilkenny Castle the seat of the Duke of Ormonde. This suggests that he was a house painter rather than a decorative painter; however, no other painter's name is known, who could have been responsible for the many paintings above chimney-pieces and door-cases, which formerly adorned the house:[2] its ruins were removed in the 19th century. Trotter was employed until at least 1672 at a yearly salary, despite the frequent quarrels he had with employees on the estate. In that year he travelled to London, to receive the instructions of the Countess for the necessary works to be done at the house, which at that time included the laying out of the grounds.[3] After July 1672 his name does not recur in the *Ormonde Papers*. He may be identified with the Robert Trotter who received in 1681 the monopoly of auctioning paintings in Dublin.[4] In an account book of an unidentified Dutch merchant living in Dublin, a 'Mr Trotter' was paid £3 for marbling three chimney-pieces in 1685.[5] Painters active in Ireland in the 18th and 19th centuries with the same name are possible descendants of Trotter.

[1] NLI, Ms 2503, *ff*.
[2] NLI, Ms 2521.
[3] NLI, Ms 2503, *ff*.
[4] Gilbert, Ms 67, p. 611; I am indebted to Dr L. M. Cullen for drawing my attention to this source.
[5] NLI, Ms 3137.

TUCKER, ANDREW (fl. 1624–?1638), carpenter and builder, who was patronized by the 1st Earl of Cork. From 1624 onwards he either copied existing buildings for the Earl, or prepared new designs. Part of his time he devoted to minor works in Co. Waterford such as the building of a storehouse at Lisfinny in 1626–7,[1] and carpentry at Lismore Castle during the same period,[2] and earlier, at a lodge in its park in 1624.[3] The fact that he, often in collaboration with other craftsmen, signed contracts for the erection of whole structures, makes it clear that he acted as builder and contractor. From the surviving ruins of Ballyduff Castle in Co. Waterford it is apparent that he was building in a rather ornate early 17th-century fashion by using intricate quoins around the windows and at the corners of the building. Tucker is last mentioned in the Earl of Cork's records on December 5, 1637. He may be identified with the Andrew Tucker who left a prerogative will dated August 14, 1638. In it he is mentioned as of Hospital, Co. Limerick. He left his wife Anne, his son John, and a posthumous child, a moderately large estate, which included several farms. Tucker's sister is identified as the wife of Sir John Browne Kt of Hospital. Tucker himself might have been illiterate for he signed the will with his mark.[4]

[1] NLI, Ms 6897.
[2] NLI, Ms 6897; *Grosart*, series 1, II, 191, 234.
[3] *Grosart*, series 1, II, 145, where named only as Andrew.
[4] Genealogical Office, W.P. 65 (will abstract).

BALLYKNOCK, also CASTLEKNOCK CASTLE, ?CO. TIPPERARY. In June 1625 the Earl of Cork agreed with Thomas Allen (q.v.), Allen's son and Andrew Tucker for the building of this castle as an almost complete copy of the Lodge in the park of Lismore Castle (NLI, Ms 6897; *Grosart*, series 1, II, 159, 160).

BALLYDUFF CASTLE, CO. WATERFORD. The Earl of Cork agreed with Tucker in May 1627 for building this castle, for which the latter received a last payment in 1629. Ruined (NLI, Ms 6897; *Grosart*, series 1, II, 214).

SHANNON PARK, also BALLINREA, CO. CORK. The joiner John Jackson and Tucker were sent in 1636 to take a 'module' of the Lord President's house at Doneraile, Co. Cork to build a similar structure for the Earl of Cork's son Francis (later Viscount Shannon). Dem. (*Grosart*, series 1, IV, 210).

ASKEATON CASTLE, CO. LIMERICK. In about 1636 Tucker and the Earl of Cork drew up a 'plott or modell' for a new building at Askeaton, after which Tucker was paid on several occasions for work executed there up until 1637 (NLI, Mss 6899, 6246; *Grosart*, series 1, IV, 210; V, 37).

BROGHILL CASTLE, CO. CORK. In January 1637 John Jackson and Tucker set out the new castle at Broghill, the building of which seems to have been in the hands of Tucker who was last paid on December 5, of that year. Dem. (NLI, Ms 6899; *Grosart*, series 1, IV, 210; V, 37).

V

VEALE or **VEEL,** WILLIAM (fl. 1636). He is first mentioned for his work on the chapel and the new stable at Trinity College, Dublin, in 1636.[1] A person of the same name was granted lands in Co. Laois in 1641, while his name recurs in 1641 and 1642 for repairs at Dublin Castle, and for other services.[2] A William Veale was assessed in 1665 for property in Keysars Lane in Dublin.[3]

[1] TCD, MUN/P/2/1, f. 8.
[2] *CSPI*, 1633–47, *ff.*
[3] *57th Report of the Deputy Keeper of the Public Records in Ireland*, 1936, 532.

W

WALSHE, JOHN (fl. 1609), mason from Waterford, employed by Sir Richard Boyle in 1609, for making two chimney-pieces and windows for Boyle's house at Youghal. Six years later he is mentioned as the plasterer and mason, who finished for the same patron a chimney-piece cut by Richard and John Hamond[1] (q.v.). His work does not seem to have survived.

[1] Chatsworth, Lismore Ms 3, f. 10; *Grosart*, series 1, I, 67; series 2, 131.

WESTCOMB, THOMAS (fl. 1624), mason, who worked for the 1st Earl of Cork. See under Allen, Thomas.

WESTLEY, DR JOHN (fl. 1651–?1687), architect who probably was of English parentage, and married a daughter of the English architect John Webb sometime after 1652.[1] He is first noted as a student in the Faculty of Arts at Christ Church, Oxford in 1651, where he received his M.A. on July 24, 1652. Two years later he matriculated at Cambridge University. He went over to Ireland before the end of 1656, for a Mr Westley's appointment as *Examiner* of the Court of Chancery in Ireland was disputed at that time.[2] The office of *Examiner* was confirmed to Westley on September 24, 1660, and in that same month Charles II instructed the Duke of Ormonde to promote him to the office of Master in Chancery.[3] This office was awarded to him on March 1, 1661, and he held it until 1682. His immediate superior in the Court of Chancery, the Lord Chancellor Sir Maurice Eustace, sent him in December 1661 to England with a draft of the additions to Phoenix House, the royal lodge near Dublin;[4] many years later Westley recounted that he travelled to Whitehall with a, presumably, wooden model (which cost £100) of Phoenix House.[5] Apart from his work on the royal residences in Ireland and the house for Sir George Lane, all in the early 1660s, little is known of the extent of his architectural practice. He seems to have been his own contractor. He may have designed the former country seat at Blessington, Co. Wicklow,[6] which was built for his superior Michael Boyle, Lord Primate and Lord Chancellor, but in the absence of any known designs by Westley, attributions are difficult to make. As an architect he competed with William Dodson (q.v.), who was later favoured by the government for work at the royal residences. In November 1669 Westley, together with Miles Symner (q.v.), Samuel Molyneux II, and Ralph Wallis were considered to report on proposed alterations to St Patrick's Cathedral, Dublin.[7] After this date Westley's architectural career remains obscure. He may easily have made use of the expertise of his father-in-law John Webb. In 1652 his wife received from Webb's kinsman Inigo Jones a legacy of £200.[8] Because of this relationship Westley may easily have had access to John Webb's designs, and Inigo Jones's drawings and annotated books, which, together with a collection of original drawings by Andrea Palladio had been bequeathed to Webb. Any impact this revolutionary Renaissance art may have made on Westley's works remains unknown. That the relationships with the Webb family remained close, is probable from the fact that Westley's daughter Elizabeth is mentioned in 1672 in her grandfather John Webb's will.[9] Possibly through Westley, the Earl of Orrery (q.v.) commissioned from John Webb the scenes for his play *Mustapha*, which was first performed in London in 1665.

On January 26, 1661 Westley received an Ll.D. from Trinity College, Dublin. He was personally involved in the redistribution of lands following the Restoration in his function as Auditor of the Court of Claims.[10] From 1661 onwards he acted as a messenger between the Irish House of Commons and the Irish House of Lords, which must have brought him in contact with most of the Irish nobility. He owned several estates in Ireland as early as 1659. In the 'census' of that year he is noted as of 'Both the Belan's', Co. Kildare, where he had a residence. Evidence is lacking, however, that he built there. In the acts of Settlement and Explanation he was granted a number of estates, followed in 1668 by a grant of lands in Co. Dublin, which he sold in the same year.[11] The office of Master of Chancery presumably caused him to live the major part of his life in Ireland. In 1672 his house in St Bridget's Street was valued for the parish of St Bride's Church at £26.[12] Westley made his will at Belan, Co. Kildare, on April 9, 1687, apparently surviving his wife. He mentions as beneficiaries his daughter Elizabeth, and John Warburton and Stephen Ludlow (Clerk of the Court of Chancery, and ancestor of Lord Ludlow). An abstract only of Westley's will survives, so that his wealth and architectural heritage remain unknown.[13]

[1] Bodl., Carte Ms 31, f. 440.
[2] *CSPI*, 1647–60, 615–7.
[3] Bodl., Carte Ms 41, f. 37.
[4] Bodl., Carte Ms 31, f. 373.
[5] BL, Add. Ms 15893, f. 243.
[6] Only known from an engraving (BL, K. 55.47).
[7] St Patrick's Cathedral, Dublin, Chapter Minutes, 1660–70, p. 372[v].
[8] J. A. Gotch, *Inigo Jones*, London, 1928, 220.
[9] PRO, Prob. 11/340, pp. 298–9.
[10] *HMC, 10th Rep. App. V*, 12.
[11] *CSPI*, 1666–9, 529; NLI, D 11286.
[12] NLI, Ms 5230, f. 13.
[13] Geneal. Off., Betham Coll., n.s. vol. 4.

DUBLIN CASTLE. In 1661 Westley and Ralph Wallis (Clerk in the office of the Master of the Rolls) were paid £150 for repairing the lower courts (*HMC, Ormonde*, n.s. III, p. 395). In March of the following year he offered the Duke of Ormonde his services for the erection of new buildings in Dublin Castle, saying that John Webb could give him directions (Bodl., Carte Ms 31, f. 440), but instead the Irish Surveyor-General John Paine (q.v.) was given the job.

PHOENIX HOUSE, CO. DUBLIN. Westley travelled to London in Dec. 1661 to show the Duke of Ormonde the plans for the additions to this royal lodge. Whether his designs or those of the Earl of Orrery (q.v.), were accepted remains uncertain. Westley supervised part of the rebuilding, (possibly assisted by Randall Beckett (q.v.)) but was replaced, for unknown reasons, by William Dodson (q.v.). Before 1665, he requested approval of his accounts. (*HMC, 9th Rep. App. II*, p. 163), but even in 1686 he had not received the £500 2s. 9d. which he claimed was due to him, in addition to the £1,500 which he already had received (BL, Add. Ms 15893, f. 243–7). Dem.

SIR GEORGE LANE'S HOUSE. In 1664 Westley prepared plans and estimates for a house to the value of £2,000 for Sir George Lane (who was secretary to the Duke of Ormonde, and later became Lord Lanesborough), in competition with William Dodson (q.v.) (BL, Add. Ms 45941A, f. 65). This possibly refers to Lane's country house Ratheline, Co. Longford, which was renovated in 1666–67 (now ruined).

WHALLEY, WILLIAM (fl. 1630), carpenter and builder, who contracted with the 1st Earl of Cork and Thomas Roper, 1st Viscount Baltinglass (q.v.) to build for the Earl a gallery and three tenements and stables at a house in Dame St, Dublin, which the Earl had just purchased from Lord Caulfeild. Whalley executed these works probably in brick after the design by Viscount Baltinglass. Because of litigation regarding payment that followed he was imprisoned. The interior of the gallery was finished by Edmund Tingham[1] (q.v.).

[1] *Grosart*, series 1, III, 176. Whalley's petition for release from prison is in BL, Harl. Ms 430, f. 91.

WHINREY (also **WHINNERY**), **JOHN** (fl. 1678–1730), a mason who had a very extensive practice in Dublin. He was admitted as freeman to the City of Dublin in 1678. About two years later he was paid for a sundial for the newly built St John's Church,[1] but there is no evidence that he was responsible for building the church. In 1685 he charged the City Council £6 16s. 3d. for laying hearths in the Tholsel.[2] Between 1693 and 1698 he received a total of £177 14s. 7½d. for repairing the front of the Blue Coat Hospital, and the cutting of the King's and City's arms.[3] He also supplied building stone for St Catherine's Church in 1681,[4] and a total of 32 tons of stone from Whitehaven presumably for the new building on the south side of Trinity College. This range was erected in 1698, probably after the design of William Robinson (q.v.); Whinrey measured the stonework on July 3, 1699.[5] In 1702 he received over £116 from the Surveyor-General Thomas Burgh (q.v.) for the building of the steeple of the Royal Hospital, Kilmainham,[6] after the design of William Robinson. Burgh also paid him four years later for making the steps leading to the hall and the terrace walk of the Hospital.[7] Whinrey again followed designs from Robinson when he did the stonework for the rebuilding of St Mary's Church in 1703. The next year Burgh surveyed Whinrey's work, but Whinrey was forced to sue the parish to obtain the £300 still due to him as late as 1727.[8] Although only Robinson's design for the east window of the church is mentioned in the Vestry Book, it seems likely that Whinrey followed Robinson's directions for the other windows as well. The absence of a unifying scheme for the exterior of the church suggests that the integration of the whole was left to Whinrey, with unsatisfactory results. From this time onwards, Whinrey's periodic association with Thomas Burgh was consolidated. He is mentioned in Burgh's accounts of 1703 in relation to the repairs at Chichester House.[9] Burgh's accounts for 1705 mention payment to Whinrey for stonecutter's work delivered to Dublin Castle, the Bagnio, the Council Chamber, Chapelizod House, and the Stores of war, and in 1707 Whinrey received £55 1s. ½d[10] for stonecutter's work at Dublin Castle. At Trinity College, Dublin, he was paid small sums for work in 1707 and 1708, and in 1710–11 several amounts probably for all the mason's work on the new laboratory of the College. Another payment was £23 1s. for stonework for a [?re] building of the Provost's House.[11] For unexplained reasons Whinrey's work at the College was discontinued and masons later employed there were Moses and Hugh Darley, and William Caldbeck. Whinrey's name is mentioned elsewhere in connection with small commissions. Between 1709 and 1710 he and a Mr Constance were paid for fixing and inscribing a stone with Queen Elizabeth's arms at the Tailor's Hall.[12] The *Egmont Papers* mention that in 1713 a 'Whinnery' supplied three stone pedestals for Sir John Perceval, probably for the garden of Duncarney, Co Dublin.[13] A large commission for Whinrey was his stonework for St Werburgh's Church for which he received at least £533 3s. in about 1715,[14] when the designer was Thomas Burgh (q.v.) and the overseer Richard Mills (q.v.). The last known work done by Whinrey was at the

Royal Barracks in Dublin in 1723–5,[15] presumably again under the patronage of Thomas Burgh (q.v.). One of Whinrey's pupils was the bricklayer Richard Coulett, who obtained the freedom of the City of Dublin in 1700. Whinrey's residence in 1702 was in [?St Mary's] Abbey St and was assessed at the valuation of the parish for £7.[16] Whinrey lived probably until old age. He signed his will on January 16, 1730, and died the same year. His wife Mary had borne him four sons, William, Thomas, Nathaniel, and Samuel, and one daughter Anne.[17] His sons Nathaniel and Samuel also became masons, possibly trained in their father's workshop; both were admitted to the freedom of the City of Dublin in 1722.

[1] *Gilbert*, I, 52.
[2] *CARD*, V, 373.
[3] King's Hospital, Ms Account Book, pp. 245, 363.
[4] PROI, M 5122, p. 204.
[5] TCD, Ms MUN/P/2/8, f. 38.
[6] PROI, RHK 1/1/1, f. 285.
[7] PROI, RHK 1/1/1, f. 333.
[8] St Mary's Church, Dublin, Vestry Book, pp. 23, 33, 140 *ff*.
[9] *Commons Jour.*, 1703–13, 666.
[10] PRO, W.O. 55/1984. Payment in 1705 amounted to £45 5s. 1d.
[11] TCD, Ms MUN/P/2 [see index of this Ms collection].
[12] *JRSAI*, 1918, *8*, 43.
[13] BL, Add. Ms 47047, p. 20.
[14] TCD, Ms 2063.
[15] *Commons Jour.*, 1723–30, 335.
[16] St Mary's Church, Dublin, Vestry Book, p. 12.
[17] Geneal. Off., Betham Coll., n.s. vol. 31, pp. 158–9.

WILLIS, DIGGORY (fl. 1635), mason who contracted in 1635 with Christopher Wandesford, Master of the Rolls, for alterations at the Castle of Kildare, Co. Kildare.[1]

[1] H. B. M. McCall, *Story of the Family of Wandesforde*, London, 1904, 275.

WINTER, GEORGE (fl. 1627), mason, employed by the Earl of Cork in making turrets and a garden wall at Lismore Castle, Co. Waterford in 1627, for work on the gable ends of the castle in the same year, and on a store house for iron at Kilmackoe, Co. Waterford.[1]

[1] NLI, Ms 6897; *Grosart*, series 1, II, 175.

	CLERK OF THE WORKS	DEPUTY CLERK OF THE WORKS	COMPTROLLER OF THE WORKS	MASTER CARPENTER
SUPERINTENDENT OF THE CASTLES 1607–1613 Sir Josias Bodley	1600–1612 Samuel Molyneux	–1603 Richard Hawett	1606–?1660 Sir Francis Annesley	1619–?1649 John Bannister
DIRECTOR-GENERAL & OVERSEER OF THE FORTIFICATIONS & BUILDINGS 1613–1617 Sir Josias Bodley	1612–1625 Samuel Molyneux & Tristam Gawen	c. 1601–2 Thomas Rookewood (At Loughfoyle)	*office discontinued*	
1618–1634 Sir Thomas Rotherham & Nicholas Pynnar	*office discontinued*	*office discontinued*		
1634–?1644 Nicholas Pynnar				
1644–?1648 John Paine				
OVERSEER OF THE PUBLIC WORKS ?1653–1660 Randall Beckett	*office discontinued*			1661–?1673 John Mills
DIRECTOR-GENERAL OF THE KING'S FORTIFICATIONS AND PLANTATIONS 1661–?1670 John Paine (initially with John Hallam)				*office discontinued*

Table 1, Part 1: THE ORGANIZATION OF THE IRISH ROYAL WORKS IN THE 17TH CENTURY.

SURVEYOR-GENERAL OF THE FORTIFICATIONS AND BUILDINGS	DEPUTY SURVEYOR-GENERAL
1670–1684 William Robinson	
1684–1687/8 William Robinson & William Molyneux	fl. 1692 William Spike
1690–1700 William Robinson & William Molyneux (d. 1696)	
1700–1730 Thomas Burgh	

Table 1, Part 2: THE ORGANIZATION OF THE IRISH ROYAL WORKS IN THE LATE 17TH AND EARLY 18TH CENTURIES.

Index of Persons and Places

Index

Index

Index

Index

Tucker, Andrew, 3, 13, 40
Tunney, Co. Antrim, 51
Tyrconnell, Richard Talbot, 1st Earl and titular Duke of, 76, 85, 89, 106

Valencia, Island, Co. Kerry, 15
Valentia, Henry Power, 1st Viscount (1st creation), 108
Valentia, Francis Annesley, 1st Viscount (2nd creation), 13, 14, 74, 116
Van Nost, John, 79
Vanbrugh, Sir John, 46
Vanhomrigh, Bartholomew, 77, 90
Vanhomrigh, Hester, 91
Vaughan, Sir John, 20, 47, 59, 84
Veale, William, 111
Vermuyden, Mr., 50
Villiers, Sir William, 62
Volterra, Francesca Da, 36, 54

Wakely, family, 39
Wallis, Ralph, 112, 113
Wallis, William, 55
Walshe, John, 3, 68, 42
Wandesford, Sir Christopher, 63, 115
Warburton, John, 113
Waringstown, Co. Down, 80, 88
Waterford,
    Barracks, 42
    St. Patrick's Fort (Citadel), 22, 25, 42, 86, 87, 100
Wattson, Mr., 29
Webb, John, 5, 26, 112, 113
Webb, William, 26, 72, 82, 104, 107
Webbe, John, 103

Wentworth, Sir Thomas,
    see Strafford, 1st Earl of
Westcomb, Thomas, 13, 112
Westley, John, 4, 5, 6, 7, 20, 26, 28, 50, 51, 72, 77
Whalley, William, 98, 114
Wharton, Francis, 69
Wharton, Robert, 35
Whinnery, John, 34, 114–15
Whinrey, Nathaniel, 115
Whinrey, Samuel, 115
Wibault, Jacques, 33, 41
William III, 16, 31, 41, 64, 89–90
Willis, Diggory, 115
Willoughby, Anthony, 25
Wills, Michael, 32, 33, 37, 38
Winter, George, 115
Winwood, Sir Ralph, 24
Wolseley, William, 90
Worsley, Benjamin, 104
Wotton, Sir Henry, 85
Wren, Sir Christopher, 64, 65
Wren, Robert, 92, 93
Wyche, Sir Cyril, 42
Wynter, Sergeant, 4

Yorke, Edmund, 85, 87
Youghal, Co. Cork, 112
    Alms House, 52, 68
    College, 57
    North Abbey, 85
    St. Mary's Church, 27, 52
    Schoolhouse, 68
    Town Walls, 26
    Uniacke House, 68
Young, Paul, 55

126